Praise for **THE GHOSTS OF MEDAK POCKET**

National Bestseller

Winner of the Dafoe Prize

"In addition to a stirring account of the battle, Off provides the historical context an uninitiated reader needs to understand the origins of the bewildering and precarious situation Canadian soldiers faced while peacemaking in Croatia. . . . Carol Off has written a first-class account of Canada's soldiers in action. Her prose is lively and her tone impassioned. Combining credible secondary sources with a large collection of first-hand accounts, the best evidence of all, she has made a solid argument for a reassessment of Canadians' attitudes toward peacekeeping."
—*The Globe and Mail*

"Carol Off's careful analysis of the events in Medak Pocket and her compassionate portrayal of those who served there is required reading." —*Canadian Defence Review*

"Carol Off has done the nation an invaluable service with *The Ghosts of Medak Pocket*." —*Literary Review of Canada*

"For the soldiers who served in Medak Pocket, I can only hope that Off's book will bring them some relief and sense of justice."
—*The Gazette* (Montreal)

CAROL OFF

MEDAK POCKET

The Story of Canada's Secret War

VINTAGE CANADA

VINTAGE CANADA EDITION, 2005

www.randomhouse.ca

Quotation from "Dedication" from *New and Collected Poems 1931–2001* by
Czeslaw Milosz copyright © 2001 Czeslaw Milosz Royalties, Inc.
Published in Canada by HarperCollins Canada Limited. Used by permission.

Library and Archives Canada Cataloguing in Publication

Off, Carol
The ghosts of Medak Pocket : the story of Canada's secret war / Carol Off.

Includes bibliographical references and index.

ISBN-13: 978-0-679-31294-9
ISBN-10: 0-679-31294-3

1. Medak Pocket Operation, Croatia, 1993.   2. Canada. Canadian Armed
Forces. Princess Patricia's Canadian Light Infantry—History.
3. United Nations—Peacekeeping forces—Croatia.   4. Canada—Armed
forces—Croatia.   5. Genocide—Croatia—History—20th century.
6. Yugoslav War, 1991–1995—Atrocities.   7. Croatia—History—1990–
I. Title.

DR1313.42.M33O44 2005   949.703   C2005-901323-0

Book design by CS Richardson

Printed and bound in Canada

2 4 6 8 9 7 5 3 1

To the memory of Ivo Knesevic
November 18, 1943–March 4, 2002

THEY USED TO POUR MILLET ON GRAVES OR POPPY SEEDS
TO FEED THE DEAD WHO WOULD COME DISGUISED AS BIRDS
I PUT THIS BOOK HERE FOR YOU, WHO ONCE LIVED
SO THAT YOU SHOULD VISIT US NO MORE

—Czeslaw Milosz, "Dedication"

CONTENTS

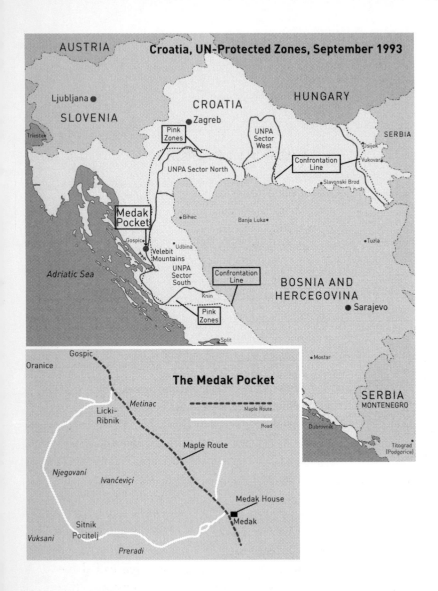

A NEW WAR DAWNING

*Fate is the same for the man who holds back,
the same if he fights hard.
We are all held in one single honour,
the brave with the weaklings.*

—The Iliad *of Homer*

RUDY BAJEMA GOT UP BEFORE DAWN on September 9, 1993. He wanted a moment of quiet and solitude before the bustle of the day in order to wish his mother a happy birthday. There was no way to talk to her directly, so he just thought about her, hoping mental telepathy would convey his feelings. Somehow he knew she'd get his message. And so Bajema was already wide awake when the first shell slammed into the ground at six-thirty.

A mortar explosion near their living quarters was nothing new for the soldiers of the Second Battalion of the Princess Patricia's Canadian Light Infantry. They had been dodging indirect fire ever since they moved into an area called the Medak Pocket, where they were guarding a ceasefire line between two hostile divisions of seasoned fighting forces: Serbs on one side and Croats on the other. Both of the forces had benefited from the training and expertise of what until recently had been one of the great military machines of Europe: the Yugoslav National Army. Now they were using the considerable skill they had acquired as a unified force in order to kill each other. The Patricias had long ago come to the realization that the cease-fire line they were assigned to guard was a barrier that existed only in the imaginations of international diplomats. The surprise on this particular morning was that the first shell was followed immediately by another one that came in almost on top of the Canadians, and shook the building.

Lieutenant Tyrone Green, a university student from Vancouver, consulted his compass after the first mortar explosion to determine which of the two adversaries was on the offensive this time. The second shell knocked him off his feet. He ran through the barracks that housed his soldiers, sending out the alarm. "Artie, artie artie!" he hollered (incoming artillery shells), while more mortar bombs smashed into the ground around them. As they scrambled out of their sleeping bags and jumped into their boots, grabbing their weapons, the peacekeepers knew, with a mixture of exhila-ration and terror, that they were no longer incidental bystanders at someone else's battle—they had become one of the targets.

Green dashed out to the yard and climbed into his armoured vehicle. His platoon had been in what they called Medak House for just over a week—not long enough to set up a proper com-munications system. The mobile radio in the vehicle was all he had. Green called Charlie Company headquarters to report this new development; by now the shells were landing all around them with the rhythm and the urgency of a major offensive operation. Charlie Company's Nine Platoon was suddenly in the middle of a war. To the young Canadians, the rules of engagement, if there were any, were as incomprehensible as the long, complicated Balkan history that had led up to this terrify-ing moment. Rudy Bajema had got his birthday greetings out just in time.

* * *

Eight kilometres south of Medak House and two kilometres straight up a mountain from the Canadian battalion's base camp in Sveti Rok, Sergeant Rod Dearing and his section of Charlie Company's Eight Platoon were deep asleep in and around their bunker. It was a standard war-zone shelter, its dirt walls and ceiling shored up by pit props, netting and prayers. The soldiers had dug into the stony ground of the Lika Highlands of Croatia, overlooking the villages and pastures on the Serbian side of Medak. A few metres away, precariously perched on the brow of a hill, they'd scooped out a second bunker to use as an observation post. Twenty-four hours a day, the Canadians peered out from that position into the deep valley below them, watching the comings and goings of soldiers as well as civilians.

Living in an earthen bunker with several other men might not be everyone's idea of pure joy, but Dearing loved being outdoors, surrounded by the dense oak forests of the Lika Highlands. The moors, valleys and woodlands of central Croatia resonate with dark, bloody history and an even darker mythology. Legends of clan warfare and revenge killing twist and turn through local folklore like the maze of goat trails that crisscross the empty hills.

To the north and east of the bunker and lookout, long spurs of the Austrian Alps tumble down into the interior of Croatia and merge with the Dinaric Mountains, which roll up from the southeast in a single rocky backbone. The green expanse of the Medak region's pasturelands flows away to the south and squeezes between foothills. Through a gap in the white rock of the Velebit Mountains to the west, the soldiers of Eight Platoon could sometimes see the blue water of the Adriatic, not more than twenty kilometres away.

It was early September and the woods were just beginning to turn gold and red. The setting reminded Dearing of his boyhood home in Armstrong, British Columbia, where he and his friends had played and explored, and where he'd acquired his love of the outdoors. A steady diet of *G.I. Joe* comics and a love of the Canadian war stories he learned in school—whenever he could sit still long enough to read—had filled him with the single desire to be a soldier. He'd joined the Rocky Mountain Rangers as soon as he was old enough to be a soldier in the reserves.

At twenty-eight, muscular and fit, Dearing was exactly where he always wanted to be. He was living in nature. He was a soldier. But he was in somebody else's country, caught in the middle of someone else's bloody war.

Dearing was the first one to hear it. The opening salvo of rocket artillery whistled through a jag in the Velebit foothills, fifty metres above their heads, and plowed into the valley below. "That woke us up," Dearing recalls. And then the Croatian army vented its full fury on the Medak Pocket. It sounded like a freight train passing overhead; this barrage just wouldn't stop. "We tried calling in shot reports to figure out what direction it was coming from, but there was just so much of it, it was impossible to figure out." From his vantage point, Dearing watched Serbs retreating to the south, away from the source of the rocket artillery. The Patricias were embedded on the Serbian side of the action, and he couldn't really see the Croats on the other side of the front line, but the attack was definitely coming from the Croatian direction.

He didn't report any of the Serbian troop movements on his radio. The Croats would have intercepted his calls and then used the information to pick out more targets. The Canadian peacekeepers were already having trouble maintaining a working relationship with the volatile Serbs who believed the United Nations force was really working for their enemy. The Canadians weren't about to risk provoking new accusations that they were providing intelligence to the Croatian army.

Dearing watched the horizon light up with orange flashes. It was like a thunderstorm rumbling over the foothills. He'd been imagining and reading about scenes like this for most of his youth, and had always wanted to see a battle close up. The reality was both fascinating and frightening. As he and the other wide-eyed young Canadians peered down into the valley below, they suspected they were observing the preparations for a major battle. But they were also staring into something larger, the unfathomable maw of Balkan history.

* * *

The stretch of Lika Highlands that now lay before the soldiers of the Princess Patricia's Canadian Light Infantry is among the great geopolitical fault lines of history. The word *krajina* means "the frontier" and it has been the stage for many battles over the centuries, as the great empires of the West and the East confronted each other.

The first state of Croatia emerged in the tenth century from a scattering of tribes clinging to the Adriatic coast and the broad Pannonian Plains of the interior. Their land became the Croatian Kingdom, governed by Roman Catholic Slavs. Over time, modern Croatia emerged as two long, thin limbs of territory that hug the landlocked state of Bosnia in a firm—at times strangling—embrace.

In the fourteenth century the dark shadow of the Ottoman Empire fell across the Balkans. Hungarians, Bulgarians, Serbs and Bosnians all collapsed before the advancing Turks. In the late fifteenth century, disaster struck. In one of the odd coincidences of history, it fell on September 9, 1493—the exact date on which, five hundred years later, Rod Dearing stared down into the Krajina battleground.

On that day in 1493, the battle of Krbavsko Polje rumbled across a wide field on the Lika Highlands, twenty kilometres to the northeast of Dearing's bunker. The entire Croatian nobility was all but wiped out in that single encounter, and with it went the last hope of any indigenous Croatian leadership for several more generations. It is tempting to think that the Croats of 1993 chose the date to commemorate that decisive event, but no written record or even any chance remark supports that conclusion— perhaps it was the ghosts of Croatian nobility themselves that inspired the Croatian generals to go on the offensive on that day.

The Ottomans swept through Croatia from 1493 until well into the 1600s, looting houses and churches, murdering tens of thousands of peasants and laying waste to the entire country. The Croatian way of life, with its Slavic customs and Roman Catholic faith, would not recover for centuries. But the Ottomans inadvertently set the stage for the formation of a fierce military, which developed gradually over the next two centuries. The Croatian territory became a crucial bulwark behind which the mighty Hapsburg family assembled its European empire: the power that would ultimately block and drive back the Ottomans.

The Hapsburg Empire, at war with the Ottomans across the continent, established a series of forts and military outposts along the Croatian border with Turkish-held Bosnia, which eventually became garrisons. The Lika Highlands formed a critical part of this fortified front line, called the Vojna Krajina (the military frontier). There was no commerce or business allowed, no serfs or peasants—only an industry of defence and a population of soldiers.

For the Hapsburgs, the tribal history of the region was of little interest and no consequence. They wanted the Krajina settled and defended by people of bellicose disposition and proven skill at arms. One particularly warlike tribe, called the Vlachs, was especially welcome. They were Orthodox Christians, ancestors of the modern Serbs, and over time they would earn considerable autonomy from both the Hapsburg governors in Vienna and the feudal lords of Croatia. Eventually, they laid claim to the Krajina as their homeland. It was that claim the Patricias were now caught in.

Whether the Canadians knew it or not, a long arm reached out of the Middle Ages and into the hills of the Lika Highlands and shook Rod Dearing and the others from their slumber on the morning of September 9, 1993.

* * *

Rudy Bajema had been keeping track on the calendar. They were only weeks from returning home, but now he wondered if he was going to die here with his platoon in Medak House before he got there. Bajema had been on peacekeeping duties in Croatia for nearly a year. After his first six-month rotation he had decided to return for another round because he and his wife had separated. He really had nothing to go back to, and in these final weeks his courage had been running low. Now all at once he was riding the biggest adrenaline rush he'd had since he arrived, along with all the other Canadians inside their makeshift barracks.

The platoon quarters were on the lip of the tiny village of Medak on the Serbian side of the front line, and close to a dozen of the hamlets sprinkled throughout the area. In keeping with the martial traditions of the Krajina, the villages were tucked away, connected by roads and paths that only the villagers could properly navigate.

The Medak Pocket region was a strategic enclave on the border of the territory that the Serbs of Croatia had claimed as their own separate country, calling it the Republic of Serbian Krajina. "Pocket" is a military term, referring to a salient, or bulge, in a line. The Medak bulge thrust the Serbian front line deeper into Croatian-held territory than elsewhere and it gave Serbian soldiers a convenient position for launching attacks on the Croatian military headquarters in the nearby town of Gospic.

The Pocket was a major irritant for the Croats. The Serbian villagers of the region for their part were particularly vulnerable to counter-offensives from Gospic. Firing back and forth had been a regular feature of life and death in the region since the so-called ceasefire had been signed. The only thing that now protected the Serbian civilians from being completely overrun by the Croats was the tenuous moral authority of the international community. Now that authority was seriously under attack.

* * *

Lieutenant Tyrone Green was in charge of the soldiers in Medak House. He had been appointed commander of Charlie Company's Nine Platoon just for this mission—an unusual distinction, since Green was a reservist from the Seaforth

Highlanders of Vancouver on loan to the Patricias. He had ordered his men to build sandbag walls as soon as they arrived on the first day of September. But they hadn't completed the fortifications. On the morning of September 9, as they ducked shells, he knew their defences weren't going to be enough.

Since the mortar barrage began, Green had new orders: the platoon was to hunker down, observe and not fire back unless fired upon. That might be difficult. If they were to hold the position, they would need more sandbagging and a lot of luck. During lulls in the shelling, the soldiers struggled to reinforce the walls and to remove the glass from the windows. Green privately wondered just how long this could last.

Corporal Glen Peters scribbled little notes in a diary he kept: "Major Croat offensive. Built up walls. Kissed the ground. Four hundred rounds fell in our area, as close as twenty-five metres."

Peters was a twenty-one-year-old reservist from the Princess Louise Fusiliers out of Halifax. He became an infantryman when a heart defect scuttled his lifelong dream of joining the air force. His parents had been nervous about this mission to Croatia but they didn't stand in the way when he left his studies in social sciences at St. Mary's University and departed with the Patricias. Over half of the battalion were from the reserves—the highest militia deployment for Canada since the Korean War. The Canadian Forces were operating at maximum capacity in the early 1990s. There were no more regular soldiers to send on the many peacekeeping missions that had mushroomed around the world. The reservists—weekend warriors— had to fill the ranks.

Now Peters, the student from Halifax, was among the young soldiers in Medak House watching in horror as civilians of the region streamed down the road past them, following the retreating remnants of the Serbian army. The Serbs had piled all their belongings into wagons, tractors and the trunks of old cars. The soldiers escaping with them were poorly equipped, decked out in unmatched bits of camouflage clothing and carrying their AK47 assault rifles (the paramilitary weapon of choice) over their shoulders as they rode out on trailers pulled by trucks. They were injured, dispirited and clearly outgunned. The tanks, personnel carriers and weapons they had were relics of the once mighty Warsaw Pact.

But the most astonishing moment of the day for Peters was not the shellfire and the refugees, but the surprise arrival of a local woman who had been coming daily to make lunch for the platoon. During one deafening barrage, Peters and his companions looked up from the floor and through the dust they saw her standing there. *"Dobar Dan!"* she greeted them, sunnily, as she reported for her lunch detail. Peters thought she must be crazy, but a more likely explanation is that she so badly needed the cash the Canadians gave her that she was willing to face death for it.

* * *

Two hundred kilometres to the north, in the Croatian capital of Zagreb, another battle was going on, a war of words. Diplomats from Europe, the United States and the United Nations had been urgently dispatched to find out exactly what the Croatian president Franjo Tudjman was up to. The international community had assumed that the Croatian war was under control and that things would be quiet now that the UN peacekeeping force had been deployed. But a major offensive was underway in Medak Pocket, and they wanted to know why.

The president deferred the inquiries to his chief of defence, the portly General Janko Bobetko. Bobetko was a fierce Croatian patriot, but unlike some of the country's more ardent nationalists, he'd fought with the partisans against the fascist regime that had ruled Croatia during the Second World War, and he had supported Tito. His military credentials were impeccable, at least from a Croatian point of view.

The international diplomats and UN bureaucrats implored the general to stop his offensive into Medak, but he refused, claiming with a straight face that Croats were shooting only in self-defence. The international delegation in Zagreb had received eyewitness reports from Rod Dearing and his section of soldiers and from Tyrone Green in Medak House that challenged Bobetko's version, but the general wouldn't budge. He knew what he knew, even if it was a lie. Croatian military leaders had grown tired of diplomats. And they were even more fed up with pesky peacekeepers whose mission kept getting in the way of their national aspirations and destiny.

***

Bobetko's troops had attacked the Pocket with artillery for half of the day. Then Croatia's infamous special forces under the merciless General Mladen Markac began a classic pincer movement down from the Velebit foothills. The big guns fell silent as the Croatian infantry, with its tanks, worked its way into the territory during the afternoon, meeting very little resistance. General Markac's units had spent a year in those mountains, waiting for this moment, and his forces knew the geography well. Bobetko declared, "We were in a position to not only pound Medak but to totally break it up." What Bobetko never admitted, but what every Croatian soldier throughout the ranks knew, was that the objective of the action was not just to eliminate the military bulge in the front line and retake territory that belonged to Croatia. It was to kill or drive out the people who lived in it. The operation was classic ethnic cleansing.

***

Major Bryan Bailey feared for the lives of his troops. He had prepared the soldiers of Charlie Company himself, and he knew that even the reservists, who had sometimes seemed so hopeless during the exercise drills back home, were now more accustomed to shelling than most seasoned Canadian soldiers. But Bailey couldn't make sense of what the Croats' objectives were.

In many respects, he was an unlikely commander. Bookish, introspective and soft-spoken, he talked to his men and would listen attentively to the opinion of even the lowest-ranking soldier in his company. But a passion for competitive shooting had lured him into the army at a tender age and, at thirty-one, he was very young to be commanding a company. Bailey was on his second rotation in Croatia, which suited him: it was good for his career, and besides, he was curious about the region. Bailey loved to travel, especially to places as steeped in history as Croatia. But it wasn't going down well domestically; his wife was expecting their third child and she wanted him home.

Bailey's main concern was for the thirty-six soldiers of Charlie Company's Nine Platoon in Medak House. The Croats were poised to take the town of Medak, and Bailey knew their tanks could come rumbling into the village any time now and roll right over his men. He ordered Nine Platoon to double their anti-tank teams with Carl Gustav rocket launchers and patrol the area during lulls in the mortar attacks. But he realized how thin their ranks were. If the Croats really came after them, they had neither the manpower nor the firepower to defend themselves. Rod Dearing and Eight Platoon up in the hills were keeping Bailey informed as best they could. But their lookout was high up in Serbian territory, too far from the Croatian side for them to discern the shape and size of the battle plan.

Bailey had spent days driving the hills in his Iltis jeep, getting to know the landscape and seeing what the Serbian soldiers in his area of responsibility had in the way of arms. But he didn't know anything about the Croats in his area. They had made themselves inaccessible, refusing to meet him and not allowing him anywhere near their headquarters in Gospic. Now he was starting to realize why the Croats had been so uncooperative. They had been planning and preparing for this attack.

Late in the afternoon on the ninth of September, Bailey was attempting to drive the short distance from the platoon house to the Serb brigade headquarters when a tank appeared before him with its gun barrel swivelling his way. He froze. Bailey had no idea whose tank it was. Both sides used the same equipment; only the markings were different. This could easily be a Croat machine, and if so it was the end of him—and possibly the end of Medak.

He gambled. Leaping from the jeep he started shouting the names of Serb commanders that he knew. He was lucky. A Serb officer emerged from the tank and after listening to him babble for a moment, let him through. He drove on, nerves jangling and intestines threatening to turn his lunch to liquid.

Bailey met with the Serb brigade commander under a barrage of shellfire: "He was either extraordinarily brave or extraordinarily used to what was going on. A round would come in, you would hear it and you knew it was going to be close. And I would drop to the ground and he wouldn't." Eventually Bailey convinced the battle-hardened officer that it would be a smart move to at least conduct the conversation on the lee side of the building.

* * *

As daylight failed on September 9, the United Nations forces learned that local villages were falling one by one into Croat hands. First Divoselo, a village whose population had produced seven Serbian generals and where the heartbeat of Serbian nationalist aspirations in the Krajina had ticked for centuries— or so the Croats believed. The next village to fall was Licki Citluk, right next door, a village Bryan Bailey had visited only a week before. The two hamlets were draped down the side of the Velebit foothills, within shelling range of Gospic. They were also less than ten kilometres away from Medak. General Markac's tanks and infantry soldiers were coming nearer. The Patricias would soon have to decide whether to run or fight. But they were supposed to be peacekeepers. What were the rules? It wasn't at all clear what the world expected of them.

* * *

As the man in charge of the Canadians, Lieutenant Colonel Jim Calvin wanted very much to impress his UN commanders in the field. Calvin is a small but compact man with a large temper and an aggressive command style. A prominent vein in the middle of his brow becomes more pronounced—to the alarm of his men—when he is under a lot of stress. Today, it seemed the vein might pop.

Calvin had a lot to prove. He had taken a ragtag group of soldiers from a total of sixty-six different regular and reserve units from all over Canada and transformed them into a unified battle group. The Second Battalion of the Princess Patricia's Canadian Light Infantry had a reputation for fierceness, augmented by the fact that they garrisoned and trained in the uncompromising cold of the Manitoba winter. Calvin was from Oshawa, Ontario, and his soldiers were from all over the map of Canada, but somehow, regional distinctions were folded into a single personality, that of the Patricias' tradition. Never say die. Never surrender a weapon. Whining is disgraceful. Follow orders—no matter how fraught with peril. These rules of conduct were the battalion's pride and Calvin wanted the senior leadership of the UN to see what they were made of.

He was prepared to lead his 860 soldiers wherever he was told they were needed. But on September 9, 1993, they were exhausted and only weeks from going home. Calvin had just moved the soldiers into the Krajina and the battle group was spread out over twenty-five hundred square kilometres.

General Jean Cot, the no-nonsense French officer who was the commander of the United Nations Protection Force for the former Yugoslavia (UNPROFOR), had singled out Calvin and his Canadian soldiers to be his SWAT team, the only contingent of peacekeepers he claimed he could rely on. And now was the time to call on them. Cot's recommendation would have been more of a compliment if the other national contingents under his command in Croatia hadn't been pathetic. His own French countrymen were in Croatia and Bosnia in large numbers and they had considerable skills. But they were mostly listless and unmotivated conscripts and their officers openly defied orders to do something about it. Cot couldn't persuade them to stand up to the Serbs and Croats who, for their part, spent almost as much energy trying to get rid of the peacekeepers as they spent trying to get rid of each other.

The war had reignited like a prairie grass fire, and it was breaking out all over the very combustible Krajina. The UN in New York City and the international diplomats in Zagreb were worried that Bobetko's operation would wreck the entire UN mission in the Balkans. Cot was desperate, and he thought the Canadians might be willing, or crazy enough, to take on an assignment that no other contingent wanted to touch. Colonel Calvin looked as if he might be the kind of gung-ho soldier who could save the Krajina, the UN mission and Cot's reputation, all at the same time.

By the end of the day on September 9, 1993, hundreds of shells were falling on the Canadian soldiers in the Medak Pocket. The civilians in the region were fleeing for their lives, just ahead of the infantry attack. Croat soldiers had moved in following the artillery barrage to begin the widespread extermination of any civilians left in the area—a zone that was supposed to be under UN protection. Colonel Calvin and his troops were about to be confronted by an exercise in ethnic cleansing. Would they risk their lives to stop it? Or would they run away?

CHAPTER ONE

HOMELAND CALLING

What happens to a dream deferred?

Does it dry up
like a raisin in the sun
Or fester like a sore—
and then run? . . .

Or does it explode?

—Langston Hughes, "Harlem: A Dream Deferred"

IN THE CENTRE OF ZAGREB is a large, sweeping, open square, a space of elegant flagstones with a fountain. Trg Jelacica (Jelacic Square) is the hub of the Croatian capital. If you arrange to meet someone in Zagreb, chances are it will be here, at one of the bright, Viennese-style cafés. If you have business elsewhere in Zagreb, you can always get back to Jelacic; a half-dozen of the city's tram routes pass the square. People throng the space every day, meeting friends and lovers or buying flowers from market stalls, but on special occasions commemorating the great events of Croatian solidarity, the normally crowded pavement is packed with thousands more people.

The square's centrepiece is a giant statue. A bronze figure on horseback in full-dress uniform, with an eagle feather stuck in his jaunty hat, is poised to charge into battle. His sword is at the ready; his look is determined. This is Josip Jelacic—among the greatest folk heroes of Croatia and the man who perhaps best symbolizes Croatian nationalist aspirations. Ban (Governor) Jelacic promised the Croats he would lead them from their centuries of dark feudalism into autonomy and nationhood. And though by the time of his death in 1859 Croatia had actually sunk deeper into imperial bondage, Jelacic helped to inspire Croats to believe they could become a nation.

He is a worthy hero—unassuming and sincere, though not very bright and certainly lacking the Machiavellian sophistication it would have taken to wring concessions from Croatia's rulers—an autocratic and self-interested series of Austrians and Hungarians who controlled the country's destiny for centuries. Jelacic embraced a Croatian nationalism that did not exclude its minorities, not even the Croatian Serbs.

Before he was lured into national politics, Jelacic was a soldier. He was the seasoned commander of the Austrian-backed forces in the Krajina, where, by the nineteenth century, there existed more military culture than actual military purpose. He was unmarried, lived frugally, and was worshipped by his troops, who were both Croat and Serb.

To Jelacic, the sharp, cordite-reeking air of the Krajina was the breath of life itself. He had no interest in the perfumed corridors of the Austrian nobility or in the intrigues of what was then called "Civil" Croatia—a fragmented feudal state whose constituent parts were scattered over the Dalmatian coast and onto the Pannonian Plains and administered separately by outside powers. But a political and cultural revolution was underway in Civil Croatia—part of the sweep of revolutionary ideas through all of Europe in the mid-nineteenth century. Revolutionaries were issuing manifestos, newspapers were available to most people, democratic ideas from France were reaching students and intellectuals all over the European continent. There was a rising cry from southern Europe's burgeoning bourgeoisie and intellectual class for more political autonomy from the great empires. They demanded constitutional governments with laws that were codified and not based on the whims of nobles. The

Croatian rebels wanted an end to serfdom and a new system of universal taxation. But most significantly, they wanted recognition for their newly emerging cultural nationalism. This was the first stirring of the *Volksgeist*—a desire to reorganize states according to ethnicity, language, religion and history. The intellectual elites of Croatia not only shared in these emotions and ideals but were among its leading proponents. The growing middle class yearned impatiently for their own unified national homeland while the poor dreamed of liberation from feudalism.

The House of Hapsburg, based in Vienna, controlled Austria, Bohemia and Hungary, but within those larger entities the Hapsburgs ran the affairs of numerous national and linguistic groups: Croats, Serbs, Slovaks, Germans, Czechs, Magyars, Poles, Slovenes, Romanians and Italians. The *Volksgeist* fever was infecting each and every one of them. The brilliant and cunning foreign minister, Prince Metternich, managed the Hapsburgs' disparate territories with an eye to maintaining a strategic advantage over powerful competing forces in Europe. Not surprisingly, he had deep misgivings about the rise of nationalism and he presciently warned that it would lead to "the war of all against all." But his bureaucratic response to the romantic idealism of the nationalists only fanned the flames of their revolutionary passion.

The Hapsburgs decided to grant many of Croatia's demands, believing Croatia's soft nationalism would provide a counterweight to the Magyar rebels in Hungary and their more insistent campaign for full autonomy. The emperor happily appointed Jelacic, who was after all a loyal guardsman of the Austrian court, to the position of Ban of Croatia and counted on the Croats coming on side if Vienna had to suppress the national aspirations of the Magyars by force.

Though appointed by Vienna, Jelacic was the overwhelming favourite of Croats. When he arrived in Zagreb to take up his new post, he was greeted with joy bordering on hysteria. He rode into the city on a white horse, dressed in the costume of the governor—red and white with silver decorations and eagle feathers in his hat. He took the oath in the square that would later be named after him, surrounded by thousands of his countrymen, all anxious to get a glimpse of their national saviour. Church bells pealed and cannons boomed all day long. A grand outdoor feast with displays of fireworks ended the historical event.

Jelacic took control of the Sabor—Croatia's parliament— and immediately abolished the last remains of feudalism in Croatia, while imposing a tax on the nobility. It was the birth of the modern state that would take Croatia into the twentieth century. The Triune Kingdom was established, answerable to the Sabor, and the Krajina became an integral part of Civil Croatia. For the first time in its history, members of the government spoke Croatian in their own parliament. They had achieved their sovereignty-association.

By mid-summer 1848, Jelacic had given himself dictatorial powers and declared war on Hungary, to the enthusiastic cheers of his fellow Croats and the only slightly better concealed relief of Vienna. Jelacic was back in his element as a warrior chief. He led his Krajina army into Hungary, crossing the Drava River before dawn on September 11, 1848. The campaign was officially supported by the Hapsburg emperor and it was well supplied. But to the Hapsburgs, Jelacic's army was a disappointment. The Krajina warriors were impatient fighters with a hit-and-run military style, whose only field of operations had been the rugged frontier. Ultimately the Hungarian rebellion was subdued by a massive mobilization of over 100,000 Russian troops.

The Hapsburgs had never been fond of nationalists, and now, having supressed the Magyar uprising, the empire cracked down. Five hundred Hungarian rebel leaders were executed, then steps were taken to quell the nascent nationalist movements in all the other Hapsburg territories, including Croatia. A new emperor, the teenaged Franz Josef, had taken over the Austro-Hungarian Empire. His career would begin in turmoil and end in an even greater crisis with his nephew's assassination in 1914. Within a year, Franz Josef and his henchman Alexander Bach reversed the reforms the previous emperor, Ferdinand, had con-

sented to in Croatia, with the exception of the abolition of feudalism. Eliminating feudalism had marginalized a corrupt local
nobility; in the new system all tithes and taxes went directly to
Austria.

By 1850, Croatia had less autonomy than before its national-
ist movement started. The Sabor was stripped of its power over
Croatian political life except for a few areas in education.
Pleading by Jelacic—who had been ceremoniously decorated by
Franz Josef while the court mocked him behind his back—failed
to restore the modest Croatian autonomy they had gained.
Instead of living out a long life in a new nation called Croatia,
Jelacic despaired, and died less than a decade later, in 1859, not
yet sixty years old. His despondent figure would come to symbolize Croatia's stillborn dreams. When he died, Croatians immediately planned a gesture to at least symbolize those aspirations: a
majestic statue to adorn the newly christened Jelacic Square.
There was a strong feeling that a local artist should create the
work, but typically for Croatia's paradoxical nationalism, the
commission went to a famous sculptor in Vienna.

**

Winston Churchill once described the Balkans as a region that
produced more history than it could consume. The word *balka-
nize* long ago entered the English language to describe the kind
of political fragmentation that generates mutual animosity and
destructiveness.

Any attempt to draw a clean narrative line through the last
few centuries of Balkan history would have to distort the facts.
The dense tangles of overlapping and scattered cultures in the
region, complicated still further by overgrown thickets of imperial ambition and conquest, have turned Croatia and its neighbours into enigmas whose political objectives are, more often
than not, inscrutable to outsiders.

But starting in the nineteenth century and continuing
through two world wars, a socialist revolution and a bloody struggle

for nationhood, there is a clear line of purpose one can draw through Balkan reality: a rising ethnic Slav awareness. It sometimes pulled the disparate people of the region and their histories together and at other times set them against each other in horrible battles. And it would repeatedly suck the outside world into its centre of gravity.

* * *

When the Krajina became an integral part of Croatia in the late nineteenth century, the official Serbian population of Croatia increased sharply. This was not, in itself, a problem since Croatian Serbs did not see their dual identities as a conflict. But Serbia's own self-consciousness was growing and the ultra-nationalist parties there began to appeal to the Serbian minority of Croatia to regard much of Croatia as part of the neighbouring state of Serbia. Wherever Serbs lived was Serb land. There were many who claimed Croats were really Serbs.

Hard-line Serbs, who were becoming increasingly powerful in Belgrade, dreamed of a Greater Serbia that would assimilate most of the Slavic national communities. Any discussion of a pan-Slavic state or "Yugoslavia" had appeal to Serbian nationalists only if it was understood that all of its citizens would be Serbians first, regarding their other allegiances as provincial, not national. Incendiary Serbian newspaper articles published in Zagreb argued that Croatia wasn't really a country at all and that the Croat language was actually Serbian.

Serbia's ambition to create one large state out of all the lands where Serbs lived was alarming not only to the smaller nations whose territory would be annexed but also to the Austro-Hungarians, since Serbs lived almost everywhere in the empire. Tensions between Serbia and Vienna continued to build as Serbia successfully expanded into Albania and Bulgaria, managing to double its territory in the process.

But Serbia's activities would explode in 1914, in one violent moment that would prove fatal for two of the three empires then dividing Europe and much of Asia. In June of that year a young Bosnian Serb by the name of Gavrilo Princip, acting with the full knowledge and support of Serbia, went into the streets of Sarajevo and shot the heir apparent to the Austro-Hungarian throne, Archduke Franz Ferdinand. Princip was a member of a secret Serbian society that called itself "Union or Death," and his weapons had been supplied by the chief of Serbian military intelligence.

As the Austro-Hungarian Empire prepared for war with Serbia, the Roman Catholic priests and bishops of Croatia and Bosnia-Herzegovina, who were loyal to the Austrian emperor, denounced the Serbs. Mobs in the streets of Zagreb destroyed Serbian shops. The differences between Serbs and Croats, until then only a matter of religion and the written language (Serbs use the Cyrillic alphabet, Croats the Roman) were fast flaring up into a dangerous and permanent conflagration, stoked in large part by the Catholic Church.

When Austria declared war on Serbia the leaders of all the major nations of Europe and the West made dire and dreadful predictions: it would be a horrible disaster, a war unlike any in human history. They were right. Russia, Germany, France, Great Britain and its commonwealth and ultimately the United States became players in a conflict that would lead to the redrawing of the map of Europe and the destruction of the lives of millions. It would also set in motion the geopolitical forces that would lead to a second world war, and to scores of minor conflicts that during the ensuing century would claim the lives of more than 200 million human beings.

* * *

Long before the First World War was over, a delegation of Croats from Dalmatia began travelling the world, lobbying for support for a project to be called Yugoslavia. They wanted a union of Croatia, Serbia and Slovenia, in which each state would be an equal partner.

Almost a half million Croats had emigrated to the United States and Canada, escaping poverty and war. The Yugoslav Committee was the first to appeal to the diaspora of Croats, a vast resource that future Croatian leaders would call upon to great effect. A large part of the diaspora lived in the United States, and Croats believed Washington, considering the American tradition of republicanism and rebellion, could be persuaded to adopt their cause and help them forge a nation. It was a fatal miscalculation and one that led the Croats to make further false steps.

In the early twentieth century, two distinctive strands of Croatian nationalism emerged: one emphasized similarities among the Slavs and advocated the union of South Slavs into a single entity: Yugoslavia. The other strain of nationalism pursued a separatist goal: an independent Croatia, though still associated with the Hapsburg Empire. A union of Croats, Serbs and Slovenians was an idea that had been around for a long time. It was the flower of the pan-Slavic nationalism of Jelacic and his followers in the nineteenth century. But there was always the tug in the opposite direction: the consciousness of difference, the suspicion of the other. Slovenes spoke their own language, but they were Roman Catholics, like the Croats. Serbs and Croats spoke the same language, but they were not of the same faith and they used a different alphabet. How could the three possibly find common purpose, common history or a common poetry?

Among Serbian politicians, the differences were more pronounced. Hard-liners of the Serbian National Radical Party didn't care about Croats and Slovenes but only about the Serbs who lived in those territories. Any union of South Slavs would have to serve Serbian self-interest; no concessions or compromises would be made. They had suffered extraordinary losses in Balkan wars over the centuries and those defeats had hardened Serbian resolve into a kind of victim culture. Serbs believed, essentially, that the world was full of their enemies.

Croatia had a less fraught past, though it too was certainly shaped by successive wars. Croats had originated the idea of a federal Yugoslavia, even though many chauvinistic Croats regarded Serbs as primitives conditioned to look eastward toward Byzantium. Croats, especially those from Dalmatia, had enjoyed centuries of arts and sciences from the West, particularly the Italian peninsula, and they thought themselves more cosmopolitan than the Orthodox Slavs.

But such differences were mostly superficial and (contrary to much current writing on the subject) there was not a deep antagonism between most Serbs and Croats. In the aftermath of the First World War, the idea that they could find common ground was attractive to many South Slavs. And there was an assumption that representatives of the world powers—especially the United States president Woodrow Wilson—would endeavour to make it work. They were dead wrong.

The players who would determine Croatia's future began to emerge after the First World War, and the stage was being set for the major events of the twentieth century. These events would have less to do with the dreams of ethnic nationalists than with the rigorous ideology of two Germans—Marx and Engels—and their *Communist Manifesto*. It was during the 1920s that the Communist Party of Yugoslavia first appeared, with its charismatic leader, Josip Broz, soon to be better known as Tito.

The seventh son of Croatian peasants, Tito had been an officer in the Austrian army during the First World War. He was captured by the Russians in 1915 and came under the influence of the Bolshevik Revolution. He eventually joined the Red Army. Tito returned to Croatia in the 1920s where he was eventually picked by Moscow to lead the Communists of Yugoslavia.

The Communists debated whether they wanted a truly federal Yugoslavia or a larger union of Balkan states, but they were more distracted by the appearance of a new enemy, one destined to become a deadly threat to both the Communists and the Serbian-controlled Kingdom: fascism.

An agitator named Ante Pavelic founded a movement inspired by Italian fascism and dedicated to the violent overthrow of the

Yugoslav state. It was called the "Ustashe," meaning uprising. It would introduce a new strain of virulent ultra-nationalism in Croatia, and set the stage for further political violence.

* * *

Ante Pavelic was born in Bosnia-Herzegovina, but he had a sentimental, folkloric attachment to the Lika Highlands of Croatia, his parents' birthplace. His extreme right-wing politics came from the Italian dictator Mussolini and the aims of his Ustashe rebels were "to liberate Croatia from alien rule and to establish a completely free and independent state over the whole of its national and historical territory." These objectives were to be achieved by whatever means necessary.

While Pavelic's ambitions were for Croatia, he drew much if not most of his support from outside of Croatia, in the Bosnian region of Herzegovina, where large numbers of Croats had settled before the final borders of Croatia had been established.

Herzegovina is an inhospitable region of glaring limestone cliffs and barren soil. It is one of the poorest areas of the Balkans, robbed and brutalized by successive generations of insatiable nobility. The Croat population in Herzegovina is said to be more "Croatian" than they are in Croatia, a product of their isolation from the homeland. At the time of Pavelic's rise to prominence, an extreme ethnic nationalism had infected the area.

Pavelic fled to exile in Italy after Yugoslavia's King Aleksander banned all political parties. Mussolini allowed him to set up training camps for Ustashe cells. Pavelic sent agents provocateurs to help create anti-Serb disturbances in Croatia — including the Lika Uprising of 1932. In 1934, working with Macedonian extremists, he arranged the assassination of King Aleksander, whose laws had sent him into exile in Italy. Ustashe terror was well established long before the outbreak of the Second World War — as was the framework of its adversary, Communism.

The two Croats, Tito and Pavelic, were steeped in entirely different political visions. They embodied the deep contradiction of Croatian aspirations: to be part of something larger while longing for the tribe. Each offered an extreme solution to the troubling problem of identity in Croatia. The fact that they hated each other—and that their followers even more passionately hated each other—is part of the foundation on which modern Croatian history is built.

* * *

Though Yugoslavia declared itself neutral in 1939 at the beginning of the Second World War, German troops entered Zagreb on April 10, 1941 and established the Independent State of Croatia. Ante Pavelic returned from exile to become the equivalent of Croatia's führer, head of Hitler's puppet regime on Croatian soil. Pavelic began with only a few hundred supporters, but the Independent State of Croatia became an extension of Hitler's war machine. The only policy that distinguished it from the Third Reich was the ferocity of its campaign to exterminate Croatia's Serbs as well as its Jews.

Herzegovina's inhabitants supported Pavelic and the Ustashe, and with Hitler's agents planting the perverse values of the European Fascists in the Balkans, the Simon Wiesenthal Centre estimates that the Ustashe killed 30,000 Jews, 29,000 Romas and 600,000 Serbs over four years. The Ustashe's education minister stated that the goal of the Croatian government regarding Serbs was to convert one-third, expel one-third and kill the rest. At the Nuremberg trials the Ustashe slaughter of Serbs was spoken of as genocide. The savagery was enough to make even the Nazis cringe: the Germans called the Ustashe attack on Serbs "the peak of abomination."

The Serbs who managed to escape the pogroms had moved into the hills of the Krajina, where they rekindled the fighting tradition of their frontier ancestors. Large numbers of the Krajina fighters joined Tito's Partisans, the Communist-led anti-Nazi campaign conducted out of Belgrade. But other Serbs in the region had different plans. Called Chetniks, they were Serb nationalists and fiercely loyal to the Serbian royal family. The name Chetnik had first surfaced in the nineteenth century to describe the Serbian guerrilla units who fought the Ottoman Empire.

The two distinct Serbian organizations in Croatia—the Partisans and the Chetniks—initially worked together to resist the Pavelic regime. But they eventually turned on each other, engaging in a vicious civil war even as they were still fighting the German occupiers and their henchmen. The conflict within a conflict was even bloodier and it revealed the central schism of Serbian identity, just as Tito and Pavelic revealed the schism of Croatian identity.

The civil war thwarted efforts by Yugoslavia's allies to get a foothold in the Balkans. Under Winston Churchill, the British government had high hopes for the Chetnik forces in Yugoslavia: they were anti-Communist, anti-Nazi, and they supported the Yugoslav royal family. But in 1943, Churchill began having doubts about the anti-Nazi convictions of the Chetniks when they formed an alliance with the Italian forces occupying southern Croatia. Eventually, Britain learned, the Chetniks had also started making deals with the Germans.

Meanwhile, the zeal and fighting skills of Tito's Partisans continued to impress the pragmatic Churchill. Tito wasn't much of a military strategist, but he'd been able to inspire and unite by far the largest part of the Balkan resistance movement.

Croatia had the most cohesive force of Partisans in Yugoslavia; it was largely made up of Serbs who were deeply motivated by the genocidal attacks on their population and by a loathing of the Chetniks. Nazi-occupied Croatia had eighteen brigades; there were four in Lika alone.

In the spring of 1943, Britain sent Petar Erdeljac, Pavle Pavlovic and Aleksander Simic, Serbo-Croatian–speaking Canadian soldiers, into the Partisan heartland of Lika to make the first Allied intelligence contact with Tito's fighting force. Their reports established, once and for all, that for the Allies the Partisans were the one truly reliable liberation movement in Yugoslavia. In September, the famous British commando, Fitzroy Maclean, made contact with Tito himself to form an alliance. The Canadians thus laid the groundwork for power to move into Tito's hands when, after the war, another Yugoslavia rose from the ashes.

This new state was united under Communism, with Marshal Tito at the helm. The second Yugoslav state more closely resembled the pan-Slavic ideal that early Croatian nationalists had envisioned: it included Serbia, Croatia, Bosnia-Herzegovina, Slovenia, Macedonia and Montenegro. Each republic was to have equal power in a rotating presidency.

Throughout the 1950s, Tito's agents worked to reinforce the legitimacy of the new Yugoslavian state by crushing any residual nationalist aspirations. In Zagreb, Tito ordered the statue of Jelacic removed, and the square was renamed Republican Square. The bronze statue was stored, out of sight, in a government building and then was dismantled and hidden away in pieces in various basements. Croatia was finally part of a union of South Slavs but the price had been high: Croats had to give up their identity as Croats.

As Tito organized the apparatus of power, he sought out loyalists with impeccable party credentials to be his leaders. Among them was an ambitious young man born in Tito's home village. His father had been the local leader of the Croatian Peasants' Party in rural Croatia, and Franjo Tudjman had been steeped in left-wing politics since childhood. He was not yet out of his teens when he joined the Communist underground and helped to publish a Partisan newspaper. He eventually rose through the ranks to become Tito's youngest and best-educated general. He was eventually appointed a commissar in the liberated territories of eastern Croatia, near Bosnia. It was a bureaucratic post, but nonetheless one that clearly illustrated how much Tito trusted him.

Tudjman found himself near Herzegovina, the Ustashe heartland. In the immediate post-war period, large numbers of Croats were fleeing into the hills or escaping abroad to Canada and the United States. These were the supporters of the extreme ethnic nationalism of Ante Pavelic.

In one small Herzegovinian town, Siroki Brijeg, the passionate hatred of Serbs, Jews and Romas burned with special intensity: the place is of historical note for the number of Ustashe leaders it produced. Andrija Artukovic, who had personally ordered the execution of the town's Serbs, was educated, along with other Ustashe organizers, at the large Franciscan monastery in town. Artukovic acquired enormous power as right-hand man to the Ustashe leader, Pavelic. The town of Siroki Brijeg was so loathed as a fascist symbol that the Communists changed the town's name to Listica, and shut down the monastery.

The Herzegovina Croats detested Tito, but they also feared him, and with good reason. After the war, the Partisans killed an estimated 250,000 people in concentration camps, death marches and summary executions because they were seen to be enemies of the newly constituted Communist republic of Yugoslavia.

In one infamous episode, fleeing Ustashe veterans, along with some German soldiers and civilians—more than 100,000 in all—were turned back from Bleiberg at the Austrian border by British forces, and delivered into the hands of Tito's Partisans. Many were murdered on the spot; others perished in captivity or on forced marches the Croats called the "Way of The Cross," after a Roman Catholic religious ritual commemorating the passage of Christ through Jerusalem on his way to Calvary and crucifixion.

According to some estimates, as much as three-quarters of the population of Herzegovina fled to other countries in the post-war years. Large numbers of them made their way to North America. The Ustashe leadership took advantage of the "rat-lines" (underground escape routes) organized by sympathizers, to escape to Argentina along with such notorious Nazis as Adolf

Eichmann and Klaus Barbie. Eventually, a number of the Croat Ustashe settled in the United States and Canada, blending in with the waves of Croatian immigrants arriving in the post-war years. Far from fading into obscurity, the ultra-nationalists regrouped in the new world and began plotting their eventual return to Croatia. They would resume working on the Croatia that Ante Pavelic had dreamed about.

In 1945, as the fascists fled Yugoslavia, a child was born in Siroki Brijeg who would one day help lead the extremist movement back to Croatia. His name was Gojko Susak and he would be instrumental in transforming that same Franjo Tudjman into the father of the long-dreamed of independent state of Croatia.

* * *

In the 1960s and '70s, intellectuals in the capital cities of Yugoslavia's republics began once again to have national identity crises. Yugoslavs had prospered economically under Tito's dictatorship and many were convinced that the repression of national identities was necessary in order to end the cycles of violence and create a united front. Only that, they believed, would prevent the post-war superpowers of the West from overrunning them. But they also hoped they could continue to have their national identities and still be part of a successful union of South Slavs. Their aspirations were no different from those of many nationalist leaders of the nineteenth century who wanted autonomy but within a strong union.

In rural Yugoslavia, nationalism was also intense, but far more raw and xenophobic than the intellectual version of the urban centres. In the villages and farm communities of Yugoslavia, children grew up in households where grandmothers told horror stories of finding family members hanging from trees during the war, or watching their fathers force-marched away to death camps. These were not the wholesome stories Tito would have preferred: his national slogan was "brotherhood and unity."

The appalling slaughter of Serbs under the Ustashe, following centuries of war, had overwhelmed Serbian consciousness in a way that Tito could never reverse. Croats had not suffered loss on the same scale, with the exception of the horrific Bleiberg massacre after the Second World War, but they too had their legends of struggle and injustice. It was, perhaps, too much to expect that in a few short decades people would be able to set such tragic national identities aside.

Tito had decided, as soon as he took power, that the only way to ensure that ethnic and religious differences didn't overwhelm the state with divisive emotions was to punish any display of them. Western governments had hoped Yugoslavia would live up to its promise to be a democracy. And Tito did satisfy many of their concerns. He was able to separate Yugoslavia from the Soviet bloc and to avoid the excesses of Stalinism. But Tito's Slav union could only succeed, he believed, if he crushed all internal dissent.

Tito had thousands of nationalist leaders jailed in the 1970s, including a group of Croat moderates who were part of a movement called Croatian Spring. Borrowing the name from the (temporarily) successful Prague Spring in Czechoslovakia, these Croats lobbied for a Croatian autonomy that they claimed would not be in conflict with the country's socialist values. They wanted to stay in Yugoslavia, an economically viable, relatively luxurious socialist state with a powerful army, universal education, health care and the most open media of all of socialist Europe.

Croatian Spring was the secular, intellectual nationalism that might have kept the more poisonous, and mostly rural, version in check. But Tito rejected it all, repressing moderates and extremists with equal vigour. Prominent among those arrested and imprisoned was Franjo Tudjman. He had become a historian and outspoken nationalist, but Tito blocked his message, breaking up any organization within which Tudjman might have encouraged dissent.

Beyond the reach of Tito's police and censors, however, a more virulent strain of Croatian nationalism was actually growing stronger. This was the extremist nationalism of the diaspora.

*∗∗

There are very few statistics on early emigration from Croatia, since most who left stated they were from Austro-Hungary or the short-lived Kingdom of Yugoslavia, but it is safe to say that over the twentieth century, Croats left their homeland by the hundreds of thousands.

From the late nineteenth century until the First World War the immigrants came from the poor villages of rural Croatia. Serfs who had been given ownership of their land by the Hapsburgs often chose to sell their depleted plots and depart. These first migrants were illiterate and itinerant. Some went to Europe and Australia but principally they gravitated to the job-rich areas of North America, where they could easily pass back and forth over the Canada–U.S. border looking for work.

The United States began to limit and control immigration in the 1920s, and subsequent waves of Southern Europeans more typically made their homes in Canada. They settled in the mining communities of northern Ontario, in Timmins and Sudbury, in the sparse farmlands of Saskatchewan and Manitoba and in the logging camps of British Columbia.

If they had any interest in politics at all it was generally in the Croatian Peasants' Party (CPP) founded by Stjepan Radic, the celebrated peasant politician. Radic, who had supported a federation with the Serbs but was assassinated in the Yugoslav parliament for challenging Serbian supremacy was, besides Ban Jelacic, the closest thing Croats had to a national hero. Croats in Winnipeg started a branch of the CPP and it spread across the country.

The other organization Croats joined was the Croatian Fraternal Union, which is actually the oldest Croatian diaspora organization in the world. The CFU began as a support network for workers but became a continent-wide political and cultural organization. Many of the the early Croatian émigrés were miners and forestry workers: they were interested in labour unions and their political organizations in the diaspora tended to be socialist. These Croatian-Canadians had little interest in the political turmoil back home or in the divisive extremism of the Croatian right wing as it developed over the 1930s. They identified themselves as Croats but generally had good relations with the Serbs of North America who spoke the same language.

The next wave of Croatian immigrants was different. Following the defeat of the Axis powers in the Second World War, tens of thousands of Croats poured out of the newly consti-tuted Communist Yugoslavia and headed for any country that would take them. Among these desperate migrants was the entire Ustashe leadership.

Ante Pavelic, who had been Hitler's puppet, comfortably installed himself in Buenos Aires, where he launched the Croatian Liberation Movement (HOP). His friend Maks Luburic, the notorious former director of the Jasenovac concen-tration camp, operated out of Spain, where he was able to estab-lish the Croatian National Resistance movement better known as "Otpor" (meaning resistance). Both HOP and Otpor were supported by the far-flung diaspora.

After Ante Pavelic's death from natural causes and Maks Luburic's brutal assassination (his body was slashed in dozens of places and his head was bashed in with a crowbar) the extreme movements they had founded continued to flourish and even acquired a veneer of legitimacy. Pavelic's son-in-law took over HOP and in 1960 moved its operations from Buenos Aires to Toronto: its newspaper, called *Independent State Croatia*, contin-ued to publish from its new Canadian base, agitating for the down-fall of Communist Yugoslavia. Otpor too eventually set up shop in Toronto, at a meeting hall on Dupont Street. Following the mur-der of Maks Luburic, Otpor members insisted the organization was under new management and had nothing to do with the for-mer Ustashe, but the strident Otpor magazine was filled with the same language as HOP's *Independent State Croatia*. The two movements seemed very much alike, especially when the radical fringes of Otpor began to engage in acts of violence and terrorism.

Membership in both organizations swelled over the post-war decades, thanks mostly to Marshal Tito and his repressive regime back home. Anti-Communist, pro-Church Croats escaped Yugoslavia and arrived on Canadian shores full of the anger and vengefulness of political exiles. Between 1945 and 1971, 120,000 Yugoslavs came to Canada, an estimated two-thirds of whom were Croats. Croatian-born immigrants in Canada soon outnumbered Canadian-born Croats of the previous generation by a ratio of two to one: by the 1980s, between 200,000 and 250,000 people who called themselves ethnic Croats lived in Canada.

The new wave of Croats was more urbane, more ambitious and more politically driven. They took jobs in Canadian cities and built their own successful businesses from the ground up. They moved into vast, sprawling suburbs and accumulated wealth as rapidly as they could. They regrouped in communities with strong Croatian Catholic churches and community centres.

Their continuing identity as Croats was powerful — and much encouraged by the Canadian government. In 1971, Canada declared itself officially multicultural and Ottawa began to offer millions of dollars to ethnic communities in Canada to preserve their immigrant identities, a well-meaning policy that unfortunately exacerbated the problem of the angry émigrés who weren't even trying to fit into the society of their adopted country.

The federal government funded language schools and folklore centres but unbeknownst to them they also paid for publications disseminating the message of the radical right wing. The federal support was naïve and often foolish: city halls in Toronto and Waterloo allowed Croats to fly the flag of the wartime Ustashe's Independent State of Croatia on the anniversary of the defunct state's foundation in 1945.

While most of the new wave of Croats sought the pleasures and comforts of middle-class Canadian life, an activist minority was much more militantly political than past generations of Croatian Canadians. Their anti-Tito, right-wing ideology was at odds with the left-leaning, union-supporting views of the older diaspora. It was the old guard that ultimately lost out: over the years the CPP and the Croatian Fraternal Union slowly disappeared.

***

Among the new wave in Canada was twenty-four-year-old Gojko Susak. The lean, lanky emigré was a bundle of energy and anger, with a permanent scowl on a face hooded by dark, bushy eyebrows. His wife, whom he met at Sunday Mass in Ottawa, said she found him, initially, to be a very strange man. He left Siroki Brijeg as soon as he was old enough to travel and, as with everything about Susak, there are many versions of the story of how he arrived in Canada. The official version—as published in Croatian government propaganda after he became the most powerful minister in the new Croatia—tells of his escape over the Alps into Austria, where he was helped by Franciscan monks to travel secretly to the New World. However, since Yugoslavia freely allowed people to work abroad in the 1960s, it seems more likely that two of Susak's brothers, already in Ottawa, sponsored Gojko to join them.

Susak went to school in Ottawa, and got a diploma in commerce. He washed dishes at a Scott's Chicken Villa on Bank Street and eventually became the co-owner of Tops Pizza, a local restaurant. He and his Canadian partner sold the restaurant in the 1970s for the princely sum of $20,000, according to Susak's official biography, but other sources say it was sold at a loss. Susak went on to work in the construction industry as a house painter (in the mythology, Susak is described as an interior decorator). He bought a new split-level house on Walkley Road, the main artery of a banal strip of new suburbs in Ottawa, and drove an inexpensive car. His neighbours called him Jerry.

Like other Croatian nationalists in Canada, he worked hard to make money but spent most of his spare time on Croatian community work. For Susak, his homeland was his heartbeat, and an independent Croatia his obsession. He joined up with anti-Yugoslavia Croats in a series of protests: among them a hunger strike on Parliament Hill and later, a little piece of agit-prop theatre in front of the Yugoslav embassy, where they painted the name TITO in red on the side of a piglet and placed it in a coffin-like box. They left the squealing creature in front of the embassy where the humane society rescued it.

Susak also started a sports club called Jadran and an after-hours language class for Croatian children (though Serbian and Croatian are almost identical languages, right-wing Croats claim Serbs and Croats speak different tongues).

Susak was also heavily involved in the establishment of the Norval Community Centre, a 140-acre sprawl of soccer fields, picnic areas and sports facilities with a few modest buildings for meetings and living quarters for visiting Croatian priests. It's located just outside Norval, Ontario, a village better known as the place where Lucy Maud Montgomery wrote her final *Anne of Green Gables* books.

The centre's innocuous appearance and romantic location belies its central role in the Croatian national movement: it was eventually taken over by Croat émigrés who were prepared to do anything, even go to war, to achieve their goals. In fact, the reconstituted idea of an independent state of Croatia was born at the Norval Centre.

Much of the vision forged there, including the plan to claim the Herzegovinian part of Bosnia as Croatian territory, came from Susak, along with a handful of other Croatian-Canadians who hailed from the Siroki Brijeg area. Among them was Marin Sopta, a close friend of Gojko Susak who was the best man at Sopta's wedding. Sopta was part of a smaller group of Croatian national-ists who believed language classes and street protests were not enough in pursuit of a Croatian homeland. Violent resistance to the Tito regime might be necessary, and Susak readily agreed.

Sopta's uncle was already in Canada and working for the extreme Croatian nationalist cause when the young Marin arrived. Sopta is a charming, dimple-faced man whose infectious enthusiam and youthful energy—combined with the impeccable pedigree of his ultra-nationalist uncle—quickly propelled him to leadership among the most radical of the diaspora activists. He had the veneer of legitimacy as a graduate of York University with a job in a dentist's office. He picked up the passion of his uncle's nationalism and learned its coded language from the Otpor newsletters of Maks Luburic's Croatian Resistance Movement.

That euphemistic language had been forged by Maks Luburic: the goal was "national reconciliation." The unstated ambition—that the new Croatia would include a vast tract of territory that included Herzegovina, much of Bosnia and even some of Serbia, and that it would be a nation for ethnic Croats—rarely turns up in the written material. But, according to Mate Mestrovic, a professor of history and a moderate Croatian-American community leader from the United States who visited the Ontario facility frequently, it is what the insiders discussed in their meetings at Norval.

Sopta also learned how to rationalize the Ustashe's dirty history as a Nazi puppet regime by claiming that Croats had only wanted the Nazis to be their vehicle toward independence. Sopta insisted that Optor had no love for Hitler and no desire for Croatia to become the agent of fascism. The Ustashe, according to Sopta and Otpor, was simply misunderstood. Sopta and the others—including Susak and the membership of the Norval Centre—were able to compartmentalize the brutal killing committed by Ustashe forces, in particular that of Luburic who ran the notorious Jasenovac death camp, and to recast the Ustashe Croats and other nationalist supporters as victims and not perpetrators.

Sopta had help from another prominent Croatian-Canadian, Ante Beljo, an electrician from Sudbury and an old high-school chum of Susak's from Siroki Brijeg. Beljo's role seems to have been to help rewrite the history of Croats as victims. He claimed that Croats had suffered a genocide after the Second World War and he managed to inflate the numbers of victims of the already horrific Bleiberg massacre by including among them not only the dead but also everyone who was "forced" to leave Croatia, including himself.

While Beljo revised the historical record, Marin Sopta proved himself to be an effective speaker. He rose through the ranks in the 1970s and '80s to become the leader of Otpor, presenting himself as a political moderate in an organization with a militant extremist fringe. Sopta glossed over Otpor's politics with the inspirational language of the freedom fighter, while the Otpor fringe became increasingly well known to the police for acts of sabotage, terrorism and murder.

The targets of the fringe were principally members of Tito's Communist Federation: in the 1960s, Yugoslav diplomats throughout Europe were assassinated by agents the authorities believed to be members of Otpor. In Sweden in 1972, one of the first hijackings of an airliner in history was blamed on Croatian extremists, and in the same year a bomb on a Yugoslav airliner killed twenty-six people.

A bomb that police suspect was planted by one of the Croatian extremist groups went off in a storage locker of La Guardia airport in New York City in 1975, killing eleven people and injuring seventy-five others; in September of 1976, Otpor members, including an employee of the Croatian embassy in Washington, hijacked an American TWA jet, resulting in the killing of one policeman; and in 1978 scores of people were injured and two murdered by Otpor gangs trying to extort "donations" from Croat Americans to finance their cause. A Croatian priest who was a leader of the Croatian Fraternal Movement received a bomb in the mail, carefully concealed in a book and designed to detonate when opened; he survived.

Nine Croats were arrested and six convicted under the new American laws called RICO—the Racketeering, Influence and Corrupt Organizations Act. The fifty charges against the men were for a range of crimes. One of those arrested was Drago Sudar, picked up at his Toronto home in June of 1981, where the Peel Regional Police Department found a number of timing devices and batteries related to bomb-making. Court documents from the trial show that Sudar was teaching others how to make bombs, including the notorious book bomb.

Prosecutors also presented testimony concerning a trip made by Sudar and his associates to Elliott Lake, Ontario, to the site of the Dennison uranium mines, where three of them took receipt of bags of dynamite, with manufacturing markings from CIL.

According to court documents the men took the dynamite to Toronto, where, working in the garage of a group member, they concealed the explosives inside the doors of a car for transportation to the United States.

The trial took place in New York City; Sudar had been extradited to face the charges. He was sentenced to twenty years in prison while his partners received sentences ranging from twenty to forty years. Prosecutors said all of them were members of Otpor.

In an interview for this book, Sopta admitted the convicted men could have been in the ranks of his organization, but members didn't exactly fill in application forms. Otpor was banned in Germany and under constant police scrutiny in Canada and in the United States. Sopta himself was watched by the Royal Canadian Mounted Police—and people who were active in the organization kept a low profile. Sopta also claims, as do many Croat nationalists and some neutral observers, that Otpor had been infiltrated by Yugoslav secret police who were trying to discredit the cause by committing crimes in the name of Croatia.

Sopta became a member of the executive of Otpor in 1982 and its leader in 1987, just after the trials—and the violence—came to an end. Sopta says he wasn't involved in any of the criminal activities. But he beams with joy at the mention of the Croats who hijacked the TWA plane in 1976: "They were my heroes," he declares.

* * *

Marshal Tito's death in 1980 was officially mourned by millions in Yugoslavia but cheered by thousands of exiled nationalists. After the funeral, all the repressed and dormant nationalist movements within Yugoslavia fearfully re-emerged and began to form very tentative political parties. After decades when anyone who even talked about Croatia's aspirations would be arrested, nationalist pride had been so cowed in Croat society that there was not much of a spark. But in the diaspora, there was a giant bonfire.

Croatian leaders and intellectuals made their way to Canada and the United States throughout the 1980s, hoping to court the dynamic Croat émigré population. Canada had particular allure, as its multicultural policy enabled the emigré population to maintain the purest and most uncompromising nationalist sentiments in the entire diaspora.

Franjo Tudjman, with his distinctive mane of silver hair framing his hawk-nosed face, became a familiar character in the New World after he began to make connections in the diaspora. Tudjman had cleverly cultivated the Catholic Church in Croatia as a source of potential support for his political aspirations, and through its hierarchy he had made a very important contact in Father Ljubomir Krasic, the head monk at the Norval farm where the Herzegovinian friars in exile had set up shop. Krasic introduced Tudjman to the man from Ottawa who could grease his political wheels: Gojko Susak.

Susak organized and helped to finance Tudjman's first tour in 1988, taking him to various universities and social centres across the country and introducing him to Canadian politicans, including British Columbia premier Bill Vander Zalm and the federal cabinet minister Tom Siddon. Even though Yugoslavia had lost its dictator, Tudjman knew that Yugoslav secret agents had penetrated many of the nationalist organizations abroad. His message in Canada was muted: he talked vaguely of "the national project."

Although Susak helped to sponsor the visit, initially he wasn't sure that Tudjman was the leader to take them to the New Jerusalem. Tudjman had been arrested during Croatian Spring, which gave him some nationalist credentials, but he had also been a general in Tito's army. Susak explained his reservations in a 1996 interview that appeared in the Croatian publication *Hrvatsko Slovo:* "Imagine how hard it is for someone from Siroki Brijeg, who lost the family, to meet a former general of [Tito's Partisans]. It wasn't easy to accept him as the right person." But in the same interview, Susak described his motivation for supporting the Tudjman visit: "For years, depending on how long ago we had left Croatia, as if from a cage or over a wire fence, we peeked into Croatia," he said. Franjo Tudjman was the first politician to cross the wire fence and meet the diaspora.

Marin Sopta says his initial encounter with Tudjman was love at first sight. He understood Tudjman was reluctant to speak publicly, but in private conversations, Tudjman emerged as the man to lead them. Sopta and Tudjman differed only over the timing and the means. Tudjman didn't believe Yugoslavia would collapse; he hoped that Croatian autonomy could slowly emerge through federal devolution. Sopta and Susak were confident that Yugoslavia would inevitably break apart, and that full independence could then be established quickly, through bloody conflict.

Susak finally decided on Tudjman, he says, after long conversations with the future president about his program. Tudjman had taken up the Otpor philosophy even if he distanced himself from the Otpor name: the only hope for a Croatian victory was in uniting both right-wing and left-wing Croats. The Ustashe supporters and the Partisan supporters would have to sit in the same room and find common cause. Susak and the Norval crowd were convinced that they could unite all Croats in the diaspora. It was up to Tudjman to bring them together in Croatia. The common enemy that would unite Croats, they believed, was their old nemesis, the Serbs.

Tudjman returned for two more visits to Canada and the United States, and became increasingly involved with the radical side of the diaspora. John Caldarevic, a moderate Croatian nationalist in Toronto who was looking to help the cause, gave Tudjman a place to stay on his first visit, but later declined requests to host him. The Norval group—Susak, Sopta, Beljo and Father Krasic—took over. They were under police surveillance and Caldarevic told a number of people he didn't want to associate with extremists. Increasingly, Tudjman did.

* * *

In 1989, the entire socialist experiment of Europe came tumbling down with the Berlin Wall. For many countries in the Soviet bloc, this was the moment they had waited for and dreamed of. But in Yugoslavia, the mood was much darker; a severe economic depression had gripped the country in the late 1980s. The federation's currency plummeted and unemployment soared. This was a new and frightening phenomenon for Yugoslavs, and in these insecure times, the people looked for leaders to guide them. In Serbia, a banker turned nationalist politician named Slobodan Milosevic, was whipping the Serbian population into a political frenzy, pushing their nationalist buttons and warning the Serbs that the Ustashe was rising again.

Milosevic had never been a member of a Serbian nationalist group or even spoken about their cause in the past. He was well known as an ambitious politician, who had first attempted to make himself into a new Tito, casting himself as a leader of all Yugoslavia. That strategy had not met with much success, and he then shifted to a Serbian nationalist platform, suspecting that the Serbs still believed that they were the true inheritors of the land and that if he could drag the dark, murky sediment of xenophobic Serbian nationalism up from the bottom he could dominate Yugoslav society. For him, it would be the surest route to power. Milosevic's openly expressed ambition was for the establishment of Greater Serbia: even the words inspired fear and loathing throughout the non-Serbian population of the country.

In the late 1980s, Yugoslavia's central control was in tatters and the final blow to its unity was the fall of the Communist Party. The one-party state was finished. Political parties had begun to organize well before its demise and they now rushed to fill the vacuum. The Sabor in Zagreb declared Croatia would hold free multi-party elections within the year. A new era of Croatian nationalism was born.

***

In February of 1989, Franjo Tudjman met with a number of former members of the Croatian Spring movement at the Zagreb Writers' Club. They drew up the program of a new political party that they thought could win in Croatia—heavy on the national question, light on everything else—and they called it the Croatian Democratic Union (HDZ). They chose Tudjman as their leader. Only a few years earlier, these activities would have landed them all in jail. Tudjman was back in Canada soon after the meeting, and in the excitement of the new post-Communist reality, diaspora crowds thronged to see him. Even for those not politically active in Canada, the collapse of Communism in Europe generated romantic and sentimental ideas of their homeland.

According to Croatian moderate Mate Mestrovic, the principal movers and shakers behind Tudjman among the diaspora were hardcore nationalists from the Otpor group of Marin Sopta. "They were mainly Croats from Herzegovina and less developed parts of Croatia. Most of them were less educated people from poor families and they never adjusted to their new countries. The fact is that some of them did get very rich, but even the wealth they acquired didn't help them adjust to the new country. They were dependent on their roots, their village, and they were devoted to the idea of an independent Croatia. These are the people who financed Tudjman's campaign." Though Susak always tried to distance himself from the radical organizations, Mestrovic cites Susak as being instrumental to Otpor.

Tudjman was able to secure support from former Communists as well as nationalists inside Croatia by promising that if he was elected there would be no reprisals against anyone for their past Tito affiliations. Tudjman even succeeded in getting the support of former Yugoslav secret police chiefs by promising they would keep their jobs in a Tudjman Croatia. In this way, he was able to balance the interests of socialist Croats against those of militant right-wing emigrants. Tudjman quite deliberately ignored a third group: Croatia's minority Serb population, who had lived in Croatia for six hundred years at least.

Tudjman attempted to keep a certain distance from any direct association with the Ustashe. The journalist Marcus Tanner, in his book *Croatia: A Nation Forged in War*, describes one of Tudjman's visits to Toronto. At one gathering the organizers had invited Srecko Psenicnik, Ante Pavelic's son-in-law, who had continued Pavelic's HOP party in Canada. When Tudjman's aides from Zagreb realized who he was they hastily rearranged the seating arrangements to keep Tudjman as far away as possible from any Ustashe associations. But such associations were of less concern to the Soptas and the Susaks. The politics of the diaspora radicals were frozen in time: they had lived in Canada for decades and had not shared in the gradual normalizing of ethnic relations in the give-and-take of Yugoslav society over those years. Susak, Sopta, Beljo and the others saw Croatia's future through the filters of their own anger at having been, according to them, driven out of their country.

These were heady times for Croat nationalists. Susak and a large number of other Canadian Croats headed back to Zagreb for the first convention of the HDZ party in February of 1990. Ante Beljo remembers the wildly exhilarating moment of getting on to the Air Canada plane that was leaving for Zagreb. None of them had set foot in Yugoslavia since they had all fled in Tito's time, but now the homeland was calling. As they passed through customs unobstructed, they knew for sure that the wall was down, even if Croatia was still a part of Yugoslavia.

The HDZ convention lasted for two days. Tudjman supporters had rented the biggest music hall in Zagreb and 2,500 delegates jammed the convention, including Croats from North America, Norway, Germany and Australia. Susak and the others from Canada (many originating from the Siroki Brijeg region of Herzegovina) were euphoric. The Croatian media went on the offensive, claiming the Ustashe was back in town. Tudjman dealt with it head-on, declaring in a speech that "our opponents see nothing in our program but the claims for the restoration of the independent Croatian state. These people fail to see that the state was not the creation of fascist criminals; it also stood for the historic aspirations of the Croatian people for an independent state. They knew that Hitler planned to build a new European order." The crowd was wildly in favour of this clever dismissal of the charges. They all sang the Croat nationalist songs that would have landed them in prison the last time they had been in Croatia. And the émigrés returned home to raise the money necessary to put Franjo Tudjman's HDZ party into power.

Despite a heavily revised and modernized program put forward by the Croatian Communists, many voters were looking for any party that spoke to their newly revived national pride and made them feel less vulnerable to Belgrade. Tudjman knew how to appeal to his listeners; he masqueraded as a democrat, and some were fooled, but not many in Croatia missed the neo-Ustashe tinge to some of his remarks. In one campaign speech he said, "All people are equal in Croatia, but it must be clear who is host and who is guest." If Croatia's minorities weren't frightened by that statement, they surely were when Tudjman remarked publicly, "Some say my wife is Serb or Jewish. I am happy to say that she is neither Serb nor Jewish."

He made the off-the-cuff remark at a rally and the pro-Yugoslav media pounced on it, not without good cause. Croatians would cast their votes in the first free elections for the government of the republic, which was still part of Yugoslavia, held in two rounds, in April and the beginning of May 1990. The HDZ launched a slick, up-beat and modern campaign that was new to Croats. Posters and banners proclaimed, "God in Heaven and Tudjman in the Homeland." There were now dozens of HDZ branches in North America who took donations for the party. Canadian Croats Susak, Beljo and Vinko Grubisic returned to Croatia to help run the campaign with a fleet of fax machines and a small army of students from Canada—bright-eyed young Croat nationalists who believed they were realizing the dream of their parents. Sopta went to Croatia as well but he also worked the Canadian front, raising money and trying to avoid tangles with the RCMP, who were still asking questions about the activities of Otpor.

Though it had failed to garner a majority of the votes, and won no support among minorities, the HDZ won the most seats. The country was still largely divided. And even after the emotionally charged election, Tudjman did little to dispel the perception that his government was only for Croats. Streets and towns that had once been named after Serbs were changed to Croat names, some of whom were Ustashe; the Square for the Victims of Fascism became the Square of Great Croats; and the memorial at the Jasenovac concentration camp from the Second World War would henceforth represent all Croats who died in the war, including Ustashe; the checkerboard flag that had represented Pavelic's Nazi puppet state was returned as the flag of Croatia; and the constitution was rewritten with no recognition of Serbs as a "constituent people." Serbs were fired from their jobs in government and the police force as Croats claimed they only had the jobs in the first place because they were Serbs. Tudjman had someone locate the dismantled bronze figure of Josip Jelacic and put him back together again. The reassembled statue of the Ban was installed in the (once again) renamed Jelacic Square. But the statue points its sabre in a different direction now. Jelacic is no longer charging toward Hungary but toward Serbia.

***

Most important for Susak and his circle of Herzegovinians, Tudjman proclaimed that Croatia was not limited to its historical borders: a large part of Bosnia, meaning Herzegovina, must be included in the dream. These were ideas that had been forged in Norval and Toronto on Tudjman's trips abroad. They had gone from fireside musings to a call to arms. Tudjman laid the groundwork for the horrors that would soon befall the non-Croats of Herzegovina and the revenge that Susak and his group had longed for. Tudjman's nationalist zealotry helped to blind Croats to where all of this was leading. Serbian leader Slobodan Milosevic, for his part, was whipping up emotion among Serbs in Croatia. It wasn't hard to reawaken the old fears and hatreds.

In 1990, Tudjman made an emotional appeal to a crowd of 20,000 Croats in Toronto to come back to Croatia and help rebuild their nation. Susak was among the most prominent of the scores of Croats who did that: he gathered up the pieces of his twenty-year life in Canada and moved "home" to Croatia—although Susak was really from Herzegovina.

Tudjman made Susak his minister in charge of the Croat diaspora, whose numbers very likely rivalled the population of Croats who still lived in Croatia. In the rewritten constitution, the emigrants were given the right to actually vote in subsequent elections, whether they returned to Croatia or not. Other Canadians joined Susak in the cabinet: Rosie Tomasic resigned from the Ontario Provincial Police to become Tudjman's head of security; Ivica Mudrinic took over telecommunications in Croatia; and Ante Beljo, who had worked as an electrician at INCO in Sudbury (but was now described in HDZ literature as an engineer), became the secretary general of the HDZ in Zagreb.

Eventually Susak's Ottawa house was sold, and his wife and children joined him in Croatia. According to a *Saturday Night* magazine article about Susak, the neighbours were impressed by his new image when he returned for his family: better suits and a bigger car. They had a vague sense that he was now a big man in Croatia, but didn't know much more than that. They recognized Susak as someone dedicated to his country, his church and his family—and the three were inseparable.

In Croatia, the rapidly shrinking independent media dubbed Susak "Pizza Man" and made many unsuccessful attempts to interview him, while the Tudjman government-controlled media published mythologized portraits of Susak and the other ministers, supported by fabricated histories.

Just in case Tudjman's antics were not intimidating enough, Milosevic's state-controlled media also fed a steady stream of propaganda into Croatia, reminding the Croatian Serbs of past pogroms. Belgrade TV pumped out hours of old Second World War propaganda films and archives, evoking in horrendous detail the kinds of things that might be in store for Serbs in an independent Croatia.

The campaign had a particularly powerful effect on the Krajina, where groups of armed Serbs, calling themselves

Chetniks, began to mobilize and build up an arsenal of weapons in the Croatian areas. They blocked roads—in what was called the log revolution, since they laid trees in front of traffic—and they took over police stations. With enormous help from Milosevic in Belgrade and the Yugoslav national army, the Krajina Chetniks began to organize a powerful opposition to the emerging Croatian state, threatening to ruin the celebrations of Croats around the world as they moved toward a plebiscite on independence from Yugoslavia.

* * *

Gojko Susak was not interested in trying to bring down the temperature in this ethnic pressure-cooker—quite the opposite. *The Death of Yugoslavia*, the highly respected book and documentary TV series by Laura Silber and Allan Little that chronicles the break-up of the federation, describes just one of the acts of provocation for which Susak is held responsible.

In April of 1991, Susak and some of his companions visited the police chief in eastern Slavonia, in the old Pannonian part of Croatia. Josip Reihl-Kir was of mixed German-Slovene descent but saw himself as a loyal Croat. He also saw himself as a professional police officer whose job it was to try to keep the skittish countryside safe and under control. Reihl-Kir didn't like the look of Susak and his friends and he suspected they were up to no good, but they were high-placed members of the Croat government and he was obliged to do their bidding.

Together, they took a night drive through the farm fields to the outskirts of Borovo Selo, a Serb-dominated town near Vukovar on the Danube, where Chetniks had formed their first base. It was within shooting distance of Borovo Naselje, a Croat village. Reihl-Kir had been trying to keep the peace in this particularly volatile region for months and he watched in horror as Susak and the others took out a shoulder-mounted rocket launcher and lobbed three missiles into the village. No one was killed or injured but Susak had deliberately lit a fuse with this act of provocation.

At the time Susak denied taking part in the act, though he bragged in later years that he had fired the first shot in Croatia's war of independence. He later gave a flak jacket to one of the men who had accompanied him on the excursion, in recognition of his new role as a combatant. A few weeks later, some newly recruited Croat policemen returned to Borovo Selo in the dead of night to attempt to strip the town of its Yugoslav flags. Two of the policemen were injured and two taken prisoner, which provoked, in turn, reprisals from other militant groups.

Tudjman had little control over these skirmishes, which were quickly escalating into real, violent clashes. He had hastily assembled loyal Croats into police forces but the new recruits were bold young men without much training or experience. Their credentials were principally that they believed in the Croat nationalist cause and they could handle guns.

But Croatia was still a part of Yugoslavia and Milosevic held a monopoly on power in the federation. From Belgrade, he watched and waited for the moment when the escalating violence in Croatia would justify sending the JNA (Yugoslava National Army) to "intervene." It was an order he clearly looked forward to issuing.

Reihl-Kir began to see that his task was hopeless. He asked the minister of police for protection and requested a transfer to Zagreb. "We are losing control down here," he told his superiors, adding that hard-liners like Gojko Susak had taken over. The minister told him he was being "childish," although he did agree to transfer him out of eastern Slavonia. But by the time the permission came, it was too late: Reihl-Kir was murdered by extremists in Tudjman's HDZ party the day before he was to leave. "It is a striking commentary," says authors Silber and Little in *Death of Yugoslavia*, "that Kir's moderation, his conciliatory approach to the Serbs, had cost him his life, while Susak's activities, stoking tension and provoking conflict, were to win him one of the most prominent places in Tudjman's government."

The provocations and fights were turning into all-out battles, as Franjo Tudjman called his plebiscite on the question of

Croatian independence on May 19, 1991. Given the charged emotional atmosphere of the time, the vote was a success for Tudjman and Croatia declared its statehood in June.

The Serbs, for their part, announced the formation of a new entity, called the Republic of Serbian Krajina (RSK), claiming an area that eventually comprised a third of Croatia, going way beyond the original Krajina. They boycotted the referendum and held their own plebiscite on whether the RSK should, itself, separate from Croatia. Even without the reported vote-rigging and intimidation, the proposition would have passed.

Tudjman made Susak his trusted adviser as the Yugoslav National Army moved in, ostensibly to protect the minority Serb population but really to join forces with the Krajina rebels. Within months, soldiers of the RSK with assistance from ruthless paramilitary brigades from Serbia called Arkan's Tigers and the White Eagles had expelled or killed the entire Croatian population of the Serb-held areas—85,000 were driven out of the Krajina alone. The rebel army was well supplied by Belgrade and well led by a new upstart colonel by the name of Ratko Mladic. The term "ethnic cleansing" was invented at this time to describe what the Serbs were doing to Croats, but Tudjman's new police forces caught on quickly and soon they had "ethnically cleansed" tens of thousands of Serbs out of their territory. In its first act as an independent nation, Croatia descended into ugly, brutal ethnic war.

Tudjman claimed to be shocked by how quickly his country had slid into bloody conflict and at times his dismay seemed genuine. He fired his defence minister, Martin Spegelj, for suggesting that Croatia should declare war against the Serbs and deal with the Krajina before it could really get organized. Instead, Tudjman did nothing while Chetnik forces, backed by the JNA, devoured whole sections of Croatia.

Why didn't he declare war? The common theory, for which there is considerable evidence, is that Tudjman thought he had a deal with Milosevic: that the two leaders had pledged they wouldn't get in the way of each other's nationalist aspirations and then they would divvy up neighbouring Bosnia between them.

Tudjman was said to have expected to get Herzegovina, the territory for which the leaders of the émigré Croats hungered.

But now Tudjman was in a jam, because he was losing ground and had no army of his own. His only option was to quickly mobilize the local militias or homeguard—called the domobrans—and the regional police forces. But he was up against the JNA tanks, armoured vehicles, modern weapons and a mountain of ammunition. Tudjman needed money and he needed heavy weapons. He had little of either. He turned to his new defence minister, Gojko Susak, and his contacts in the diaspora.

* * *

Back in Canada, Croat immigrants were obsessed with events in their newly independent country. Southern Ontario's rich network of ethnic radio programming took on new significance. Shows like *Sounds of Croatia*, which appealed to homesick Croats by playing familiar music and giving the sports scores in the Croat language, became lifelines. The show tapped right into the newscasts of Radio Zagreb and people followed every development as Yugoslavia descended in to war. People stayed home to listen to the broadcasts or left their workplaces to go out to their cars to listen. When the JNA tanks were rumbling toward Zagreb, two thousand people went to the Croatian Club in Toronto to monitor the alarming event.

Rival Serbian radio programs gave their equally emotional version of the other side of the story and people from both communities called station owners to complain. Some of the editorial commentary was obviously inflammatory but other provocations were more subtle: a song with patriotic lyrics or an innuendo in a news story might be found offensive. Communities of Serbs and Croats who had long lived together as fellow Slavs, and had probably shared a loathing of Tito's Communists, now became enemies. Those who had no interest in the political intrigue of the Balkans suddenly became politicized. And people began to pour money into the cause.

The Croatian National Fund was established, with Susak as one of its controllers. Money was deposited in the Croatian Credit Union in Toronto, and into other banks all over the world, then transferred to accounts in Switzerland. The final tally on what the diaspora contributed has never been revealed. Susak says that the first wave of donations, responding to a letter he sent out, solicited US$15 million, though the figure was probably closer to $50 million, according to reliable Croatian media. Marin Sopta says the contribution during the war years was more like $200 million.

Much of it was raised through small events and campaigns on the Croat radio programs; even children sent in the contents of their piggy-banks. The Croats in Canada were in a state of shock as they watched their former villages and cities being destroyed and heard of relatives reduced to refugees as they were ethnically cleansed from family homesteads. They donated money for blankets, medicine, food and clothing for the people shivering in the dark throughout the war. But undoubtedly the lion's share of the funds went to purchasing arms. Did people know that? Susak's letter to the diaspora spelled out that Croatia was undefended and that it needed weapons.

Susak refused to make a distinction between soft and hard military aid. In 1991, he told CBC's *the fifth estate*: "Everything we use is for defence purposes. Whether I buy a piece of clothing, or toothpaste, or whatever with it—you can say it's for war purposes." Susak only shrugged for the cameras when he was asked if the money was used to buy guns.

One of the Canadian fundraisers, Dick Besic, was more blunt about it: "We do not ask the government what the money is spent on. It could be arms, it could be food, it could be buying trucks, airplanes. If they use the money for arms, it's up to the Croatian government. Not us."

In 1991, the international community determined that the best way to keep the violence from escalating was to impose an arms embargo on all Yugoslav territory, past and present. Canada and the United States led the initiative, which was endorsed by a UN security council resolution. Well-intentioned the embargo may have been, but the effect was devastating for the fledgling republic of Croatia. The JNA was the fourth largest force in Europe before the war began and all of this military might was now in the hands of the Serbs. The Croats and later the Bosnians would have to smuggle in whatever they could get. Croatia needed money to buy arms on the black market and it needed undercover agents. Canada was able to provide both.

A businessman from Hamilton, Ontario, named Michael Yurkovic was arrested in Germany while he was in the midst of what German authorities believed was an attempt to buy nearly ten million US dollars' worth of weapons. Yurkovic argued that he was only trying to purchase uniforms for the Croatian Army. He was released after a month in jail. Mark Belinic from Alberta was caught in Phoenix, Arizona, attempting to buy state-of-the-art weaponry left over from the Gulf War; a sting operation in Miami picked up four men from Chicago who were haggling with undercover police over the price of missiles and guns. They were attempting to buy US$12 million worth of M-16 rifles and Stinger anti-aircraft missiles, the weapons of choice of guerrilla armies. One of the men caught in the police operation was connected with a prosperous construction contractor in Windsor, Ontario, Roko Juricic, who was a mover and shaker in the Croatian fund-raising community. Juricic admitted that one of the men had stayed with him and that he'd called from Miami the night before the attempted purchase; still Juricic claimed he wasn't involved. But when asked if he supported the arms smuggling he said he had no problem with it. He summed up the feelings of many in the militant diaspora when he told *the fifth estate*: "If I see my cousins dying, kids dying, my mother is there for already six months and I can't go to her, she cannot come out. And I see this monster Serbian Communist doing those things, I would give everything to give them something to defend themselves."

The boldest case of all involved the wealthy Toronto businessman Anton Kikas, who ended up spending three months in a Belgrade jail before the Serbs traded him for one of their captured generals. Kikas was an old friend of Susak's and he had been one of the founders of the Croatian National Fund of Canada. He always gave generously of his own money and had raised a million dollars to endow a Chair of Croatian Studies at the University of Waterloo. But he went one step into the great unknown when he collected an undisclosed amount of money from private sources, chartered a Ugandan Airlines plane and loaded it with weapons purchased in South Africa, which he then attempted to get to Croatia. It was a brazen initiative—and there were probably countless successful operations like it during the war that no one ever heard of. For reasons Kikas says he will never quite understand, his chartered flight was diverted to Belgrade where his weapons were confiscated and he was arrested.

Marin Sopta says he was proud of what Kikas attempted to do, but in Zagreb, Susak and Tudjman tried to discourage the amateur gun-running. All they could usually get were rifles and bullets, and the negative publicity that came from the exposure of the weapons' purchases put the image-conscious Zagreb administration in a bad light. Most of what Tudjman needed he could purchase easily in the chaos of the Communist east bloc as it fell apart, awash with heavy weapons and armoured vehicles. Russian mafia bosses were willing to sell whatever Susak's heart desired.

The dirty war sank to a new low in the fall of 1991, when Arkan's Serbian paramilitaries moved in on the eastern Slavonian river port of Vukovar. The beautiful old Austro-Hungarian city on the Danube would become Croatia's Stalingrad. The siege of Vukovar lasted three months. Serbian paramilitaries, with JNA support, pummelled the town into rubble, killing dozens of civilians daily. Most of those who survived—and there were a few—hid in their cellars, hungry and cold, for the duration of the attack. The brutality set the tone for what was to come in the Balkans. Bodies lay in the streets for weeks since no one dared risk collecting them; hundreds of people went to the hospital where they huddled in fear as bombs dropped on them; all those able to escape did so. The international community kept insisting on a negotiated settlement and a ceasefire, while it scrambled to avoid having to intervene to protect the civilian population. Still, in a final Serbian assault in November, Vukovar fell.

Within hours, Croats climbed out of their holes into streets that were lined with corpses. They headed to the hospital where the Red Cross was going to help them depart. But before the aid workers could arrange their safe passage, the Serbs rounded up all the hospital inmates, including the sick and wounded. They were taken out of town, shot, and dumped in a mass grave. When war crimes investigators opened the grave a few years later, they found hundreds of bodies, including men still in hospital gowns and one with a catheter tube still attached to his penis.

Other people were killed in the streets where drunken Serb paramilitaries roamed with pockets full of loot. When the few Croatian survivors were finally removed from Serb-held Vukovar, Serb civilians screamed "Ustashe murderers" at them as they were escorted out of town by foreign-aid workers.

Tudjman and his "Pizza Man" defence minister were losing the war. At Tudjman's behest, foreign negotiators put pressure on Milosevic to agree to a complete ceasefire. Before Christmas, they had worked out the arrangements for a force of international peacekeepers to come to Croatia and supervise the war's end. All parties agreed.

But a third of Croatia was under the control of the rebel Serbs, the country was cut in half and dysfunctional. With fresh memories of murdered civilians seared into their brains, Croats awaited the arrival of the peacekeepers.

CHAPTER TWO

NO PEACE TO KEEP

Victims can be victims and not be innocent.

—David Rieff, A *Bed for the Night*

St. Mark's Square in Zagreb is a landmark rich in powerful symbols of Croatian history and nationalism. The centrepiece is the Catholic church—a Gothic structure, undistinguished except for its extraordinary roof, whose steep slope is like a painted canvas composed of brightly coloured ceramic tile. The pieces are arranged to depict the coat of arms of Croatia in a three-part image that represents the three historic regions, Dalmatia, Slavonia and central Croatia, along with the emblem of Zagreb. The roof is a strong political and historical icon and one that strikingly reminds visitors of how closely church, state and national identity are tied together here.

On all sides of St. Mark's are the buildings and institutions of the Republic of Croatia, facing toward the church as if supplicant to it. The government office building is on one side, and the Sabor is on the other. For a thousand years of Croatian history, it seemed that these indigenous institutions would never truly be central in Croatian society. Croatians were controlled by outsiders; religious and political independence was always just beyond their fingertips.

In the sixteenth century, a serf by the name of Matija Grubec was executed in St. Mark's Square after he led a poorly equipped peasant army into battle against the feudal Hapsburg landlords. Before he was dispatched, Grubec was mocked as "king" of the peasants and crowned with a ring of red-hot iron. In the 1940s, the square was festooned with the swastikas and flags of Nazi Germany when Ante Pavelic led Hitler's puppet regime. The Roman Catholic church and all institutions of religious or national identity were shunned and all but closed down during the Communist rule of Marshal Tito.

In 1991, Croatians were masters of their own destiny for the first time. But the taste of independence wasn't as sweet as many had expected it would be.

Stipe Mesic was finding it very bitter indeed. Mesic is a burly man with a fleshy face and a full head of closely cropped salt-and-pepper hair. He is a bon vivant—a man who loves good food and wine but who, as a Tito-era politician, also dutifully swallowed a lot of unpalatable policy. Mesic was the last president of Yugoslavia, or at least, he should have been the last president. Serbian representatives in Belgrade, led by Milosevic, shut Mesic out of the office in 1990 when he attempted to take his place in the rotating leadership of Yugoslavia. It was Croatia's turn and Mesic was the man appointed by the Sabor to take the job, but Milosevic and his cronies wouldn't allow it. Mesic never became president; instead, Yugoslavia began to fall apart.

Mesic had been a member of Croatian Spring, the liberal democratic movement put down in 1971 when many of its members, including Tudjman, went to jail. Mesic was a soft nationalist and shared the view of many Croatian intellectuals that an independent Croatia had to include not just the Serbian minority but also Muslims, Jews, Hungarians and Slovenes.

Croats like Mesic who had lived in Tito's Yugoslavia had evolved with it. They had worked to heal old rifts between ethnicities or to simply gloss over them in the interests of harmony. But Mesic was concerned that the diaspora Croats were returning from abroad with the bile and anger of the Second World War preserved in their hearts and minds as though their ugly personal experiences had happened only yesterday. This was not the foundation on which Mesic wanted to build a nation.

Mesic had joined the anti-fascist Partisans as a very young man and had been a dedicated socialist under Tito. Now he was in a government with hard-liners like Gojko Susak and he knew that they were gradually gaining control over the presidency.

As Tudjman changed the names of public places in Zagreb to honour historical figures with Ustashe connections, Mesic became increasingly alarmed. But he remained passive even when the president restored the statue of Ban Jelacic in the central square, an act that was as much a provocation to the socialists as it was a boost for national pride. Mesic wanted to believe that his old Communist Party colleague Tudjman and the HDZ party that he had helped to form were just placating the people who could pay his military bills.

* * *

In the darkest hours of the winter of 1992–93, Croatia was broken, spiritually and physically. The boomerang-shaped territory of the Republic of Croatia was severed in crucial locations: first in Slavonia, where Serb-held areas blocked the famous Yugoslavian highway of brotherhood and unity; and in Dalmatia, where the Serbs held the Maslenica bridge, cutting communications and travel links between Dalmatia and the rest of Croatia. The Serbs also held the airport at Zadar and a very important hydroelectric dam at Peruca—for all the good it did them; none of these facilities could function without the rest of the grid. Croats had lost badly, but it wasn't clear what the Serbs had won.

If anything, Croatian-held areas were slightly better off than the Krajina. In the capital, life had regained a veneer of normalcy. Zagreb's cafés were open and a few restaurants served quite passable food. People in a number of industries had gone back to work. Outside Zagreb, though, Croatia was badly wounded, first by the devastation of the once stunning old port city of Dubrovnik at the southernmost point of Croatia and then by the pall of evil that hung over Vukovar at the opposite end. Between those two points lay a wasteland of smashed lives and dreams.

Chetnik paramilitaries had not only cleansed Croats from the Krajina but had also tried to erase any sign of their existence. They went so far as to remove the stones of the churches they had destroyed. Similarly, in Croatian-held areas, not a single Orthodox church was in operation by January 1992.

Paramilitaries roamed the streets in a drunken stupor, failing to realize what, if anything, they had accomplished. In town after town, village after village, soldiers destroyed everything, but— even more depressing—they destroyed it over and over as the armies shelled or shot up buildings that had already been obliterated. If levelling a village didn't already appear to be a senseless act, the repeated destruction of structures that were already rubble could only be construed as madness.

Thousands of refugees flowed in a steady stream out of the Krajina into the rest of Croatia, while Serbian refugees headed to Serbia. At least 20,000 people were dead or missing, 2,642 of them from Vukovar alone.

The Serbian para-state within Croatia, with its capital in the grubby railroad town of Knin, was completely isolated: there was no trade, commerce, industry or business. The entire Republic of Serbian Krajina could exist as a state only with the support of Belgrade. The Knin leadership dreamed of a RSK university and a new, exclusively Serbian age in the Krajina. In reality, the area was almost deserted by civilians.

The Croatian historian Ivo Goldstein says the self-styled Republic of Serbian Krajina would have had a bleak future even without the military threat from the Croats, unless Serbia itself absorbed the economically depressed para-state. The Krajina was hemmed in on all sides, and the Serbs inevitably faced poverty and emigration. To survive economically the Krajina needed its Croat neighbours. But Croats and Serbs were no longer prepared to do business with each other.

By early 1992, Milosevic was growing weary of his Knin tribe. Desertion rates from the Yugoslav National Army were very high. Many soldiers failed to grasp the meaning of the project for a Greater Serbia or why they should be in Croatia, on an ill-defined front line, fighting for the survival of something called the Republic of Serbian Krajina. As the coffins returned home, Milosevic's government had a hard time hiding the death toll and, increasingly, Serbian mothers wanted to know what was happening to their sons.

The Krajina Serbs now held any area in Croatia where there had been a significant Serb population before the war, and which now—of course—had only Serbs. They wanted more territory, and pushed Belgrade to help them continue their campaign, but to no avail. Milosevic was turning his attention elsewhere, principally Bosnia, where he was helping to turn up the heat to fuel another war for Greater Serbia. Without back-up from Belgrade and continual JNA reinforcements, the Serbian Army of the Krajina was fairly puny. They had enough military *matériel* to hold the areas they had already occupied but could do nothing more. Nor did the Croats have the military might to attack and regain their land, at least not yet. By 1992 the war had ground to a stalemate, with both sides unable to make any further inroads into each other's territory. Only the occasional firefight broke the boredom of the deadlock.

* * *

Cyrus Vance was seventy-four years old when he was appointed to find some kind of enduring solution to Croatia's bloody conflict. The affable but restrained Yale graduate was an old-style diplomat who had served as Jimmy Carter's secretary of state until they fell out over the U.S. hostage crisis in Iran. Vance had worked on the toughest files: détente with the Soviet Union, the Camp David agreements on the Middle East and U.S. attempts to normalize relations with China. But he was now entering the black hole of Balkan politics, from which few escape unscathed.

The United States had little interest in the goings-on in the former Yugoslavia and considered it Europe's business. James Baker, the U.S. secretary of state, summed up American indifference when he declared that the U.S. had "no dog in that fight." The United Nations didn't have the resources to respond to the political turmoil that was erupting all over the former Soviet sphere of control in Europe, and Europe was also at a loss to know what to do about the post-Communist republics that were dissolving into civil war.

Germany, with its long historical experience of the Balkans, eventually cajoled the European Community into recognizing Croatia's independence. Europe's few qualified Balkan-watchers knew that this was a risky move that would almost certainly push Bosnia to also seek independence. The Muslims and Croats in Bosnia had good reason to expect a bleak future within a Serb-controlled Yugoslavia under Slobodan Milosevic. And the Bosnian Serbs had already declared they would go to war if Bosnia tried to secede from the union.

The fact that Cyrus Vance was an American appointed by the United Nations gave him at least the appearance of having the support of both the UN and the United States. On January 2, 1992, Vance persuaded President Tudjman and the Krajina Serbs, under the influence of Milosevic, to sign a ceasefire agreement. There had been more than a dozen ceasefires already, but this particular deal proved to have more staying power. Vance thought he could build a durable peace agreement on its back.

The plan was signed the following day in the Bosnian capital of Sarajevo, a place chosen because the United Nations considered it, quite mistakenly, to be a neutral oasis in the crumbling federation. It was yet another demonstration of how little the UN understood the situation, since Bosnia was already well on the way toward its own savage war, and within days of the Croatian agreement, the Bosnian Serb leader Radovan Karadzic declared the independence of another Serbian splinter republic in Bosnian territory, as the Krajina Serbs had done in Croatia. Karadzic declared that "rivers of blood" would flow if Bosnia followed Croatia's lead by attempting to separate from Yugoslavia.

Vance pushed on and, with the ceasefire holding for the moment, came up with a plan for stabilizing the Krajina region. He mapped out four UN Protected Areas (UNPAs), which would be demilitarized and patrolled by UN peacekeepers. There would be two safe areas, called Sector East and Sector West, in Slavonia; two others, Sector North and Sector South, would be marked out in the Krajina. The UN peacekeepers would protect local populations while all JNA and Croatian army troops withdrew. The demilitarizing would mean that all paramilitaries within the UNPAs' well-defined borders would also have to leave or surrender their weapons to the peacekeepers.

During weeks of intense negotiations, Vance had gotten to know the parties well enough to understand what it was going to take to persuade both Serbs and Croats that they were getting what they wanted. Milosevic was still mistakenly regarded in many foreign circles as a besieged leader who was attempting to keep Yugoslavia together. He claimed he was only trying to protect Serbian minorites in Croatia, and he put on a good display of opposition to the Vance Plan, claiming it didn't go far enough to achieve peace. But in the end he agreed to it. Milosevic had, after all, achieved most of his military objectives in Croatia already.

The Vance Plan would freeze Serbian military gains in Croatia until new international boundaries could be drawn, which Milosevic hoped would incorporate all the newly seized territory into a Greater Serbia. The international community, including Europe, the United States and the United Nations, had taken the principled position that the borders of the republics must not be changed by force and that aggression would not be rewarded. But Milosevic was sure that such lofty principles would have little staying power when it came to dealing with the Balkans, and that in the end pragmatism and expediency would prevail.

Franjo Tudjman quietly applauded the Vance Plan for many of the same reasons as his nemesis Milosevic. Tudjman too wanted his forces freed up for the coming war in Bosnia. The real strength of the Vance Plan was that it made all the strongmen feel like winners and brought the shooting to a stop. The installation of peacekeepers would, in effect, sanction the status quo, allowing Serbs to strengthen their hold on areas they'd seized during the fighting. Tudjman believed the plan would give him time to negotiate the return of Serbian-held territory to Croatian hands, or failing that, time to regroup and take it back by force after the Yugoslav army withdrew.

* * *

With the leaders in agreement, each for his own reasons, the Vance Plan was ready to proceed. Approximately 30,000 Yugoslav army personnel had been trapped in their barracks in Croatian-held areas of the country and were down to their last food rations. The Vance Plan called for the release of these hostages (one diplomat reported that the Croat government had sent cases of dog food to a JNA barracks when the soldiers pleaded that they were on the verge of starvation) and their safe passage back to Serbia.

Milosevic needed those soldiers for his further adventures. The end of hostilities in Croatia allowed him to move troops into strategic positions in the Bosnian Krajina, adjacent to the Croatian Krajina (during Hapsburg times, they had been part of a single entity); he also installed in Bosnia a newly promoted general who had made a name for himself in Knin. General Ratko Mladic would further distinguish himself as an extraordinarily ruthless commander of the Bosnian Serb army, and would ultimately be indicted for crimes against humanity and genocide for the extermination of 7,000 Bosnian men and boys in Srebrenica (the general is still at large at the time of this writing).

The end of war in Croatia also meant that the vicious Serbian paramilitaries, the White Eagles, Arkan's Tigers and others, could now redeploy to Bosnia, having so successfully honed their skills at ethnic cleansing in Croatia.

The Vance Plan would eventually create as many problems as it solved. But at least, for the perplexed and distracted international community, it gave the appearance that something was being accomplished.

* * *

On February 21, 1992, the United Nations Protection Force— UNPROFOR—was born, with a call to deploy 14,000 international soldiers to Croatia.

In Ottawa, Prime Minister Brian Mulroney had a personal stake in the former Yugoslavia. His father-in-law was an anti-Titoist Serb and his wife, Mila, had been born in Sarajevo and the Mulroneys had honeymooned in the Balkans. The prime minister volunteered peacekeepers even before he was asked for them. UNPROFOR initially was to get forces from sixteen different countries: Canada provided an infantry battalion of nearly 900 troops and a combat engineering unit. Over the coming years, thousands of Canadians would rotate through UNPROFOR and its NATO equivalent, leaving hardly a Canadian soldier who had not served at least once in the former Yugoslavia.

While Canada was eager to play peacekeeper and Mulroney revelled in the role of an international statesman, his government was busy slashing budgets in all departments, not least among them Defence. The belief that the end of the Cold War would produce a "peace dividend" was at best illusory. Instead of peace the end of the Cold War produced dozens of small nasty wars that had been held in check by the over-arching balance of nuclear terror between superpowers. The bloody confrontations in the Balkans would require a new order of military commitment, no less onerous and certainly no less expensive than the Cold War. It was a commitment Canada was increasingly less capable of making.

Mulroney's popularity at home had been seriously on the decline in 1992, but his stock was up internationally. He was on the short list of people being considered for the soon-to-be-vacant job of secretary-general of the United Nations, replacing Boutros Boutros-Ghali. He had a strong personal friendship with President George Bush Sr., as he had with Bush's predecessor, Ronald Reagan. But unlike the American leaders, Canada's prime minister believed in playing an interventionist role on the world stage.

Mulroney was one of the first foreign leaders to identify Slobodan Milosevic as the villain in the Balkan break-up. He pushed for a robust military response to the crisis, but in the absence of support for such an intervention from Europe or the United States, the only thing Mulroney could do was send a peacekeeping force.

What Mulroney and the other international players failed to realize, or at least to acknowledge, was that the peace plan they had negotiated would only serve to entrench the conflict in a particularly deadly phase. It was into this perilous morass that the Mulroney government committed the services of a Canadian military establishment that had been seriously compromised by budget cuts.

As Canadian soldiers headed off to the former Yugoslavia, Canada already had peacekeepers in Cyprus, the Golan Heights, Cambodia, El Salvador, Kuwait, the Western Sahara and Nicaragua. Their pay was barely adequate, but they got bonuses for UN service and so hundreds of them volunteered for back-to-back missions, often destroying their home life and health with these lengthy stays overseas. Canadian officers began to warn their superiors about what they called the "tempo" of the operations and the burnout factor.

* * *

Though the UN force was assigned to Croatia, Boutros-Ghali decided to headquarter the mission in Sarajevo for reasons of economy. The Security Council was committed to the operation and had agreed to send one of the largest peacekeeping forces in UN history, but Boutros-Ghali had little interest in the Balkan break-up. He thought if the UN mission was based in Bosnia it could do cheap double duty. The presence of a few dozen Blue Berets would comfort Bosnians who feared that Radovan Karadzic might be serious about "rivers of blood" flowing on their streets. Boutros-Ghali's decision meant that the headquarters was a day's drive (through conflict zones that would soon be utterly impassable) from the UNPROFOR troops and their equipment.

The UN appointed Lieutenant General Satish Nambiar of India as force commander and a Canadian, Brigadier General Lewis MacKenzie, as chief of staff at the UN forces' head-quarters in Sarajevo. With 1,400 soldiers in the mission, Canada was the second-largest player after France. MacKenzie and Nambiar arrived in Belgrade on March 8 and had their first les-son in Balkanization within hours. They couldn't fly to Zagreb because Belgrade would not allow it. They couldn't drive from Belgrade either: the "highway of brotherhood and unity" no longer functioned. In a gesture that the old Hapsburgs would have enjoyed, the UN commander could only make the trip into Croatia by flying to Austria and then driving to Zagreb.

Nambiar and MacKenzie were warmly received in Croatia. MacKenzie was pulled aside by Croatia's minister of communi-cations, Ivica Mudrinic, who explained that he was from Mississauga. Just the night before, Mudrinic had called Croatian community leaders in Canada with the good news that Canadian soldiers would soon be on the ground. MacKenzie wasn't sure how to deal with this national appeal, since the UN force was supposed to be neutral.

* * *

The Canadian troops, along with the other fifteen contingents of international soldiers, began to arrive in April. From Sarajevo General MacKenzie could travel overland to meet with them in

Zagreb. But all travel and movement of foreign troops and their equipment had to pass under the eyes of Serbian leaders and have Belgrade's approval.

The Canadian Forces called its contribution to the UN mission Operation Harmony, though as they soon discovered, Operation Discord would have summed up the assignment better. Ottawa's military down-sizing was already in full swing, and the Canadian Forces had to cobble together battle groups from units all over Canada instead of assigning cohesive battalions of men and women who had trained and worked together.

Lieutenant Colonel Michel Jones led a contingent of 850 soldiers from the First and Third Battalions of the Royal 22e Regiment (the Van Doos), The Royal Canadian Regiment and other Canadian units scattered across what was left of Canada's old NATO deployment in Europe. A separate regiment of field engineers, whose main job would be clearing mines in the four protected areas, was assembled mostly from Canadian units in Germany, where the big Canadian base at Lahr was being dismantled. Colonel Jones was assigned to Sector West. His battle group shared the area with soldiers from Argentina, Jordan and Nepal, none of them with significant peacekeeping experience. Very few countries took peacekeeping as seriously as Canada. Other Western powers saw it as a nuisance, or at best an opportunity to influence events to advance their own interests. Most developing countries saw peacekeeping as a quick way to get hard currency from the United Nations.

The Argentinian battalion was north of the Canadians, in an exclusively Croatian area, while the Nepalese and Jordanian soldiers were farther south and had only the Serbs to contend with in a strip of territory that hugged the Bosnian border. The Canadians got the worst of it—they were smack dab in the middle of the contested territory. They were the only peacekeepers among all contingents in Croatia who actually had a hostile front line in their area of responsibility. In some places, the Serb and Croat forces were only a matter of a few hundred metres apart. It was no accident: the UN commanders knew that the Canadians formed one of the few competent battalions in the force and had come trained and well equipped.

Colonel Jones set up Camp Polom near Daruvar, formerly a JNA base. Before the war and the ethnic cleansing began, this part of Slavonia hadn't been counted as either a Serb- or a Croat-dominated area; in fact, it had probably the richest mix of ethnicities in all of Croatia. Czechs, Poles, Hungarians, Italians and Slovaks and more than a dozen other ethnic minorities had all been attracted to the area's fertile farmlands over the centuries and had commingled easily.

The centre of Canada's responsibility was Pacrac, a small Slavonian town that was probably one place in the region where Serbs had been the majority before the war. Pacrac was a major flashpoint for the conflict and became one of the first places outside the Krajina to endure a siege by Serb forces.

Almost exactly a year before the Canadians arrived—at the outset of the Croat-Serb war—Serbian paramilitaries had raided the Pacrac police station and declared that the town and its environs would from now on be the Autonomous Region of Serbs (soon to join the Republic of Serbian Krajina). Franjo Tudjman sent two hundred of his newly formed and highly motivated special police to Pacrac to put down the Serb rebellion. He was successful.

The Belgrade media excitedly reported that 20,000 refugees had fled the area. The fact that Pacrac's entire pre-war population was no more than 10,000 didn't get in the way of the story. Serbian television reported that forty people, including a priest, had been killed, and one of the largest Belgrade dailies put out a special edition to mark the Pacrac "massacre." Page 1 reported the murder of the unfortunate priest, while page 2 featured an account in which he was only wounded. On page 3 he was quoted, alive and well. An official Yugoslav government communiqué reported that no one had been killed in Pacrac, but it was too late. The Serb military leader in Croatia, Jovan Raskovic, was already inflaming a public rally with the assertion that war had been declared against Croatian Serbs.

By the time the Canadians arrived in the spring of 1992, the Croats had been beaten back to a line just north of Pacrac. The Canadian battalion under Michel Jones was now supposed to restore and sustain peace in the volatile neighbourhood. The UN's job was to ensure that both the Yugoslav and the Croatian armies withdrew and that all weapons were removed from the demilitarized zone. The peacekeepers were to guarantee the safe return of refugees, and according to the Vance Plan, police forces in the UN zones were supposed to return to their pre-war ethnic mix, whatever it was. None of these objectives were ever met.

UNPROFOR was simply not large enough to protect anyone if there was any serious fighting, as of course there was. From the outset, Canadian soldiers were fired on by machine guns and mortar rounds, and threatened by ambushes and booby traps. Lewis MacKenzie visited the Canadian contingent in Daruvar shortly after their arrival to give them a pep talk. Standing on a table, he told the soldiers: "You are peacekeepers. All sides in this conflict want you here. There is a ceasefire here in Croatia, so you should not be overly concerned about your safety—you're located in a peaceful area." As MacKenzie himself tells the story, the Canadians he spoke to were being shelled less than an hour later by heavy mortars and artillery.

Living conditions for the soldiers were appalling. The peacekeeping units took over buildings that had been abandoned during ethnic cleansing and were in many cases only slightly better than rubble. Sandbags reinforced what was left of walls and only plastic kept the icy wind at bay. The entire region was littered with land mines. Raw hostility radiated from both Serbian and Croatian forces while a civilian population trapped in between them desperately hoped the Blue Berets would protect them when the war started up again. Everyone knew it was only a matter of time before that happened.

***

Following the formal departure of Croatia and Slovenia from the former Yugoslavia, Bosnia had little choice but to declare independence as well.

The beleaguered Bosnian president, Alija Izetbegovic, tried, at least in the early stages, to maintain a multi-ethnic coalition government, and his declared intent was to preserve Bosnia's multicultural nature. Bosnia was the most culturally diverse of all the former republics, particularly in Sarajevo where the population was intermingled in mixed marriages and neighbourhoods to a greater extent than anywhere else in all of the former Yugoslavia. The idea of untangling the Bosnian ethnic communities looked impossible and pointless to Izetbegovic, but Serbian paramilitaries had a different opinion, and believed they had a foolproof method — brute force.

In the first week of April 1992, the warlord Arkan entered Bosnia from Serbia with his paramilitary Tigers. They took over the border towns of Zvornik and Bijeljina, and began to systematically execute Muslim leaders. Snipers took up positions and fired randomly at civilians on the streets. Thousands of people began to flee as dozens were killed. JNA soldiers, working openly with the paramilitaries, piled bodies onto trucks to take them out of town and bury them in unmarked mass graves.

The area was strategically important to Serbia's war effort since Bijeljina and Zvornik were frontier towns, straddling land claimed by both Serbia and Croatia. The fighting for a Greater Serbia was now underway throughout the former Yugoslavia, while in Belgrade Milosevic was still posturing before the international community as a man of peace.

On April 5, the European Union recognized Bosnia's independence, as did Canada. That same day, Serb snipers positioned on top of the Sarajevo Holiday Inn opened fire on a peaceful street demonstration, killing a young woman. Soon there were roadblocks everywhere. The city of Sarajevo was quickly surrounded by a ring of Serbian tanks, artillery and mortars provided by the JNA, and the city was under siege. The poet-psychiatrist Radovan Karadzic was about to fulfill his own bloody prophecies. The siege of Sarajevo began, along with the ethnic cleansing of Bosnia, even as Lewis Mackenzie and UNPROFOR settled into Sarajevo.

First a trickle, then a stream and finally a flood of refugees poured over the border from Bosnia into Croatia as civilians fled the ethnic pogrom. The Bosnian refugees flooded areas of Croatia not already occupied by Croats who had fled Slavonia and Krajina. Muslims and Croats huddled in fear together as the grand plan for a single state for all Serbs continued to unfold, under the direction of the masterminds in Belgrade.

Within weeks of Arkan's initial attack, Bosnian Serb forces and the paramilitaries from Serbia, reinforced by 70,000 JNA soldiers, had ethnically stripped almost two-thirds of Bosnia's territory, claiming it for the newly declared Srpska Republika. Serb forces soon united the Bosnian and Croatian sectors of the Krajina and established land corridors from the Dalmatian coast all the way to Belgrade.

It was an astonishing land-grab, carried out at top speed under the noses of the international community, which tut-tutted and passed disapproving resolutions at the Security Council, but seemed unable to muster the political will to oppose the Serbian expansionism by force.

At UN headquarters in Sarajevo, General MacKenzie watched the war in Bosnia unfold on TV. In his diary, he wrote that it was riveting stuff. Boutros-Ghali believed that UNPROFOR would also have a stabilizing influence in Bosnia, but MacKenzie remained focused exclusively on the Croatia mission even as the new Serbian army encircled the city of Sarajevo and began to fire mortars into the centre of town while Serbian snipers helped to make Sarajevo the most dangerous city on earth. The UN finally realized that Nambiar and MacKenzie were right. Sarajevo was the wrong place for their Croatian headquarters, even if it was the right place to help resist the siege of Sarajevo. The UN soon began efforts to move the base to Belgrade, the only city from which the UN commanders could move freely in and out of the region. In many ways, the transfer only made matters worse.

But another alarming development was about to burst upon the UN peacekeepers. Croatia launched its own war in Bosnia.

* * *

Franjo Tudjman had been doing a bad job of concealing his master plan for a Greater Croatia. He tried to disguise his raw ambition for more territory by claiming to foreign diplomats that the Muslim population of Bosnia posed a threat to regional stability and that Croatia had to move quickly to contain an Islamic threat to all of Europe.

"The Muslims want to establish an Islamic fundamentalist state," Tudjman told an astonished Warren Zimmerman, the U.S. ambassador to Belgrade. "They plan to flood Bosnia with 500,000 Turks." Zimmerman, who spoke Serbo-Croatian and was one of the most experienced international players in the region, had initially believed Tudjman to be an honest leader who was only trying to preserve the integrity of his internationally recognized borders. This sudden departure from that moderate stance came as a shock. Zimmerman told the Croatian president that he had heard the rumours that he and Slobodan Milosevic had actively discussed the partition of Bosnia. "Tudjman admitted that he had discussed these fantasies with Milosevic," says Zimmerman. Tudjman explained that he and Milosevic had agreed that the only solution to the "Bosnian question" was to dismember the territory, because Bosnians were, after all, way down deep, under the Muslim exterior, really Serbs and Croats just like them.

Zimmerman was the shrewdest of the foreign observers in the region and he had noted that the Canadian Gojko Susak was always hovering close to Tudjman. When the president told Zimmerman that "Bosnia doesn't really exist" he was echoing the sentiments of his Canadian advisers. Croatia's manifest destiny as a greater entity encompassing all the Balkan lands ever occupied by Croatians was a vision straight out of brainstorming sessions in Norval, Ontario.

When Zimmerman replied, "But Bosnia is as real as Croatia," Tudjman's revealing riposte was that "If the two major groups [Serbs and Croats] agree, then the Muslims will be compelled to go along."

Zimmerman, aware of the startling naïveté in Tudjman's assessment, asked, "How can you expect Milosevic to respect a deal with you to divide Bosnia when he is trying to annex Croatia for himself?"

"Amazingly," Zimmerman said later, "Tudjman replied—of his sworn enemy—'Because I can trust him.'"

***

Among the multi-ethnic mix that Izetbegovic was trying to maintain in the Bosnian government was a branch of Tudjman's HDZ party, an organization that represented the minority population of 750,000 Croats in Bosnia. At the end of 1992, however, the HDZ of Bosnia unilaterally claimed a part of Bosnia to be sovereign Croat territory. Tudjman was without a doubt behind this brazen call to arms, even though he denied it. Bosnians, and many Bosnian Croats, went into a state of shock.

The former president of the HDZ in Bosnia, Stjepan Kljuc, had been a model practitioner of multi-ethnic Bosnian politics. A pudgy man who always wore a tidy bow tie, he embodied the values of the vast majority of Bosnian Croats, who believed that political autonomy was possible without ethnic division. He had voted in favour of Bosnia's separation, but when he resisted taking orders from Zagreb, Tudjman had him removed as party leader, and replaced by a former supermarket manager whose political ambitions did not include autonomy. His name was Mate Boban and he came from the town of Grude in western Herzegovina near Siroki Brijeg. Boban's loyalty to Tudjman was without limits, since he believed Tudjman and Susak would make Herzogovina a part of Croatia.

Like the other breakaway "republics"—the Republic of Serbian Krajina under Milan Martic and the Srpska Republika under Radovan Karadzic—the new self-styled Croat Union of

Herceg-Bosna under Mate Boban represented a small, largely rural and undereducated population. The leaders of these entities declared backward little farm towns to be international capitals with power over all civil affairs in their jurisdictions, from the school curriculum to the currency.

The pretensions of such "states" might have been cartoonish, but their intentions were lethal. And throughout the long Yugoslavian conflict, the self-appointed "presidents" of these tiny territories would be wined and dined in the capitals of Europe while international diplomats tried, by flattery and appeasement, to engage them in peacemaking.

As Tudjman and Milosevic conducted their own partition talks, Boban was in secret negotiations with Karadzic to finalize the gritty details of a plan for carving up the nation of Bosnia. In the project they were about to launch, Muslims would be asked to convert or leave. If they refused, they would be killed.

* * *

Croatia had initially armed the Croats in Herzegovina in order to fight the Serbs in Bosnia. The Bosnian Croats had formed their own fighting force, the formidable Croat Defence Council (HVO), which was heavily reinforced with soldiers from Croatia proper. In the beginning, Bosnian Muslims had joined the HVO—to defend Bosnia from the Serbs. But now the HVO turned against the Bosnian Muslims.

The Muslims, who were in the majority and controlled the Bosnian government, reacted swiftly, mobilizing the state's own military resources in a fierce attempt to preserve the integrity of Bosnia as they conceived it—a multi-ethnic state. The force they mustered was predominantly Muslim but had significant numbers of both Serbs and Croats. The Serb-Croat plans to break up and redistribute the population of Bosnia wasn't going to happen without a fight.

Tudjman tried to persuade the world that the Croat assault on Bosnia was a spontaneous uprising by Croats living in Bosnia, and that his government had had nothing to do with it, but the lie would eventually be exposed by gruesome evidence: "The coffins were coming back to Croatia," declared Stipe Mesic.

Indeed, the body bags were soon returning by the thousands. The Croatian general Janko Bobetko, who covertly led the Croatian campaign in Bosnia, later boasted in his autobiography that he had ordered his Croat soldiers to take off their HV insignia (that of the Croatian Army) and to put on an HVO one (that of the Bosnian Croats) as they crossed the border in order to foil the international community. He admitted to losing 9,000 soldiers, but the real numbers are known to have been considerably higher.

In Zagreb, some members of the Croatian government were extremely disturbed by Tudjman's actions. Stipe Mesic had to finally concede that the cabinet had been hijacked by the Susak vision of Greater Croatia, and he resigned from the government. In a statement, he said, "I can only say that the Croatian parliament never took any such decision [to go to war in Bosnia] and according to our constitution only the Sabor can order deployment of the army outside of Croatia." Tudjman retaliated by sending a small army of police officers to evict Mesic from his state-appointed apartment; he would be systematically harassed by Tudjman's people for years after.

Mesic wasn't the only Croatian to oppose Tudjman's territorial ambition. Anton Tus, a general and chief of staff of the Croatian Army, protested against what he considered military madness. Tus had been central in setting up the Croatian Army and without people of his expertise Tudjman had no real hope of recovering Serb-held areas in Croatia. But when Tudjman ordered him to save the failing Bosnian campaign, Tus refused. He could not fathom the reasons for attacking Bosnia. It made no military sense. As a result, he was fired. "Not only did I refuse," says Tus, "I made a statement to the press that it was an unjust war, and in fact a war against Croatia. Tudjman said I was anti-Croat."

Another general, Martin Spegelj, who had been Tudjman's first defence minister, quit his remaining post in the military. General Janko Bobetko, meanwhile, moved to the highest ranks of the Croatian armed forces. The liberal side of Tudjman's HDZ was now completely overwhelmed by the right wing. General Bobetko, along with Gojko Susak and the other Canadians, including Ante Beljo, were thrilled. Unhindered by opposition, they now warned Croats that the Muslims of Bosnia were planning to invade Croatia. This was a preposterous claim; the Bosnians were barely managing to hang on to Bosnia in the face of the Serbian and Croatian aggression.

Despite some underreported barbaric behaviour by Croats in the war, Croatia had until now enjoyed a certain immunity from international criticism. Hundreds of thousands of Muslim refugees, who might otherwise have flooded into other parts of Europe, were being absorbed by Croatia, which enhanced Croatian standing in the eyes of the world. But in 1993, the Croat authorities began to round up refugees and send them back to Bosnia, or turn them over to the HVO commanders to be used in prisoner exchanges. International sympathy for Croatia and its struggle for autonomy began to wane.

The biggest blow to Tudjman's international reputation came in April 1993 when a badly shaken British UNPROFOR officer, Lieutenant Colonel Bob Stewart, reported an atrocity in the Bosnian village of Ahmici. Shaking with rage and on the verge of tears, the British soldier spoke to a television crew that followed him into the burned-out community. In Stewart's words: "Each house was systematically taken out by squads of soldiers, who killed anyone they found . . . after that the bodies were thrown into the houses and destroyed by fire."

In May, the HVO began a systematic expulsion of Muslims from Croatia; first from Mostar, a beautiful city familiar to the world for its medieval architecture and extraordinary bridge, and eventually from the entire Herzegovina region. Susak and his gang imagined they were implementing their vision of an ethnically pure Herceg-Bosna and they cared little that the brutality of the Croatian military was destroying their reputation abroad. They also didn't seem to notice that they were losing badly in both wars—against Bosnians, and against Serbs.

The Croatian public, for its part, was having a hard time understanding just what Tudjman was trying to accomplish. Croats were grumbling about the economy and the scandalous rumours of corruption within the Tudjman regime. Inflation in Croatia was growing at 25 to 30 percent a month, and the average standard of living was half what it had been in pre-war times. Whatever Susak and the repatriated Croats were able to contribute to the war economy from the diaspora, it paled in comparison with what the Dalmatian hotels and beaches normally earned from tourists, who had of course been frightened off by the war. But more disturbing was the knowledge that Croatian men were dying in this doomed campaign even though Bobetko was making an effort to conceal the casualty rate.

Public opinion of the campaign in Bosnia gradually crystallized into bitterness and embarrassment. "From being victims in 1991 and 1992 we have turned into small and unsuccessful aggressors in Bosnia, and we have lost support around the world," said one of Croatia's mayors. Even people who cared not a whit for Croatia's reputation abroad opposed the campaign. The economic loss was bad, the waste of human lives worse, and in the end nothing would be gained by it. Croatia's fate, after all, would be the same as Bosnia's in the long run. If Milosevic succeeded in Bosnia, then he would succeed in Croatia as well. Both countries would fall victim to the grand Belgrade vision for Greater Serbia. The Croatian war against the Muslims only made Milosevic stronger.

But public disappointment in UNPROFOR was growing even faster than disillusionment with the Tudjman government. UN forces were simply becoming irrelevant to both Serbs and Croats. The UN Security Council had passed resolutions declaring that the Serb-held Krajina was an integral part of the Republic of Croatia, but resolutions had no power to return the territory to Croatia's hands. Resolution 743 called for the return of displaced people and the reconstitution of the police force based on pre-war ethnic proportions. But neither of these things happened, or was likely to happen. The UN Security Council passed more resolutions for the former Yugoslavia than for any other conflict in its history, and none of them seemed to be having any effect.

The JNA had officially left Croatia as promised, but their departure was an empty gesture, since heavily armed Serbian paramilitaries continued to operate in the areas they had controlled. Arms from Serbia were still flowing into the country. A U.S. State Department report said that Serb forces inside the UNPAs (which were officially demilitarized) numbered 15,000 to 18,000 men "with large amounts of weaponry at their disposal." Their numbers were augmented by "volunteers" from Serbia and Montenegro and from Serbian paramilitary forces in other parts of the former Yugoslavia.

"Authorities in Serbia were reliably reported to have dispatched substantial numbers of 'volunteers' to Sector North and Sector South to fight against the Croats," said the U.S. report. An elderly Croatian woman who had refused to leave Sector South was left with a meat hook through her neck and hand. Three Croatian policemen were murdered in Pacrac, an area under Canadian UN control.

Cedric Thornberry, the civilian head of the UNPROFOR, declared in late 1992 that the protected areas were pure "anarchy." It was a strong condemnation of the Vance Plan but an accurate one. The UNPAs failed in part because they offered no real solution to the Croat-Serb conflict, but even more because the entire Balkans were now descending into hell. The UNPROFOR task had been difficult enough when only Serbia and Croatia were clashing; when two more wars broke out in neighbouring Bosnia it made the mission almost impossible.

At this point Tudjman announced that he was cancelling the UNPROFOR mission and sending all the foreign soldiers packing. This was partly in response to popular sentiment, but it was also to distract attention from his own failures. The UN was able to get the peacekeeping mandate renewed despite Tudjman's bluster, but it was clear that the UN mission couldn't succeed if the Security Council failed to put any muscle behind its windy resolutions.

Meanwhile, the ring of Serbian heavy guns and snipers choked the city of Sarajevo and people had begun to slowly starve to death under the siege. The UN appointed Lewis MacKenzie to lead a relief operation. It redirected Michel Jones and his Canadian battalion from the Croatian mission to Sarajevo to open the airport so that relief supplies could get through. The assignment was difficult and encountered violent opposition. Though successful, Jones and the Canadians discovered they often had to fight, using lethal force, in order to survive "peacekeeping" in the Balkans.

When Jones's weary battle group returned to their duties in the UNPAs of Croatia, the UN had new responsibilities for the peacekeepers to take on. UNPROFOR was to take control of what were called the Pink Zones: areas outside the UNPAs where Serbian forces were stubbornly refusing to withdraw. The Pink Zones might have been better described as grey zones since the UN had no clear idea what was happening within them. If the mission of protecting the dangerous but relatively well-defined UNPAs was fraught with peril, the ill-defined Pink Zones promised to be deadly.

Happily for Jones and his battalion, their tour of duty was coming to an end. The impossible task would fall to the next rotation of Canadian soldiers preparing to enter the Balkan quagmire.

CHAPTER THREE

THE GHOSTS OF KAP'YONG

*Peace is a relative term in the former Yugoslavia. And in fact,
in 1993 it was something of a joke.*

—Colonel Jim Calvin, speaking before the Board of Inquiry
into Potential Exposure of Canadian Forces to a
Contaminated Environment, 1999

JIM CALVIN WASN'T SURE how he was going to pull this off. He
had only been the commanding officer of the Princess Patricia's
Canadian Light Infantry, Second Battalion, for a few short
months. He had arrived in the summer of 1992 and it was now
November. In some businesses, that would be long enough for a
new boss to gain some credibility, but soldiers are naturally suspicious. A commander can quite literally lead a soldier to his
death: trust, in those conditions, isn't easily won.

The magic number of years it takes to gain the confidence of
your soldiers in peacetime is said to be two, and that's exactly
how long a commander usually remains in the job before being
transferred again. There are also exceptional circumstances:
experiences that bind soldiers so tightly together that light doesn't
show between them. If such an experience happens it can sub-
stitute for the two-year stretch. But Calvin had neither of these

advantages. And now he was told by his seniors that he was to take his untried battalion into a place that even seasoned soldiers said was sheer hell: the Balkans.

Calvin was to replace Lieutenant Colonel Glen Nordick, whose battle group had landed in the Balkan pressure-cooker in early October. Nordick had replaced Michel Jones, commanding officer of the first Canadian battalion of UNPROFOR: Jones's soldiers had come out of Croatia shaking their heads in shock and disbelief. For decades, the prototype of peacekeeping had been Cyprus, the sun-drenched, mostly low-stress mission in the Mediterranean: Canadian soldiers were familiar with that kind of duty, but this was different. In the Balkans, "peacekeeping" was chaotic, volatile and deadly.

Initially, the UN had approved a limited twelve-month mandate in Croatia, but that was now to be extended. Not because the mission was working, but because no one in the international community had a better idea. The UN Security Council members had not been able to agree on an approach; European countries, and also Great Britain, had their favourites in the bloody conflict and no one country would take the lead with a commitment to really solve the matter. The United States had just elected a new president and Americans weren't showing much interest.

The UN sent in more peacekeepers, but they were having little effect. As the months passed, the hostility between Serbia and Croatia deepened. Historical grievances were being dug up by the partisan media, supported with new history and fresh grievances; the front lines became intractable. Another Canadian battalion had recently been added to those already serving in the rapidly growing UN force in the former Yugoslavia. The new troops were dispatched to Bosnia, where they found themselves in the midst of a savage three-way war. The number of Canadian soldiers serving in the former Yugoslavia was now 2,300.

Canadian Forces policy was that, normally, a soldier should have at least a year on the ground in Canada before redeploying on a mission, but many Canadian soldiers were coming home from one rotation and going right back out on another. Some units, such as engineers, were sent back because there was a heavy demand for them in these land-mine-saturated assignments. But large numbers of Canadian soldiers went out again simply because they needed the extra pay.

With Canada involved in so many missions, from Africa to the Balkans, and with battalions borrowing and swapping companies to fill their assignments, Colonel Calvin's battalion was seriously under strength in November of 1992. About 180 members of his Patricias had been taken by the Third Battalion, already in Croatia with Glen Nordick. There remained a nucleus of only 320 soldiers in the Second Battalion. Calvin needed four rifle companies of approximately 120 soldiers each to cover the huge area of responsibility he would inherit, as well as combat support and administration companies, in addition to his headquarters. He could probably pull together a hundred service personnel from the professional ranks across the country—medics, cooks and the like—and he could find an engineer troop. But he needed a total force of 860 soldiers to function as a battalion. No other regiment had those kinds of numbers to spare.

Brigade groups and even a division of Canadian soldiers numbering as many as 10,000 had trained together in the Cold War years. Brigade-level forces of four to five thousand soldiers had come together at least once a year as late as the 1980s. In 1993, after the Mulroney government's deep budget cuts had taken effect, soldiers didn't even train in battalions, since their ranks were often split up over several different missions. Canadian peacekeeping forces went into the world in "battle groups"—bite-sized, but theoretically efficient units of six to nine hundred soldiers that were cobbled together according to the needs of the mission. The Canadian government had stripped the armed forces to the bone, insisting that Canada no longer needed the fighting power. Try explaining that to Colonel Calvin as he contemplated his 350 men. Calvin's superiors told him that he would have to get the rest of his force from the ranks of Canada's reservists.

Glen Nordick had taken 120 reservists with him to Croatia; Calvin needed three times that number. It was unprecedented in post-war times for any commander to complement his force's numbers with that many "weekend warriors." "They could shoot their weapons," Calvin says of the reservists, "and they did a minor form of physical fitness training before they arrived, but that was it." Calvin had only months to get the battle group together. He was expected to be in Croatia to replace Nordick by early March. This was going to take work.

Canada has had reserves, or a militia as they were once called, since before Confederation and, for long periods of Canada's history it was widely assumed that they were the only fighting force the country really needed. The historian David Bercuson says that Canadians possess a time-honoured contempt for things military, and except in wartime rarely even think about their soldiers. Canadians and their leaders have historically assumed that Britain or the United States would defend us if we were invaded, and so our best option was to remain on the friendliest terms possible with those two countries. Bercuson says the low opinion of military affairs has prevailed since the days of John A. Macdonald when professional soldiers were considered "useful only for hunting, drinking and chasing women." According to popular opinion, they became soldiers simply because they could do nothing else of any use.

Notwithstanding peacetime sentiments, Canada was able to mount divisions of soldiers during the great wars and they became among the most proficient fighting forces in Europe. But as soon as the wars were over, Canadian governments would slash the budgets and reduce the forces to the most inconspicuous units possible. The militia never went out of fashion: Canada could always point to reservists when accused of not having the forces necessary to defend itself. By the early 1990s, Canada had about 23,000 soldiers in the army and almost as many people registered in the reserves.

In peacetime, the militia had proven themselves to be effective when they were needed for small Canadian Forces operations, but not since Korea had their employment been tested on such a grand scale. The problem for Calvin was that his soldiers had come from all over the country, from Newfoundland to Vancouver Island, and most of them had never operated together. Also, the reservists had not trained on the latest equipment that Calvin would be taking to Croatia. "They didn't have familiarity on some of the weapons that they were going to be manning. They weren't familiar with the .50-calibre machine guns." If Calvin had known how heavily he would come to depend on reservists operating machine guns he would have been even more deeply concerned. Glen Nordick was reporting back to Calvin that he should expect a lot of trouble.

***

On January 4, 550 reservists reported for duty on the frigid Princess Patricias' base in Winnipeg. With the core of the battalion and the other personnel Calvin had been able to borrow or steal, the ragtag group standing on the frozen tarmac that morning was a thousand people taken from nearly seventy different units. There were the Seaforth Highlanders of Canada from British Columbia, the King's Own Calgary Regiment, the Saskatchewan Dragoons, the Royal Winnipeg Rifles, the Lake Superior Scottish Regiment, the Nova Scotia Highlanders and the Newfoundland Service Battalion.

The soldiers-in-training were installed in the Kap'yong barracks, named for the extraordinary battle the Patricias had fought in Korea forty-two years earlier. In 1950, when the Second Battalion had been called up for duty in Korea, they were by all accounts unfit for combat. Typically for the Canadian Forces, their training and their numbers had dropped off sharply since the end of the Second World War. Canada's armed forces had gone from a strength of 500,000 to 15,000 overnight. But the Patricias were needed badly and they started immediate, intense training. Once overseas they weren't expected to have to fight, but in 1951, a few scant months later, the Second Battalion successfully fought off a Chinese attack on Hill 677; this was the battle of Kap'yong, for which they were awarded the United States' Presidential Unit Citation. They were the first regiment in Canadian history ever to receive the award.

From those first days in January 1993, Major Dan Drew, the operations officer for the battle group, wondered what he had got himself into. It was his job to take these men and a handful of women, most of them barely out of their teens, and turn them into a fighting force in a matter of months.

Drew is a soldier out of central casting: a stern-faced man with intense blue eyes, a classic military salt-and-pepper crew-cut and a physical presence like a wound-up spring. He could easily play the role of a U.S. marine or a Green Beret in a Hollywood war movie. Hailing from the bleak, brash Miramichi region of New Brunswick, Drew says he always wanted to be a soldier. Three days after finishing high school, he was in Chilliwack, British Columbia, for his training.

The commanding officer sets a certain tone for a battalion and according to Drew, Jim Calvin was no exception. Calvin is a small-framed man, with sandy hair and an open, approachable face. His demeanour is deceptive, disguising what colleagues describe as an irascible, even dangerous temper. Drew says simply: "He didn't put up with people who tried to fuck with him."

Unlike Drew, Calvin had never planned to be a soldier. Growing up in a big family in Oshawa in the late sixties, he only wanted to go to university. His father's brother, Uncle Stan, took him aside and told him about Royal Roads Military College, which had only just opened. Calvin could get a free education in exchange for putting in a few years of service. At first, it seemed strange: everyone else was growing their hair long and protesting the war in Vietnam when young Jim went off to Royal Roads. Twenty-five years later, he was commanding a battalion.

Every battalion has a personality of its own and his was already regarded as the scrappy street fighter of military units. The Second Battalion had had a reputation for aggression since the days at Kap'yong, but the Princess Patricias had an "in the field first" reputation that went back decades.

The Patricias were initially a privately funded regiment, the brainchild of a Montreal millionaire by the name of Hamilton Gault who named them after the Governor General's daughter, Princess Patricia of Connaught, who hand-made the regiment's insignia. The Patricias were the first Canadian formation to reach Europe during the First World War. From the blood-soaked battlefields of Ypres and Vimy Ridge to Ortona and Leonforte in the Second World War, the Patricias were noted as fierce, uncompromising fighters. The regiment's losses were heavy: 1,272 killed in the first war, 273 in the second, and thou-sands more wounded. The Patricias were hailed as heroes and were decorated many times over.

Dan Drew had never known training as intense as the train-ing he underwent in the Patricias in his early years: "You would have the pus whipped out of you every day," he recalls. The com-mander in those days was Lieutenant Colonel Larry Gollner, who never let up on the soldiers, pushing them until they were single-minded fighting machines. For Drew, there would never be another Gollner, but he found Calvin too was a good fit as commander of the Patricias.

Calvin claims that he inherited the battalion's character more than he coloured it, but he undeniably put his own stamp on it through those he promoted and consulted—Dan Drew among them. Drew became a major and was put in charge of Delta Company, a unit that Calvin wanted to rely on as his bedrock in the field. Another soldier Calvin singled out was Matt Stopford, a tough, inflexible man of action. Stopford's col-leagues nicknamed him Pig Pen, since he was always dishev-elled, but they knew better than to call him anything disparaging to his face: they would have regretted it. Calvin promoted him to warrant officer in Delta Company, sending a signal throughout the battle group as to what kind of soldiers he wanted.

Rounding out the fierce little nucleus of Dan Drew's company was the dark-haired, ruddy-faced Mike Spellen, a streetwise and cantankerous sergeant major who inspired fear and sometimes anger, but always respect. His soldiers would learn over time that despite his rough exterior his heart was as soft as sponge.

Calvin instructed his officers to "work their asses off," as he and Drew went off to Croatia for a week of reconnaissance. It was an alarming eye-opener. Living conditions were appalling: "The soldiers were bunking in bombed-out buildings that had no heat or lights," Dan Drew remembers, even though it was the dead of winter. The only luxury was a whisky and cigar by candle-light at the end of the day, huddled in a tent with two sweaters on.

But that wasn't the most alarming news for the reconnaissance party. Within days of arriving in Sector West, Calvin got a first-hand taste of what conditions would be like for his battalion. He went out in the middle of the night with a crew of four Canadian soldiers to check out some commotion on the Serbian side of the line. When they got close, they left the driver and the armoured personnel carrier (APC) behind, and headed out on foot. Moments later, a Serb anti-tank rocket smashed into the side of the APC. They had been ambushed. The driver, mercifully, was outside the vehicle but he was knocked flat.

"What that taught us," says Calvin, "was that we were going into a theatre where Canadian soldiers could be specifically tar-geted. This was no accident. They had drawn a Canadian APC and a group of soldiers out and they had attacked that APC."

Drew had been on peacekeeping duty in Cyprus in 1988, a place, he said, "where both parties wanted you there." But in Croatia, the job "had morphed from peacekeeping into a sort of peacemaking environment." He says that neither Canada's sen-ior defence officials nor the government seemed to realize what they were getting their soldiers into.

It's not clear whether that was true. By early 1993, plenty of significant incident reports must have reached Ottawa and the message about the level of danger in the Balkans should have been clear. Michel Jones and the Van Doos had confronted a tremendous amount of violence in both Bosnia and Croatia. There was no peace to keep.

If Ottawa knew of the conditions, the politicians never alerted the public, perhaps because they were eager to get kudos internationally for being first in the field as peacekeepers. But Canadian departments of foreign affairs and defence were also deeply distracted by another peacekeeping mission that was seriously coming apart: Somalia.

Operation Deliverance had been assigned to enter a country that was without law or central authority: the objective was to disarm the local warlords and put down their military forces. Somalia was a rare Chapter 7 mission, meaning that the United Nations had authorized the use of force. The operation was being planned and led by the Americans, and the Canadians' role was combat, not traditional Chapter 6 peacekeeping. The government and the Canadian Airborne had been apprised of the nature of their task shortly before they departed and when preparations for a more benign assignment were well advanced. However, Brian Mulroney (and then Prime Minister Kim Campbell, who replaced Mulroney) seemed eager to oblige Washington, and never questioned the change from peacekeeping to peacemaking. Nor did they verify that the Airborne was prepared for such a mission.

By January the Canadians had been in Somalia for weeks, living in tents in the middle of a deeply impoverished country that had been reduced to anarchy. Somali boys constantly broke into the Canadian base to steal food, supplies, guns and ammunition. When the soldiers managed to catch the teenagers they locked them up and kept them overnight, often treating them cruelly in order to teach them a lesson. That only made matters worse.

The thieves became bolder and the soldiers more belligerent. In February, there was a significant incident with the Canadians when relief workers in Belet Huen were attacked by Somalis bent on carrying off whatever they could. It turned into a riot. Canadian foot patrols tried to stop the mob by firing over their heads. When that failed, they fired into the crowd, killing one Somali man and wounding several others.

Some angry Canadian soldiers on the mission began to drink heavily and plan their revenge on the ungrateful Somalis. It was the beginning of a collapse of morale and principle that would affect everything in the Canadian military for years to come, including Jim Calvin's mission for UNPROFOR.

* * *

Back in Winnipeg from the reconnaissance tour, Calvin got down to work training his soldiers for a much tougher mission than they had been expecting. Calvin knew that he had to teach them how to "handle weapons under stress and protect themselves in a very dangerous situation." And he only had about seventy-five days to do it.

The troops were on the move long before first light each day in Winnipeg's winter. They would train hard all day, stop for supper, and then go back for more drills. The companies had to be sent out to facilities all over Winnipeg since the base didn't really have what was required. Delta Company had to go over to the naval armouries to work. By nine o'clock at night they were back in Kap'yong barracks, exhausted, while the officer staff would sit down and try to figure out how many of the people they were driving so hard each day actually had the right stuff to go on the mission.

Difficult as the training was, it was also thrilling. Each of the young recruits was getting a chance to see what he or she was made of; it was a new experience, and not just for the reservists. The officers and NCOs had never gone through anything as rigorous either. They all had a compelling sense that they were about to be really on their own as a battalion in a theatre of war, where they would have to make life-and-death decisions. This was the real thing. Sergeant Chris Byrne describes how the trainers drummed the lesson into their heads: "The opening statement of Dan Drew was 'Train for peace.' And then he knocked over the bulletin board there and he said, 'Bullshit. Train for war.' And we did. We trained for war."

Calvin ignored rank. He promoted or demoted his soldiers according to ability alone. It got up the noses of some of the full-time professional soldiers, but it also sent a signal to the reservists that they wouldn't be treated as second-class soldiers. Tyrone Green was one reservist who benefited. A Seaforth Highlander and a university student, he suddenly found himself in charge of a platoon of soldiers in Charlie Company. Green is a muscle-bound, rock-jawed man who inspired confidence simply with his size; he had a bulldog's singular sense of purpose. Master Corporal Rob Deans, a keen, high-energy twenty-one-year-old, also from the Seaforth Highlanders, desperately wanted to go on this mission. His best friend, Tony Spiess, was also trying out for the Second Battalion. The two young men would have been devastated if one got to go and the other didn't.

A lot of the reservists didn't have what it took. Drew found many of them out of shape or looking for a sinecure in a Cyprus-type mission. Others were arrogant, unreliable or dangerous: a few men "had to be sorted out," says Drew, particularly a group that busted up the base's pop machines. They were sent home.

***

Calvin knew they needed live-fire training, but the frozen Manitoba prairie was not the best environment to prepare for possible combat in Croatia. The base didn't even have enough equipment to outfit everyone. The training areas in Germany weren't large enough to do live-fire exercises and it was too cold in Europe for the training he had in mind. There was only one Western country that was still in the full-time business of preparing for war.

In February, Calvin took his battle group to California. Fort Ord dates from the Mexican-American war of 1846 and was one of the United States' leading infantry training centres, along with the adjacent Hunter-Liggett facility, established in 1940 on 200,000 acres of ranchland between the Pacific Ocean and the Salinas River Valley. The terrain of mountains and valleys is ideal for American "real-world" combat training and has been used by the U.S. military to prepare men to fight ever since the Second World War. It was the best location to test the mettle of the Canadians. If any of them thought they would get a pleasant winter break, they were mistaken: cold rain pounded them every day for almost two weeks. Dan Drew described the conditions as "perfect."

They lived in tents and slept in sleeping bags. They went to bed wet and trained wet. They marched out to ranges twelve kilometres away, had breakfast, and began training with weapons and live ammunition: field firing with Carl Gustav rocket launchers by night under flares. They were formed into tight teams of sections, platoons and companies. Every platoon commander had to take his troops through three live-fire attacks, and if they didn't pass, they went back to the start line and went through the whole ordeal again.

Rod Dearing found it all "wicked" and he loved almost every minute. Light infantry work was the best fit for him as a soldier. The live-fire exercises started small, with individual rifle training. It graduated to fighting in teams, then groups of four, then sections of eight or nine, working up to platoon-size ranges. They learned about interlocking arcs of fire, the correct positioning of the platoon's sections and the proper employment of all their weapons. Since Dearing would command a section of Charlie Company, the training was sure to be useful: he didn't know that within months it would be far more than that.

"We tried to prepare our guys for every situation they could run into over there," Drew remembers. He was now starting to see what kind of unit he would have. Miraculously, they were coming together. Regular soldiers like Spellen, Stopford and Dearing were developing into teams with the reservists like Green, Deans and Spiess. Calvin had arrived at Fort Ord with 550 reservists: only 385 survived the training. A lot of people, says Drew, found out that they really didn't want to be there.

But others, like Dearing, wanted to be there more intensely than anything else they had experienced in their young lives.

Dearing's company commander, Bryan Bailey, began to notice natural leaders, Dearing among them. At first, Bailey had written him off as more California surfer dude than soldier, but he could see how the other soldiers were drawn to him. "I'm sure the regimental sergeant major considered him too relaxed in terms of dress and deportment," says Bailey. But Dearing's ability to get the other soldiers to push themselves beyond their limits, as well as his uncanny skills as a marksman, put him into the class of soldiers from which soldier-legends are formed. Just when the tension levels were edging up, Dearing would throw back his head and deliver his trademark guffaw, and defuse the moment. With a few Dearings in the mix, Bailey started to believe he might end up with a formidible company of soldiers.

* * *

By the time Calvin's whittled-down battle group was back in Winnipeg for the final phase of training, the situation of the UN Protection Force in Croatia was teetering on the brink of collapse.

On January 22, Tudjman authorized 6,000 Croatian troops to overrun the UN Protected Area demarcation line in the Dalmatian area and to seize three strongholds: the Maslenica Bridge, which was the most crucial link between Dalmatia and the rest of Croatia; the airport near the coastal port of Zadar; and the hydroelectric dam installation near Peruca, all of which had been in Serbian hands since the beginning of the conflict.

This was an important victory for the Croats: the three installations were of major strategic significance. And it was also important for the morale of Croatian troops. Dispirited and despondent after losing so much territory to the Serbs before the peace agreement was signed, they were cheered by this evidence that they could win, and that Tudjman wasn't just a lapdog of the international community. But they had, in fact, violated a newly signed peace agreement. Tudjman had gone back on his word, destroying the Vance Plan—the premise on which the peacekeepers had entered the country. The consequences were alarming.

French peacekeepers had been in charge of the area around Zadar and Maslenica. Two were killed during the Croat offensive, and thirteen wounded. The French were conscripts, and lacked the stalwartness of the professional army. They had to come to Croatia to finish their required service, not to become war heroes. Peacekeepers are under command of the UN mission, but if the contributing country thinks the mission is dangerous or badly led, they can and often do override the orders of the mission. France pulled its soldiers out of the area and they refused to intervene further.

For the Serbs of the Krajina, the Croat offensive was all the proof they needed that the Croats' commitment to the Vance Plan couldn't be trusted. Under the terms of the plan, the Serbs had turned over many of their weapons; now they raided the arms caches and reclaimed all their rifles and heavy guns. UNPROFOR's leading peacekeeping unit in Sector South, the French, made no move to stop them.

Croatia threatened to explode into all-out war. Canadian and Argentinian soldiers had been vigorous in confiscating weapons in their area of Slavonia, persuading the Serbs that it was safe to hand over their arms. Now all their efforts were coming unstuck: several hundred Serbs broke into the weapons storage depot in Pacrac and tried to seize rifles and equipment. Glen Nordick's soldiers, along with the Argentinians, managed to stop them and the Serbs retreated empty-handed. But they were the only peacekeepers in all of Croatia who successfully resisted the Serbian revolt. It seemed clear that the UN's control of the situation was tenuous.

The Yugoslav army had been withdrawing from the UN protected areas according to plan, but as was now becoming evident, they were doing so in order to move on to Bosnia rather than to comply with the Vance Plan. Their departure left the Krajina Serbs vulnerable. The Croat forces were clearly buoyant after their victory: both Serbs and peacekeepers sensed a renewed spirit of Croat aggression, especially in the Lika Highlands and the villages around Medak in central Krajina.

Would the UN forces protect the Serbs in the event of an attack? Given the ease with which the Croats had just seized three crucial areas of Dalmatia, it seemed unlikely.

The January assault was a shrewd calculation on the part of Tudjman and his defence minister, Gojko Susak. The Croatian Army knew that the Serbs were weaker, now that the JNA had pulled out. They didn't know whether the international community would intervene seriously if they went on the offensive, but they gambled and won. The peacekeepers' interest in fighting turned out to be just what Tudjman had hoped it was—almost non-existent.

The United Nations Security Council made a feeble attempt to condemn the attack on the UN Protected Area and part of the fuzzy Pink Zone, but it imposed no sanctions on Zagreb. Tudjman paid no price for his audacious military act, although the operation didn't do him much good: Serb forces retreated but still remained close enough to prevent the Croats from rebuilding the Maslenica Bridge into anything more than a military pontoon. And the Serbs had sabotaged the power station at Peruca before retreating, making it unusable. Victory turned out to be not much more than symbolic.

Instead of imposing a penalty on Croatia for restarting the Krajina conflict and killing peacekeepers, the international community busied itself with attempting to craft another peace agreement. Cyrus Vance was again pulled out of retirement and this time was given a British partner, Lord David Owen. Claiming superior knowledge of the region, Owen convinced the international community that the best solution to the Bosnian crisis was to establish ethnic cantons: to literally partition the entire Bosnian republic into ethnic provinces. The idea would be dangerous enough in any country, but in Bosnia's complex, intertwined communities the idea was terrifying.

Lord Owen declared that the best one could do with tribes of people bent on killing each other was to separate them. His reading of the dark, bloody history of the region was that the South Slavs were people not capable of living together in one country.

Dismissing the impressive achievements of Marshal Tito, Owen simply asserted that ethnic strife was part of the Serbo-Croat genetic makeup. Few questioned his analysis: most people were baffled by this history-drenched and trouble-making corner of the world.

Owen rejected the suggestion that his cantonization rewarded ethnic cleansing. Others realized that his plan was unworkable. Bosnia's leaders resisted, since it would make the republic ungovernable even if it were possible to separate a population as thoroughly blended as Bosnia's. The Serbs opposed the plan because they had already gained 70 percent of Bosnian territory and they would have to give half of it back. But Croatian nationalists were elated. This was exactly what the extreme right-wingers of Herzegovina had dreamed of, because the proposed cantonization would legitimize Herceg-Bosna. Mate Boban, the supermarket manager with delusions of statehood, could then join his entity to Greater Croatia. The hardline Croatian Canadians in Norval, Ontario, had been hoping for this for more than a decade. The amount of territory the Croats would get in Bosnia wasn't huge, but the Herceg-Bosna defence force, the HVO, already had plans to take more. Mate Boban believed that all of Bosnia actually belonged to Croatia.

The Vance-Owen Plan not only confirmed that the international community would reward aggression, it also sent a signal that now was the time for all aspiring militias to take as much territory as possible. But the Vance-Owen Plan for the partition of Bosnia scared Tudjman's inner circle as well. If the international community was willing to reward aggression in Bosnia, maybe it would also raise no objections to the land grab of the Krajina. Knowing that UNPROFOR could be relied on to run away from a fight, all sides in the conflict began to think about annexing more territory.

* * *

The final phase of training in March for Jim Calvin's battle group was quick and basic. Exercises with mines, manning checkpoints, stress counselling and what the military calls cultural training, which Calvin admits was minimal: "We talked about the Serbs. We did some minor language training." Everyone had about a week off before it was time to go. "When we began our tour and deployed starting on the 26th of March, we weren't exactly fresh."

Everyone was in a state of heightened expectation and it was taboo to suggest anything might go wrong on the mission. But Lieutenant Mike Brown had his worries. He was one of the padres attached to the battalion: his job was to look out for the spiritual well-being of the troops.

Brown is a young Roman Catholic deacon, part of the small contingent ordained to perform a number of priestly functions but who are not really priests. After his seminary studies, he found himself unable to commit to the celibate existence of the priesthood. Brown had wanted married life with a family as well as a chance to work with the military. The chaplaincy offered him everything he wanted from his faith and his career.

Brown is a tall, restless man whose reddish-brown hair and beard form a woolly mat of closely cropped curls around his head. His sharp blue eyes flash with anger and then amusement in rapid sequence; he wears a wild range of emotions on his striking face. He was young, and he worked and played as hard as the soldiers. He never missed a training exercise or a rugby match, no matter how gruelling. He became close to the troops, but more as a peer than as a spiritual guide.

Brown couldn't hide how worried he was about the soldiers as they prepared for deployment. Though they had survived the rigorous drills, he couldn't get over how vulnerable they all appeared, though he might have seen the same qualities if he had looked in a mirror. When Brown wondered out loud whether the soldiers were emotionally equipped for what they might encounter, no one wanted to hear.

Brown joined a small group that went for basic training in critical incident stress debriefing, and he helped develop some peer counselling among the soldiers. "We trained some people in stress awareness and tried to explain what signs of psychological trauma the non-commissioned officers might look for," says Brown. But in the end, no one, not even the padre, really knew what they were getting themselves into and what effect it might have on the soldiers.

***

As it turned out, the deployment of Colonel Jim Calvin's Second Battalion was completely eclipsed in the annals of Canadian peacekeeping by events in the final weeks before they departed. On March 4, paratroopers with the Canadian Airborne Regiment battle group in Somalia shot two Somali men in the back as they tried to run away. The Somalis were unarmed and had not stolen anything, although that appears to have been their intention. One was severely wounded; the other killed. The army doctor, Major Barry Armstrong, did an autopsy on the dead man and reported that the Somali had been "killed by a close-range, execution-style shot after being wounded."

Then, on the night of March 16, something happened that would change the course of Canadian military history: inside the Canadian compound, Master Corporal Clayton Matchee and an accomplice tortured a Somali teenager to death, blindfolding him, beating him and burning the soles of his feet with cigaril-los. It was a crime of pure sadism and it took over two hours to perform, with Matchee and Corporal Kyle Brown taking photos of themselves in the various stages of killing the boy.

About a half dozen other soldiers came to see what was hap-pening but did nothing to stop it. The murder of Shidane Arone set off the worst peacetime crisis in Canadian military history. Bureaucrats and politicians scrambled to cover it up, only to have their attempts at secrecy explode in their faces. The incident revealed how utterly unprepared the defence department was for the scope of the work it was now doing and how completely in-effective the command structure was, from the government down to the ground. The Somali affair would colour everything the Canadian military touched for years to come.

Whatever Ottawa's stated intentions were, what it truly wanted from Operation Harmony in Croatia was a mission that would cause the government no trouble. It would come and go in as much obscurity as possible. It was an objective that Ottawa—unwittingly—shared with Zagreb.

CHAPTER FOUR

CROATIAN SPRING

*Why should I be a minority in your country when you could be
a minority in mine?*

—Vladimir Gligorov

THE MONTH OF MARCH in Croatia's interior is raw, cold and sodden. The newly constituted and freshly trained Second Battalion of the Princess Patricia's Canadian Light Infantry flew directly from Winnipeg to the recently reopened Zagreb airport. It was a bleak day with a driving rain, but the airport appeared perfectly normal: intact, untouched by war. The Croatian army wasn't even allowed near the facility and there were only a few policemen around.

The Canadians boarded buses for the three-hour drive to their new home in the Sector West zone of Slavonia. As they pulled out of the airport area and crossed the first of many checkpoints, the change in atmosphere was almost instantaneous, and very sobering. They crossed over to the dark side of the Balkan reality as they drove through the old Krajina garrison town of Karlovac. The facade of normalcy in the capital dissolved into the jagged, broken landscape of a country flattened by heavy guns.

Village after village, house after house, had been systematically destroyed. Within the rubble of one house the soldiers could see an old couple trying to cook on a broken stove, seeming not to notice that their walls and roof no longer existed; around another scene of ruin, despondent little groups of old women huddled together, exchanging their despairing news. Farm fields lay untended, because farmers feared the land mines lurking beneath them.

For Rod Dearing, it could have been a scene from an old war movie. His expectations were based on news reports, mostly from the war in Bosnia, but the pictures he had seen on television and in the newspapers didn't come close to capturing the devastation before him now. Padre Mike Brown noted that the soldiers fell silent, taking stock of their new home.

But their spirits brightened somewhat when they arrived at their camp. "We thought, okay, this is like an exercise at Wainwright [Alberta] in bad weather with a bit of tension, right?" Brown recalls. Camp Polom was situated between the villages of Lipik and Pacrac in the middle of the ancient Pannonian Plains. Lipik had been used by the Romans for its curative springs, and was still a popular spa and resort in the nineteenth century. The town was of no military significance, but in 1991 the Yugoslav National Army, augmented by paramilitary forces from Serbia, destroyed it anyway.

Pacrac is an old Illyrian city whose unique shape is defined by seven uneven angles, with seven towers marking its boundaries. In 1991, Serbian saboteurs planted explosives under the chapel of St. Josip and blew it up. Croats retaliated by forcing the Serbian priests out of town. In a familiar pattern, street fights broke out and the JNA tanks rolled in; Pacrac dissolved into intense combat that ended in a standoff shortly before the ceasefire was signed. When the peacekeepers arrived, the town was split in two, with a demarcation line drawn down its centre—Croatian Roman Catholics on one side, Serbian Orthodox on the other.

Unlike Lipik, Pacrac was a strategic location from a military point of view, because it is situated on the railroad line between

Zagreb and Belgrade just north of the intercity motorway called Dragonic Road. The Croats had control of Dragonic but Serbs held positions up in the hills and made it perilous for the Croats to use it. Pacrac was also strategically important because it was the only city in western Slavonia with a significant Serb majority before the war began.

When Jim Calvin and his battle group arrived, most of the ethnic cleansing in this region was completed. With a few stubborn and mostly elderly exceptions, the Serbs and Croats who had not fled the area had been redistributed into ethnically homogeneous communities on either side of a truce line. A lot of people were living in houses that didn't belong to them, nervously awaiting the resumption of hostilities. Their only hope for getting their own homes back and avoiding a vicious, ethnically driven bloodbath lay with the international negotiators and the peacekeepers who were moving into the area.

Serbian and Croatian forces were hunkered down in secure positions, frequently testing the limits of the UN's commitment to the ceasefire with rifle and mortar fire. The two armies were a shadow of what they had been months earlier. Most of the heavy equipment, and the war interest, had gone south to Bosnia. But they used any opportunity to harass the other side and, often, the peacekeepers.

The handover between Canadian battalions took about seven days as the newly arrived Patricias adjusted to the change from late winter in the Canadian prairies to early spring on the Pannonian Plains. "Our living conditions were very, very basic," recalls Dan Drew. " A lot of us were in blown-up houses. There were some people who lived in these little white UN bungalows, we used to call them, and we did have showers and stuff like that. But at that time I think only once every three or four days." Before their rotation was up, Drew and his company would come to regard these living conditions in Sector West as luxurious.

Colonel Calvin's battalion headquarters was located in camp, but his soldiers were scattered around in platoon and section houses out near the front lines. "The only reason we got houses at all was because they had already been ethnically cleansed," and abandoned, says Calvin. There was no glass on the windows. The Canadians installed plastic sheeting and a portable wood stove or the gas-powered but always reliable Herman Nelson heater for warmth. No privacy was possible, since they had to sleep cheek by jowl in cots and sleeping bags, but at least the food wasn't bad: local women came to cook so the bread was fresh and the meals were based on wholesome local produce—although the kitchen and eating areas soon were plagued with rats.

The soldiers worked twelve-hour shifts, but even after a long shift ended there would be other work to do. Their equipment was notorious for requiring constant repair and maintenance; the most basic vehicles and parts were in a sorry state. David Reiff, a journalist who covered the Balkan wars, once remarked that Canadian vehicles were a source of comic relief for people working in the area. An APC or jeep at the roadside with a soldier head first under the hood was almost certainly part of the Canadian contingent.

The Canadians were using gear that "should have found itself in the hands of some collector in Texas years earlier," Reiff observed. The Canadian soldiers took the mechanical challenges in stride. Fixing broken equipment and "making do" became a source of satisfaction and many soldiers were expert mechanics by the time they left the forces.

The Canadians seldom complained, perhaps because they realized that compared to other national contingents, they were reasonably well off. The Nepalese, with whom the Canadians shared responsibility in Sector West, had no vehicles at all. They carried only their personal weapons and a mere thirty rounds of ammunition each, leaving it up to the UN to equip them for the mission. Meanwhile, for every soldier they sent, the government of Nepal collected a thousand U.S. dollars per month. The UN also provided food for the Nepalese and other contingents who needed it, but some Canadian soldiers noticed the Nepalese seemed constantly undernourished. Soldiers from Western countries in addition to their salaries and bonuses were paid a small daily allowance by their own governments, which they could use to supplement the UN diet, but the Nepalese peacekeepers either had no such stipend from their government, or they were sending it to needy relatives at home.

Their poverty developed into a serious security issue when it became apparent that it made the Nepalese vulnerable to bribery by both Serbs and Croats who were seeking to bend the rules. The Nepalese often sold their gasoline and possibly even some of their food on the black market. When they were eventually supplied with eight-wheel military vehicles they didn't know how to drive them and had to ask the Canadians for assistance.

The Argentinians, who also shared peacekeeping responsibility in Sector West, were much better trained but they required a steady supply of parts to keep their few armoured vehicles functioning; the Jordanians had only about a dozen personnel carriers for their entire battalion. The UN thought that was all each battle group would need in what was, theoretically, a monitoring of a peace agreement. Michel Jones had known otherwise: he had brought eighty-six APCs, allowing the Canadian companies to be fully mechanized. For all the weaknesses of the Canadian battalion, it was the best equipped and best trained of all the peacekeeping contingents in Croatia, with the exception of the French.

The four rifle companies that made up Calvin's battle group were dispersed through the soggy farms and villages around Camp Polom. Alpha Company was situated in the middle, in the volatile area around the divided city of Pacrac. Bravo Company was spread thinly through rural areas that had been recently cleared of civilians, where skirmishes broke out regularly. Woodsmen were busy chopping in the forest, drawn back by a booming demand for firewood. The Canadians watched them warily, wondering if their woodcutting was a cover for some more sinister activity.

Charlie Company worked everywhere. They were the fire brigade of the battalion, the company Calvin would use first if trouble broke out. Delta Company was the most stalwart of the battalion and it was assigned to focus on the second most violent city, Lipik, or what was left of Lipik. They were positioned on the heights surrounding the town and on the important Dragovic Road, linking Lipik to Pacrac.

Being extraordinarily busy was probably healthy for all of them. It was a distraction from the human discomforts of living in close quarters, in cramped and primitive conditions. More important, it helped to prevent them from brooding about the ravaged landscape and human misery that they saw all around them. Birdlike old women in kerchiefs, dressed in black, rummaged in piles of refuse for scraps of food or firewood. Solitary chimneys, the stubborn thrust of a surviving fireplace, surrounded by the ruins of once-sheltering roofs and walls. Where walls remained, they were pocked and battered by the senseless rifle fire and shelling that seemed to go on and on in a manic release of destructive energy, long after all resistance ends. Ancient churches and monuments, symbols of civil permanence, were destroyed and desecrated in the savage determination to humiliate and terrify and, ultimately, erase the human character that defines a community.

This was the hard reality of ethnic cleansing, a phrase so frequently used it sometimes loses meaning. For young soldiers, nurtured in a society that draws energy and inspiration from ethnic diversity, the scenes of destruction were as pointless as they were barbaric. It would have been a relief to take refuge in the falsehood that the perpetrators of these activities were of an alien species, but they were undeniably human beings like themselves, reduced by fear and stoked by frightening propaganda to behave like sociopaths.

"You became inured to it in Sector West," says Calvin, though it's doubtful that he or any of the soldiers really did. "We heard stories all the time that people had gone for a walk or to church and when they came back, their house was gone. There were clear rumours that the police were involved in this, you know, on a major scale. Very difficult to prove. But the police were not independent individuals in Sector West. They were very much involved in all the weapons smuggling and all the activities on both sides."

Hard as all of this emotional overload was on the seasoned soldiers, it had a brutal effect on the hundreds of fresh-faced young reservists who had been brought in to augment the battalion. "These kids came to us, you know, out of units from Saskatchewan and B.C. and Newfoundland and some of them had never been out of their villages before," says Mike Spellen, sergeant major with D Company. Spellen could never get over the look of sheer innocence on the faces of the young soldiers.

They were under a "confined to base" rule for their social life, meaning they couldn't go to local bars and cafés (if such things had existed) but they had a lot of contact with local people through the "hearts and minds" campaign—an official part of the operation designed to win people's confidence. "We adopted a school," Dan Drew remembers, "and our engineers built them a jungle swing and sort of levelled the playing field for them."

"A lot of troops are just eighteen, nineteen years of age," Spellen says. "And when these guys are putting in long days— twelve- to fifteen-hour days in some cases—and there's the odd time when we're on our feet for over thirty hours because of some incident that happened. But we had eighteen-year-olds playing father to some of the local orphans and kids. The guys were, on their own time, chopping firewood. The wives and girl-friends or parents were sending stuff over, care packages, and when the guys went on leave that stuff was coming over."

Jim Calvin admits he worried about the effect the situation was having on the young men and women under his command. "We are talking about people who had not been seasoned. They were part-timers." He had trained them as best he could and thought they were capable soldiers, but he had no way of knowing how emotionally capable they were. "You have to put yourself in the paradigm of what the soldiers were facing at the time. We thought it was normal. It was not normal," Calvin says. But no matter what they encountered, they had a job to do and Calvin was far more concerned with the mission.

The soldiers tried to connect to anything familiar they could find. "I remember the boys making a tape to send to Don Cherry," says Dan Drew. "Don Cherry for Chief of Defence Staff or Don Cherry for Prime Minister, and stuff like that." But really, nothing was familiar or easy. "The Serbs were putting mines in schoolyards where kids were walking and blowing their feet off, and it was just destabilizing our sector. Okay, the Croats were accusing us of not doing our job and it was a bad situation."

＊

The principal task of Jim Calvin's soldiers was to disarm people for whom rifles and rocket launchers were now more reliable and trustworthy than most human beings—including international peacekeepers. The Croats and Serbs had two choices, under the terms of the United Nations ceasefire agreement: they could put their weapons under UN control or they could move them a safe distance away from the UN Protected Area.

The Serbs in Sector West had turned over their weapons, though they had lost considerable confidence in the UN system after the Croatian offensive on Maslenica Bridge and the airport at Zadar in January. They were allowed to periodically check confiscated ordnance and did so frequently, taking inventory of what would quickly be available if war broke out again.

The Croats had promised to move their weapons outside the UN areas rather than put them under lock and key. But they clearly hadn't put them all away, as they were still ambushing the Serbian side on a regular basis. In reality, both Serbs and Croats were playing a kind of shell game with their guns, moving them around outside of the UN areas but always keeping firepower available for quick raids on the enemy.

"The people on the ground didn't believe that peace had been achieved in any measure whatsoever," says Calvin. "There might have been a political agreement, but the people that we dealt with hadn't made peace with each other."

The peacekeepers manned a series of checkpoints and their frequent spot checks on cars and homes yielded a plentiful harvest of anti-tank weapons, pistols with silencers, AK47s, mortar bombs, grenades and a vast array of mines. It was a surprising haul of lethal material for an area that was supposed to be demilitarized but the peacekeepers probably found only a fraction of what had been concealed.

They had to follow a strict protocol for weapons seizures, getting permission from the local police (who had probably hidden the weapons in the first place), UN civilian police, and also the owners of the hideaways, who were hardly innocent bystanders. But thanks to the pressure on the combatants, Sector West eventually became the most stable of all the UN Protected Areas. The commander for Sector West, in charge of all the peacekeepers, was an Argentinian who earned the respect of the Canadians over and over again. He issued a zero-tolerance policy for arms and insisted that local police carry nothing more lethal than their pistols. Sector West became a model for peacekeeping in the area.

But that didn't mean that the local warriors didn't try to circumvent the rules. The audacity of some of their attacks was breathtaking. In the area patrolled by Bravo Company, a Serbian band of paramilitaries ambushed a Croatian police truck, riddling it with machine-gun fire. Then they quickly disappeared over the ceasefire line. The Croats accused UNPROFOR of failing to protect them but there was almost nothing the peacekeepers could do to prevent such brazen incidents. They had no control over guns and gunmen from outside their protected zones. And Serbia was covertly but steadily supplying troops and munitions to its Croatian-Serb kinsmen, in an effort to hold their gains there while Belgrade dedicated most of its forces to the war in Bosnia.

Land mines would become one of the most psychologically corrosive factors in the daily lives of the peacekeepers. Anti-personnel and anti-tank mines were strewn about in incalculable numbers. The engineers removed what they could in their area of responsibility only to later discover that new mines had been quietly replanted. Two of their vehicles hit mines in the first six weeks, miraculously without serious injuries, but the stress the mines produced—sometimes called "mine paranoia"—began to tell on the soldiers.

Then there were the booby traps. In one typical incident, a patrol was sent to investigate a weapons cache located in a suspicious bunker. When a soldier wrenched opened the door he heard the gut-wrenching click that comes from a grenade as the pin is being released from its firing mechanism. He ran in one direction around the side of the bunker while his mate ran the other way, barely escaping as the side blew out of the building.

A soldier could never forget that booby traps were a constant possibility; he or she could never become blasé about the sound of guns going off, usually at night, often close by. Was someone trying to scare them? To kill them? Calvin's officers told their soldiers they didn't have to make the distinction—they had to shoot back if they were under threat, and they were going to be under threat. "When you put almost four hundred reservists in a unit that is nearly nine hundred strong, they don't go into your special platoons. They don't man your anti-armour weapons and do your vehicle maintenance and they aren't your cooks. They are your soldiers on the front lines," Calvin says.

The rifle companies, for instance, had two-thirds of their complement from the reserves. "In the main, the reservists worked out very well," Calvin later reported to Ottawa. But it was not the seamless transition some were hoping for. The stress had people off balance, right from the beginning: it was the sheer unpredictability of it all. The hardest part, it seemed, was learning to shoot back. The reservists, especially, wrestled with that. Calvin's biggest challenge was to drill into their heads that they had a responsibility to return fire. "Soldiers must be prepared to use force to support the political aim," was his mantra, an attitude almost unheard of in traditional peacekeeping circles.

Calvin launched Operation Spiderweb, a mission designed to stop the flow of weapons into the UN Protected Area. The operation was the closest thing to an offensive that is permissible in peacekeeping. "I won't call it an ambush," says Calvin, "but we set up people to stop them coming across." Soon after Operation Spiderweb was in place the Canadians found themselves in a firefight at very close range. At only ten paces' separation they told a party of Serbs to halt, and the Serbs opened fire instead. The Canadians responded in kind.

"No one got hurt and everyone ran away," says Calvin. "Well, certainly we didn't run away but the Serbs ran away and we didn't capture anyone."

The next Serbs caught in Operation Spiderweb were actually stopped by a three-man patrol of Patricias. The five Serbs were carrying grenades, claymore mines and sniper rifles with silencers. Not exactly a hunting party. The Canadians felt pretty good about their catch even though they had to turn the men over to Serbian police, who soon released them.

"We didn't get into any sort of war fighting situations while we were there [in Sector West] but we were close to it," says Dan Drew. "It was low-intensity warfare, where we did a lot of patrolling, by day and night, on foot and in vehicles. Dealing with cross-border ambushes, where we manned a buffer zone, we had to deal with people that were like terrorists."

The Princess Patricias had to show they were ready and willing to fight if they had to. Since the French had turned and fled from Sector South when the Croats attacked, no one was too sure just how much gumption the foreign soldiers had. The Jordanians and the Nepalese certainly didn't appear ready to take anyone on. The Canadians, for their part, pursued the UN mandate with an aggressiveness that was uncharacteristic of most peacekeeping contingents.

Calvin had requisitioned much more heavy weaponry than a classic Chapter 6 peacekeeping mandate would theoretically need. His troops dug defensive trenches and conspicuously maintained them, as though they had every intention of using them. "They knew they were potentially going to have to fight the Croat army in these things."

* * *

Drenching spring rains washed the last of the snow away, and the fertile farmlands of the Slavonian countryside was showing some signs of life. Despite the obstacles, the Canadians felt they were making some progress in Sector West. One of the people best positioned to notice that was Major Craig King, the new arrival who had just taken command of Alpha Company.

Craig King is a sturdy, broad-chested man whose square face is punctuated by glasses and an untidy moustache. King was an early model of the educated soldier, holding a degree in philosophy. He was shrewdly observant and analytical and rarely betrayed his personal thoughts or feelings. In all, he was the poster boy for the kind of soldier the Canadian Forces wanted in its services. King had functioned as an operations officer with Michel Jones in Croatia before being posted to the Princess Patricias in Winnipeg. After a few short months in late 1992 — just about enough time to settle his family into their new home — he was sent back to Croatia to join Calvin's Second Battalion in the field.

King inherited Pacrac, the most volatile area of the Canadian mission, but he found the situation vastly more stable than when he had been there with Michel Jones. "The city of Pacrac was starting to burgeon a little bit in terms of population. We were getting along with the police forces on both sides." But King had been around long enough, and had observed sufficiently, to know that interludes of peace meant nothing in the former Yugoslovia.

New trouble was brewing. The leaders of the Republic of Serbian Krajina signed an agreement with their Bosnian Serb counterparts on the other side of the border, the Srpska Republika led by Radovan Karadzic. The two breakaway republics declared they would make all decisions jointly from then on. Neither para-state had a shred of official recognition from the outside world, but they believed that their manoeuvring would be rewarded in the end. They also believed that they had received covert signals of acceptance, specifically from Great Britain. Before Stipe Mesic was pushed out of the Sabor along with the other Croatian moderates, he had seen a letter that Tudjman claimed was from John Major's government in London. The letter stated that Great Britain wanted to see Bosnia carved up between Croatia and Serbia. Mesic thought the letter was a forgery and indeed, on a subsequent visit to London, discovered it was. But he also learned from high-ranking Brits that, while the letter was a fake, it accurately reflected the thrust of British policy.

Radovan Karadzic had been gaining legitimacy as the leader of the Bosnian Serbs. His mop of grey hair and white silk ascot was hard to miss as he darted in and out of limousines and conference halls in Geneva and London. He was convinced that his aggressive campaign would succeed, and the fact that the international community seemed to accept him persuaded the Croatian Serbs that Greater Serbia was within their grasp.

The diplomatic dithering and backroom games in the world's capitals rarely took into consideration the effects on the UN people on the ground and on their ability to function effectively. On June 10, encouraged by the signals they were getting from the outside, the Serbs in Sector West openly rearmed themselves in anticipation of a victorious battle. To Colonel Calvin, it was obvious that his job was to disarm them again immediately but the UNPROFOR commander for Sector West inexplicably said no and slapped a moratorium on the confiscation of weapons. This decision shocked the Canadians.

In a routine rotation of leadership, the UN had just replaced the no-nonsense Argentinian commander with a Jordanian, who decided it was not the job of UN forces to aggressively seize weapons from the belligerents, because Serbs and Croats should offer up the weapons voluntarily. The Jordanian may have been responding to signals he was getting from further up the UN food chain; it is also possible that his own government didn't want to make trouble in a region where its soldiers were posted. Whatever the reason, it reinforced the impression among the locals that UN leadership was erratic. One day, a robust and vigorous UN force would impose its will on the region; the next day, the orders would change, or a more pliant peacekeeping contingent would arrive, and one would hardly know there were peacekeepers in the area.

Calvin tried and failed to persuade the new sector commander that allowing the Serbs to rearm was a bad mistake. In a report to Ottawa he stated that there was "an immediate deterioration in the stability within the sector and calling the decision an error is putting it in the mildest terms."

Everything the Canadians and Argentinians had achieved, in many cases risking their lives in the process, began to unravel. Over the coming months even heavy artillery rolled back into the sector. This was exactly what the confiscation policy had been designed to prevent.

Calvin's battle group had been in Croatia for nearly four months and the stress was taking a toll. The renewed tension and violence made the soldiers uneasy, but sheer boredom was also wearing them down. Hours and hours of manning checkpoints—little booths the soldiers called hot-dog stands—and watching the to-ing and fro-ing of Serbs and Croats, in an atmosphere that was both dull and dangerous, had the soldiers looking for escape. Alcohol was the principal release.

Just days after the Serbs decided to rearm themselves, a barbecue for the soldiers of the Princess Patricias turned ugly when a Canadian soldier took a rifle and ammunition from a weapons storehouse and began to fire around the camp. A Canadian newspaper reported that Master Corporal Beverly Heimbecker, a full-time soldier with the PPCLI, had been aiming at Colonel Calvin and that the bullet had landed near his feet. Official reports discount that, since Calvin wasn't at the barbecue at the time. But officially, they did acknowledge that alcohol was a key factor. Major Brett Boudreau told the Canadian media that "It's very stressful here and drinking is a stress-reducing activity." Calvin conducted a summary trial of Heimbecker and sentenced her to thirty days in the brig. Without giving details, Boudreau told reporters that it was only the most serious of "several" alcohol-related incidents. Heimbecker denied that she was under the influence of alcohol when the episode occurred.

***

In June, Lord Owen threw up his hands and declared that the Vance-Owen Plan, which had already caused so much grief, was dead. He told a news conference that the war had gone on too long now for "an honourable solution" to be possible. Days later, the Republic of Serbian Krajina held a referendum in which the Knin authorities asked Serbs the unambiguous question, "Are you in favour of a sovereign Serb Republic of Krajina and its unification with the Bosnian Republika Srpska, and later with other Serb territories?" According to officials in Knin, 92 percent of the population turned out and 98.6 percent of them voted yes.

The legitimacy of the process was suspect, but there wasn't much anybody could do to challenge the results. No independent body had monitored the referendum and the quasi-state wasn't recognized by any outside authority. The results were suspect for other reasons as well: Serbs who opposed ethnic cleansing and might have voted no had been targeted as brutally as their Croat neighbours. Serbs who attempted to help UNPROFOR or to make live-and-let-live accommodation with the Croats were expelled from the Krajina.

Though the referendum had no legal authority it did carry tremendous emotional weight for Serbs in Croatia who felt that they had been abandoned by the Belgrade leadership. Joining their campaign for ethnic self-determination with that of Radovan Karadzic's Bosnian Serbs gave them a boost of confidence. But it was also a decisive provocation for Croats.

The UN had promised in its Security Council Resolutions that the Serbian-held territory would be regarded as an "integral" part of Croatia and would be returned to Croatia. Tudjman's government (having heard the same rumours as Karadzic's people) suspected that Great Britain, the leader in what was called the "contact group" talks, was taking the side of the Serbs.

Tudjman threatened to dispense with peacekeepers altogether, an idea popular with many Croats. Said one ominous editorial in a Zagreb newspaper: "The peacekeeping force cannot claim that they have fulfilled a single task for which they have been sent: traffic communications have not been reopened, instead of demilitarization there are more weapons than ever in the areas they patrol and not a single refugee has returned home. On the contrary—new ones have arrived." The criticism was harsh and inflammatory but accurate.

In June 1993, General Jean Cot took his place as the third military commander of the entire UN operation in the former Yugoslavia. Cot was a Frenchman and as arrogant as they come. But he was determined to put muscle into the UNPROFOR mandate. Major General John Arch MacInnis, a smooth, bespectacled Cape Bretoner with a gift for diplomacy, was Cot's second-in-command, and also in charge of the Canadian contingent. MacInnis arrived in Zagreb on the same day as Cot, much to the surprise of the Swedish general who had apparently not been informed that he was about to be relieved as the commander of UNPROFOR. It was a stumbling start, but typical of the UN bureaucracy.

MacInnis was replacing Canadian Major General Bob Gaudreau who took several parting shots at the mission and its leadership, proclaiming his profound frustration. In a candid interview with a reporter from the *Vancouver Sun*, he described the situation in the former Yugoslavia as "bleak. So much effort and so little gain." Gaudreau blamed the failure on the European leaders, whom he stated were responsible for finding a solution to a war that was in their own backyard but, instead, were riven with internal disputes: "Nationalist interests in Europe are at the fore. Europe has lost its focus." Gaudreau also lobbed a parting salvo at the Canadian government for not backing up the mission. "As a soldier, as a peacekeeper, I felt abandoned by the team that is supposed to provide us with the political guidance," he said. MacInnis would soon hit the same frustrating obstacles that Gaudreau did.

Cot and MacInnis were an unlikely but well-matched pair. Cot communicated to his deputy in French, MacInnis responded in English; Cot pushed the UN around and MacInnis smoothed the feathers afterward. Cot was "pure soldier" according to MacInnis. While he understood the military business better than anyone, "he never understood the UN," says MacInnis. "But I don't think the UN understands the UN." MacInnis adjusted to the UN way of doing things. Cot never did, and eventually was ordered out of Croatia by Secretary-General Boutros-Ghali. (Cot refuses to be interviewed about the subject. After blasting the UN in an article in *Le Monde* he retreated from the media.)

Cot and MacInnis were in charge of Bosnia, Croatia and Macedonia. The mission in Bosnia was a shambles, but it was still the focus of huge international attention, while the rest of the mission was being practically ignored. Cot assigned MacInnis to focus most of his time on the much neglected Croatian part.

General MacInnis had a reputation in Ottawa as a first-rate schmoozer, but his smooth, persuasive style was to be sorely tested in Zagreb. UNPROFOR had troops, many of them incompetent, from a dozen different countries. MacInnis had a dozen different and conflicting political sensibilities to contend with, and at the least sign of trouble there would be cries of alarm from politicians and bureaucrats around the globe, whose interventions and meddling were not helpful. The decision-makers of UNPROFOR itself were almost never in agreement on anything. John Arch MacInnis concluded that his time spent in Croatia "was among the worst years of my military career."

The International Conference on the Former Yugoslavia was supposed to spearhead talks for all the affected republics, but was often at odds with the five-nation Contact Group for Bosnia, which included Great Britain, France, the United States, Russia and Germany. They all had their own notions of how the UN mission should be carried out. The United States, despite having no troops in the former Yugoslavia, "didn't hesitate to make aggressive statements," MacInnis notes. "There was very little room to manoeuvre."

On top of the other difficulties were the demands of the negotiators, Lord David Owen and the former Norwegian foreign minister, Thorvald Stoltenberg, who had replaced an exhausted Cyrus Vance in the diplomatic partnership. They wanted to direct the peacekeeping mission to shore up the promises and commitments they were making during their negotiations. And then there were overtures from participating countries from Kenya to Nepal. As MacInnis says, an enormous amount has been written about how difficult the leaders in the Balkans were, but not enough ink has been spilled about the other impossible personalities who were complicating the issue from within the UN.

But MacInnis rarely interfered in the field. He was the Canadian contigent commander on the ground, but according to Calvin he operated more like a thoughtful but distant uncle. Calvin consulted him from time to time, but beyond that they had little contact. MacInnis says he left Calvin alone because he was one of the few peacekeeping commanders who knew what he was doing. With 8,000 foreign soldiers in Croatia, MacInnis was far more concerned about the Kenyans, who were treated with derision by both Serbs and Croats, and the Jordanians, who took weeks to complete any task.

"He supported me in just about everything," Calvin remembers. "If I told him that I thought it should go this way or my unit could handle this or that, he never really second-guessed me on anything. I had no problems with him. He wasn't aggressive, he wasn't pushing me to do anything different and he certainly wasn't looking over my shoulder, in terms of, you know, telling me how to do my job. So, in that regard, he was a perfect commander, really."

In later peacekeeping missions, the defence department assigned people to keep close tabs on the situation in the field, in some cases to the point of suffocation, but in the early 1990s, the focus was elsewhere. The DND was wholly absorbed in the Somalia scandal, and the commanders on peacekeeping missions found themselves pretty much on their own, with no senior officers to turn to for advice. Consequently, when Calvin was confronted with the most difficult task he would ever encounter as an officer in the Canadian Forces, he had to face it alone.

* * *

General Jean Cot had a serious problem in Sector South, the UNPA that covered the hot spots in Dalmatia and the Krajina, as well as the fuzzy Pink Zones that clung to the protected areas like sticky wads of chewing gum. When the Croats seized the key installations on January 23, the French peacekeepers who were supposed to be in control abandoned the area after losing two of their men. They refused to use force to hold their position. The Croats moved in unresisted, catching the Serbs completely by surprise and inflicting many casualties.

Serbs throughout Croatia quickly got their weapons back from UN storage (with the notable exception of Sector West under Glen Nordick) but in the south, they also repossessed their tanks and heavy artillery.

The problem for the UN mission went deep: the Serbs believed that the French had received advance notice of the operation from the Croats and had deliberately not warned the Serbs. As far as the Serbs were concerned, the French were now the enemy. There hadn't been a terribly warm relationship in the first place, but there was now a profound crisis of confidence in UN forces. The French battalion was the key battle group for all of Sector South and the only one with sufficient military hardware to do the job. But they wouldn't do it.

The French peacekeepers had retreated as far as the Krajina town of Gracac, at least twenty kilometres away from the front lines. There they remained, as far away from trouble as they could get. And so Cot, unable to persuade his countrymen to do their job, found himself with a serious lack of firepower just when he needed a determined fighting force the most.

***

In his analysis of the Croatian war, the historian Ivo Goldstein argued that "Croatian tactics and strategy were always conducted on two basic levels: negotiation, and if negotiation yielded no results, then resort to other means"—most often, force. Conversely, when the use of force no longer worked, Croatia would return to negotiations.

It seemed unlikely that the Croats would now agree to withdraw, but Tudjman, hoping for more international acceptance of Croatian territorial claims, hounded the Security Council to honour its previous resolutions. The UN body replied there could be no further talks until the Croats had returned to their pre–January 23 confrontation line, and in July it seemed possible that the Croats would sign the Erdut Agreement—named after the town where the deal was struck. The agreement was intended to ease tension in the volatile Sector South area around the key flashpoints: the Peruca Dam, the Maslenica Bridge, the area around Zadar's airport and Miljevci, a strategic plateau between Knin and Sibenik near the Adriatic Coast.

The Croats had taken all of these areas but weren't able to build on the advantages they offered. The Maslenica Bridge was only a pontoon at this point, the Peruca Dam had been dynamited by the retreating Serbs, leaving southern Dalmatia without electricity, and Zadar was surrounded by Serb artillery. But to get the attention of the belligerents and move them back to their pre–January 23 line, Cot knew he was going to have to mount a persuasive show of force by peacekeepers.

There were rumours, which Cot must have been aware of, that the Croats were about to launch a major offensive in Sector South. As he sat negotiating the terms of their withdrawal, Cot surely knew about their plans. He needed muscle in Sector South to stop them, and he needed it soon.

***

General Cot put Jim Calvin on warning that at any moment he might ask him to split his battle group and take part of it over the Velebit Mountains into Sector South. If the Croats signed the Erdut Agreement, Calvin's assignment would be to make sure the Croats retreated to their pre–January 23 limits, giving up all they had gained in their only successful operation since the start of the war. Cot was asking the Canadians to take the place of the French troops that had withdrawn. Calvin's soldiers' task was to wedge themselves between the two warring parties. They were the designated hitter for a very tough inning. "We were the ones that the force commander had tagged that if he had a problem we would redeploy and correct that problem," Calvin says. He had the hardware—it was old and dilapidated but sufficient—to defend the mission. He had trained his soldiers, and psyched them for battle; they were a tough, combat-ready unit and their leader was more than keen.

Canada had invented peacekeeping, and the world had embraced the idea, but Calvin hadn't realized how few other nations besides Canada were willing to take any serious risks on a peacekeeping mission. But he was beginning to get the idea.

He would have only twenty-four hours' notice. The journey from Sector West to Sector South was more than five hundred kilometres over extremely difficult and hostile territory. "At this point," says Calvin, with quiet understatement, " . . . things started to get very difficult."

CHAPTER FIVE

FRONTIER WARFARE

. . . In some places, even the air was dead. It was just so nothing down there. And about the only thing that sometimes cut through was the sounds of shells coming in or the good old sound of the multiple rocket launchers. When they go across a grid square, they were quite entertaining.

—Master Corporal Steve Atkins

IN THE FINAL WEEK OF JULY, Colonel Jim Calvin got the call he knew was inevitable. He was ordered to pack up and move 400 of his soldiers to the most volatile region in Croatia: the Krajina.

Part of Calvin's force was to stay back in Sector West to maintain the sensitive Lipik–Pacrac road corridor. Charlie and Delta Companies, a reconnaissance team, the anti-armour platoon and a slice of his administration company were to move down south. Jordanian and Argentinian peacekeepers would have to cover Sector West, but Cot believed the shift was necessary.

The 400-odd Canadians had to take with them everything they needed in order to live, and they would have to be in place within twenty-four hours. They had no idea how long they would be gone or when they would hook up again with the rest of the battle group.

The end of the soldiers' tour was less than two months away. The next rotation was to be in place in September; and now this. Many of the young men and women had never been away from Canada so long before, and "We were already thinking about going home," says Tyrone Green, the student from Vancouver.

Glen Peters, a reservist from Halifax, religiously kept a diary of the events of those days. He recorded that before heading south he had performed two back-to-back tours of patrol, and returned to base with just enough time to call his family and pack. It was one of the last calls home he would get to make until the end of the tour. Peters recalls they were on the road at 11:30 P.M. The commanders told the soldiers that the deployment to Sector South was temporary, but Peters noted in his journal that he sensed it wasn't. "We moved and we weren't coming back."

General Cot didn't just want the battle group to enter Sector South suddenly, he wanted it to *appear* to enter suddenly. He wanted the deployment itself to have an effect. The Canadians were to arrive all at once, aggressive, well armed and in large numbers. The idea was to startle the local population and impress upon it that the UN forces meant business. They had to travel light and be self-contained. Ammunition, hard rations, the soldiers and their kit all got on the road by July 16.

Calvin's plan was to move four columns of twenty-five vehicles each, with one launched every two hours. The convoy of more than one hundred vehicles would travel through Croatian territory first, cross the Serb-declared border into the Krajina, pass Knin and head directly for their new area of responsibility. At first the road was straightforward, crossing the low, flat plains of Slavonia, but then it became narrow and treacherous as it snaked its way through the foothills of the Alps and into the rugged highlands of Lika, where generations of warriors had fought off the Turks, the Partisans, the Nazis and the Chetniks.

Officially, UNPROFOR was to have freedom of movement throughout Croatia and not just in the UN Protected Areas. The Croats didn't agree with that. They set up roadblocks and delayed the Canadian vehicles. The Croats didn't want the

Canadians to go to Sector South. The French and Kenyan forces already in place were easy to deal with and didn't get in the way of Croatian operations in the Krajina. The Canadians had proved themselves to be less malleable.

Glen Peters wrote in his diary that they were stuck most of the night on the autobahn. "Croats tried to run us off the road," he recorded. He included a cryptic notation indicating that the side of the road was mined.

The Croat blockades were frequent enough to force Calvin to find another route over the formidable Velebit Mountains, navigating the twists and turns of the medieval roadways. They then made their way into the grimy little town of Knin, home of the last independent Croatian king and the epicentre of the Austrian-Turkish wars. Without knowing what ghosts they were stirring on their voyage, Tyrone Green remembers his feelings of trepidation as they travelled that stretch of roadway. "Things were happening so quickly. The information was still coming down on exactly what we were getting into, not knowing exactly where we were headed."

The Canadians arrived in Sector South within thirty-six hours of their departure. Cot was impressed. UN headquarters had said it would take weeks to move the battalion that far, and the senior command had suggested that the Canadians ship their kit down the coast of the Adriatic in ferries. The soldiers from other countries didn't realize how much time Canadians spend on the road. "Jean Cot was so impressed with that," recalls Calvin. "He said move now, and thirty-six hours later we rumbled through, convoy after convoy of M113s, right through the middle of the Serb heaven down there. Woke everybody up, people were running out and it was just vehicle after vehicle — M113s. You know, people pooh-pooh an M113, but it makes a lot of noise and it looks mean, eh? And they knew something had changed."

***

After the lush, humid valleys of Slavonia, Sector South was a shock. Furnace-like heat blasted off the white rock of the Velebit Mountains and temperatures reached into the forties Celsius. The landscape seemed empty of people: the majority had been forced out of the area by the intense fighting and the few who remained were invisible—they were hiding most of the time.

For the Canadians there was really no place to camp. The rock was not only inhospitably hard, it was also a haven for scorpions, snakes and vipers of all sorts. The places where previous peacekeepers had camped were in a deplorable state. They had to carve out living accommodations in the few burned-out towns around them.

Calvin began to take stock of what he had inherited. His new area of responsibility was vast, and its boundaries nebulous. The UN Protected Area was defined but the Pink Zones that he also inherited were as grey as they could possibly be. He wasn't certain how far his authority extended, and he had daily reminders that the local militias didn't think he had any. In Sector West, Calvin says, "It was an aberration to have a shooting situation. Sector South was at war."

Everyone had tanks in Sector South. Local militias with AK47s were the toughest force they had confronted in their previous territory. But with that thirty-six-hour move, everything had changed. This was a battlefield wtih heavy artillery pieces, manned by real soldiers who were clearly prepared to use them.

The Canadians soon discovered that as UN troops they commanded even less respect than they had in the Pacrac area. "They didn't trust the UN down there. . . . and the two sides didn't hesitate to target the UN, you know, with abandon, particularly on the Croat side," says Calvin. In part, the Croats targeted the UN forces because they were in bed with the enemy: "We were [billetted] on the Serb side and if we happened to get in the way of where the rounds were going, that was just too bad," says Calvin.

Calvin set up his headquarters in the ruins of a deserted town called Kijevo. All he knew was that it had once been a Croatian town, and that it was now empty. Kijevo is actually the village from which the term "ethnic cleansing" comes.

Kijevo's population was the first to be targeted for extinction in the summer of 1991. The town had been entirely Croat before the war, but it was surrounded by Serb villages, and the Knin Serbian militias, who liked to call themselves "Kninjas," determined that a Croatian village in the middle of the Republic of Serbian Krajina was unacceptable, not just for symbolic reasons but also for reasons of security. The Kninjas joined forces with the JNA in the summer of 1991, in particular with the up-and-coming young commander Ratko Mladic. Mladic had been posted by Belgrade to run the Knin corps of the JNA and he found himself with like-minded people in the renegade Krajina Serb authority. Together they launched an operation to drive people from their homes, kill anyone who got in the way and then systematically make the area uninhabitable. Houses and crops were destroyed, livestock killed, and wells and cisterns poisoned (usually with gasoline but often with dead animals). The Belgrade media gave glowing reports of the conquest of Kijevo and other Croat towns, and of "the cleansing of territory." The Western media picked up on the phrase and began to call these forced evictions "ethnic cleansing."

Over the course of the previous four months the Canadians had become very familiar with the crude science of ethnic cleansing, but at the time they didn't realize they had moved into its first laboratory. Calvin chose Kijevo simply because some rudimentary structures were still standing, and no one was there. They took over the buildings that seemed to have the least amount of damage and patched up the holes as best they could. The Canadians worked in the hot sun to dig latrines in the hard ground—Kijevo sits on stone. They nicknamed the place Camp Bedrock.

The heat was searing, and the soldiers would cool off whenever they found a cistern. They understood the risks—the wells and waterworks were undoubtedly contaminated. But there was no other source of water. Their drinking supplies had to come by way of the treacherous road from Sector West along with all the other food. A steady stream of trucks made the two-day journey to Daruvar and back several times a week and were often late.

While headquarters was in Kijevo, most of the soldiers were spread out over the vast area of their responsibility. There were two Croat villages behind Serb lines, Bruska and Rodaluce, and Calvin installed a platoon to watch out for the local people there. In addition to the few remaining Croats who clung to their homes, the Serbs would also dump other Croats into the two villages, often without any of their possessions. It was a frightening place to be, with a Serbian paramilitary training camp right next door.

Master Corporal Phil Tobicoe's platoon was based in Bruska, and what he saw was the real face of ethnic cleansing. "There was no young person in the village," he recalls. The people who remained were terrorized by bands of paramilitaries. The Canadians heard that local villagers had been robbed, raped or beaten as an example to the others. Tobicoe's mother is Mohawk, his father from the Mississauga Band of the Credit River in Ontario. His First Nations family has a long, distinguished history of serving in the American, British and Canadian armies. He would have stories to tell his parents when he got home, about a place where civilians and not soldiers were the targets. Tobicoe was immensely proud to have been promoted to non-commissioned officer for his deployment to Croatia. It had all happened so quickly: he was actually from the first battalion of the Patricias and he had had only a few weeks to prepare before deploying with the anti-armour platoon of the second. He hadn't been able to attend the training session at Fort Ord.

Tobicoe's fiancée was initially concerned about the tour but was reassured by the news that they could get married earlier than originally planned, since Tobicoe would be able to bank some extra cash during the tour. His parents were less easy to placate: his mother had lost a son to a traffic accident and couldn't bear for anything to happen to Phil.

For security reasons, he would not be able to tell his mom and dad too many of the details of the mission either on the phone or by mail. "We set up a code system," he says. "The code words were Waterford and Oka. If I said, 'It's a Waterford picnic,' that meant everything was going well." Waterford is a park that Tobicoe's family often went to. "If I said, 'It's Oka,' that meant things were very bad."

"Oka" referred to the seventy-two-day stand-off in 1990 between native people and police in the province of Quebec in which the Canadian army intervened. The bitter dispute over a sacred burial ground where local businessmen wanted to install a golf course had often threatened to explode into a mini-war and it eventually became a flashpoint for all First Nations people in North America, including Tobicoe.

Increasingly, in Bruska Tobicoe was sensing an "Oka" coming on. One day, he and the others encountered three masked men, members of either the Tigers or the White Eagles, the most ruthless of the paramilitary units that came out of Serbia. They took their orders from Belgrade, but their task was simple: kill or drive away any Croats who still lived in the Krajina.

For the Canadians, it was the first time anyone had stuck guns in their faces and threatened them with actual death. Tobicoe was carrying a C7 rifle and he told the Serbs they would be dead if they didn't put down their weapons. He had heard that the paramilitaries were generally cowards when confronted with serious armed resistance, and this unit, true to type, lowered their guns and offered the Canadians cigarettes. Tobicoe's crew kicked them out of the village. They would rather have arrested them but they had no way of holding prisoners.

The Kenyan peacekeepers who had been in charge of the area previously were easily intimidated by the Serb special units, and the Serbs had become very bold. The Kenyans told the Canadians they rarely patrolled the area because the Serbs insisted on seven days' notice before an inspection. The Canadians concluded that another reason they didn't patrol was that they were too busy with their black market operation selling alcohol and gasoline. When they came across the Kenyans making their transactions with the local people, the Canadians would make a show of taking down the names of the Kenyans and writing notes in their log books. But there wasn't much the Canadians could really do to stop them. The Africans weren't paid enough and this was supplementary income.

Master Corporal Gord Parker was the medic assigned to C Company and he was dumbfounded by the behaviour of the Kenyans. "Holy cow! What's going on here?" were Parker's first words when he saw the African peacekeepers "wandering around without weapons or equipment because if the Serbs caught them, they'd just take it away from them. When a Serb soldier came up to them, they were afraid for their lives and they just handed over everything they owned if that's what was needed to survive." Parker and the others didn't blame the Kenyans, but they had to turn things around quickly if they were going to stay. "So we arrived and it was 'Uh-uh. So sorry. That ain't going to happen.' We needed to make a show."

Captain Kelly Brett was one of only two doctors assigned to the battle group of 860 soldiers, along with a team of medical assistants numbering about thirty. The other doctor stayed back in Slavonia to care for Alpha and Bravo Companies, while Brett came with the companies deployed to the south. He is square-jawed and muscular with jet-black hair he wears parted to one side. He stands five-foot-eleven but his shoulder span and bulk make him seem larger and from all accounts he was a formidable opponent on the Canadian Forces rugby field. His friends describe him as quiet and soft-spoken, unless he is roused to anger. The situation in Sector South would provide him with plenty of provocation.

Brett was appalled at how bad the living conditions were in their new base. At the unit medical section, the area was infested with rats, which had to be cleaned out, first by removing the large amount of festering garbage, and then by burning off all that was left of the grass with gasoline.

There was a constant shortage of clean wash water and the soldiers learned how to bathe under a jerry can, which might have been refreshing if there wasn't always the threat that the water might be unsafe. Wash and laundry water had to come from the cisterns in the deserted towns and the soldiers knew enough about ethnic cleansing to wonder just what it was they were bathing in. They made their own showers, by digging a sump and putting a pallet on the ground with a bucket suspended above it. Dr. Brett ordered regular water testing, but soldiers were always looking for some way to cool off from the blasting heat and they often took chances. Steve Atkins, a medic who worked with Dr. Brett, says the soldiers were always asking, "Hey, can we drink the water here?" Atkins would tell them what Kelly Brett had instructed him to say. "Just don't. Whether you are told the water is safe or not, don't."

Phil Tobicoe remembers that in Bruska they had almost nothing to eat. "That was probably the most embarrassing moment of the tour. The locals would bring us food." It started with supplies of figs and fruit from their trees, but one woman tried to give them a chicken, so concerned was she for their fate. One of the best meals of his deployment was prepared by the old Croat women of Bruska—a feast of lamb and potatoes. Unlike in Sector West where the soldiers had been involved with people's lives, there was very little contact with civilians in Sector South. But at the dinner, the locals asked Tobicoe to join them in crushing the grape harvest. Tobicoe was vastly amused by the thought of a native of the Mississauga Nation helping to make wine in Croatia. He successfully communicated that his boots would probably not add much to the vintage should he jump into the bin.

Despite the rare good fortune of a few, the supply problems were constant; some of them were more serious than others. They ran short of bottled drinking water, on one occasion going without for twenty-four hours. Dr. Brett was anxious about the scarcity of medical supplies. He had brought far more with him than he was probably allowed to, given the stinginess of such missions. "We robbed the medical system of a lot of supplies out of Winnipeg, threw it in a ton of barracks boxes and took it over there with us. Because going through the normal channels to get the stuff we wanted to get, we would have had to fill out so many forms that the world would have run out of paper."

Despite raiding the Winnipeg medical cupboard, Dr. Brett still couldn't offer much more than first aid. There were no facilities for surgery, and he wasn't sure he could get anyone out of the area if they were seriously injured. They had five quarter-ton Chevy pickups converted to ambulances that he estimated could go about two miles an hour up a hill. "This was our emergency evacuation equipment," he says. "And that scared the crap out of us every day."

The French were well supplied and even had a surgical unit with them—an unheard-of luxury for Canadian soldiers, whose government seems to believe that peacekeeping assignments are always benign. But the Kenyans and the Poles, who were in the north of the sector, were in worse shape than the Canadians and relied on the Canadian battalion for medical support. If there was a sick soldier in the area he or she would almost surely end up at the Kijevo headquarters.

There was no point in getting settled in, even if the conditions allowed for it: the soldiers were permanently on two hours' notice to move. That meant having the rucksack packed and ready to go each morning. The orders were, "Don't get too set up. Don't bed in." The soldiers were told that as soon as the Erdut Agreement was signed they would have to move into different areas of responsiblity. It was also a message that they had to be on alert to decamp suddenly if the situation deteriorated enough to warrant a quick withdrawal. The reconnaissance platoon was constantly out scouting routes in case there had to be a sudden evacuation, while Phil Tobicoe and the anti-armour platoon was looking for overwatch positions on those routes from which they could protect the Canadians if they had to withdraw under fire.

Their patrols and reconnaissance trips were targets not just for snipers but also for heavy guns. When a unit of Canadians went down to the Peruca dam to check things out it was the first time in five months that any member of UNPROFOR had been so close to the front line and they came under a heavy shower of high-calibre machine-gun rounds. It was not an accident. The local militias had seen the French run, and they expected the Canadians would do the same.

"We had to impress upon the Serbs that we were staying. The officers would go forward. We would explain, 'We are new people. We are going to get up there,'" Calvin says. There was an element of intimidation, but also a lot of bluffing. Sometimes it worked, and often it didn't. It was the kind of boldness that was the hallmark of the Princess Patricias, but it wasn't very highly regarded by some of the members of the Second Battalion. Some of Calvin's officers began to suggest to him that the mission was too dangerous, particularly the padre, Mike Brown. He says he told Calvin that he was putting the soldiers in harm's way. Calvin didn't agree.

While supply problems plagued the Canadian battalion, there was one acquisition everyone was happy about. It's important for UN peacekeeping missions not just to be benign but to appear to be benign, and the contributing countries are limited by what they can bring in the way of weapons. However, Michel Jones had bent a few rules that proved to be not just useful but life-saving. Canada had recently acquired TOW missile systems— "tube-launched, optically tracked, wire-guided"—an impressive anti-tank weapon with great range and accuracy that is mounted on an armoured vehicle. Calvin decided the best way to impress upon the locals that they were now in a different game was to give a display of the TOWs.

He called in the Serb and Croat commanders, provided them with binoculars and pointed out some little dots down in the valley below—old, unused tanks, which had been loaded with fuel and ammunition. Calvin gave the nod and his soldiers fired off the TOWs. There were three tanks, three missiles fired and three direct hits. The Serbs and Croats got the message. According to Gord Parker, they "walked away knowing there was a professional army in the neighbourhood."

* * *

Calvin cancelled all leave except for the official United Nations passes that allowed the soldiers to return to Canada once on the tour. The pressure on the Canadian contingent was enormous: General Cot had told Calvin that the mission was coming apart and the Erdut Agreement might be the only way to save it. With only half his battle group in Sector South, Calvin needed every soldier he had. That meant absolutely no down time for most of the troops for the duration of the tour. Their large-scale satellite terminals had remained in Sector West, so the soldiers were no longer able to make routine calls home. It was hard to keep in touch with their families.

The most vulnerable of all the UN soldiers in Sector South—of any contingent—were those of Delta Company under the command of Dan Drew. While Calvin had Charlie Company and some support units in Kijevo, Major Drew and his soldiers were put under the direct command of the French contingent in Gracac, an unusual but not entirely unwelcome arrangement. Drew had a professional curiosity about working with another nation's soldiers. "We were there to reinforce the French battalion that had basically been pushed out of the area," says Drew. Being under French command "was a novel experience for me but one which I enjoyed."

The French battalion was stationed far from the action and the UNPROFOR commanders were anxious to show the UN flag as deep inside the sector as possible. They decided they wanted an observation post overlooking the much contested Maslenica Bridge. The bridge had once been a lofty span of concrete sweeping over the gorge joining Dalmatia to the rest of Croatia. But it had been reduced to rubble by the Serbs in 1991. After their UN-defying attack on Maslenica in January, the Croats had established a military pontoon bridge over the gorge and it was an occasional supply route to Zadar and Peruca. But the Serbs fired on it continuously, rendering the route almost unusable.

The commanders of UNPROFOR wanted to keep a sharp eye on Maslenica since as soon as the Erdut Agreement was signed the Croats would have to withdraw from the area. The French couldn't or wouldn't return to the position and so the job fell to the Patricias under French command. Drew and his troops headed up over the Velebit Mountains into the front-line areas of Obravac where they almost immediately came under shellfire. They had just come through the one narrow pass into the area, and Drew knew that if there was a major attack no one would be able to get up over that pass quickly enough to help them. They were robustly armed for a peacekeeping mission, but not for combat. Drew was disturbed by the weaknesses in their deployment.

Some of his soldiers had even more serious reservations. Sergeant Chris Byrne was part of the reconnaissance party into the Maslenica area and he was surprised to learn that the position they would occupy would almost certainly be fired on by the Croats. Surely, he reasoned, the military thinking behind the plan was faulty—they were going to put themselves into a position that the Croats had confirmed they would fire on. To Byrne, the whole mandate was a contradiction of his training. He remembered Dan Drew's briefing from months earlier when he knocked over the bulletin board and told them to prepare for war: that lesson played over and over in Byrne's head as he worked in Sector South. No matter how well Drew had psyched them for combat, they were not prepared for war because they were helpless against the big guns. "There were no military tactics here because we never had any support to fire back at these people," Byrne says.

Drew knew what his soldiers were thinking, and he agreed with them, but he had few options if he was going to accomplish the task Calvin had assigned to him. "We had no air cover, we had no artillery with us. We were being sniped at by people who would typically snipe at you at last light, and then by the time you could beat the weeds it would be dark and they would be gone." But Drew persevered.

Delta Company was spread out over a five-kilometre-square area but some of it was straight up and down—between the shores of the Adriatic and the ridges of the Velebit Mountains.

Drew put one platoon of thirty soldiers up in the hills, as per instructions from UNPROFOR. Theoretically, as the Croats withdrew, the peacekeepers would take over and ensure the Serbs did not re-enter the area. The intention was to keep Maslenica from being occupied by either Croats or Serbs.

Drew suspected the soldiers' position on the hill was far too exposed, and sure enough, on the first night up in that observation post, the soldiers were able to map out almost two dozen different places where muzzle flashes from automatic machine-gun fire were visible. Eventually, Drew and Mike Spellen went up to check the position and confirmed that there was nothing to be gained from having people up in the hills where they could easily be attacked. On the way up the hill, Drew and Spellen discovered a number of dead bodies. They were local domobrans or home guards whom the armies hadn't bothered to retrieve; it was impossible to determine which nationality they belonged to since they had no official uniforms.

Drew decided to pull down the lookout and order the soldiers to bring the corpses down from the mountain. Corporal Anita Kwasnicki, a reservist in her twenties and one of the few women on the tour, remembers the soldiers in her section bringing the bodies down. They were too heavy to carry and were leaking fluids, so the soldiers tried to drag them. Kwasnicki was present when they found one corpse; the soldiers tried to dig it out and accidentally pulled off one of its feet. They couldn't uncover the rest of the corpse before nightfall so Kwasnicki had to guard the appendage from wild animals in the area. The next day a team was able to reunite the foot with the rest of the body, wrap it carefully in hessian and carry it away. Chris Byrne was her section commander and he wouldn't let Kwasnicki or any of the others see the body. "The day before, he had seen several dead bodies that were being picked up and it really bothered him. So he wanted to make sure we didn't see it—even though we were all curious and wanted to take a peek." It was an oddly protective act for a soldier: to shield other soldiers from the sight of something unpleasant, especially a combat casualty.

In the interests of the Erdut Agreement, Drew and his company were ordered to open up five crossing areas between the Serb lines and the so-called January 23rd line. The area was mined and the Serbs continued to fire on them, but Drew persisted. "It was getting a wedge in the door . . . which would allow the United Nations to establish a zone of separation between the two forces." Drew and his soldiers displayed an earnest optimism about the mission, a feeling that was not shared by the French soldiers in their area. The French were fed up with the Krajina, but they did have something to share with the Canadians that was more uplifting—their wine.

***

The area held by Delta Company was heavily wooded and maintaining connections between the platoon positions wasn't easy. Drew's troops had to man their posts day and night. The company headquarters was established in an abandoned school near a ridge of land with a first-rate view of the Maslenica Gorge. But the school itself was a dump. The windows were broken and human feces was spread all over the floors and smeared on the walls. The first order of business was to muck it out and make it into a tolerable habitation for one of the platoons to live in. Various positions were established throughout the scrub and up into the hills, from which the soldiers simply recorded the shelling: how much, where it was from, what was the target. What disturbed D Company most was that as the days wore on, the shelling was getting closer and closer; sometimes it seemed they were making a record of the lead-up to their own demise. The Croats fired on them from below while the Serbs shelled them from above. The only possible strategic explanation for the shooting was that the Croats didn't want the Serbs to dig in behind the peacekeepers. And the Serbs thought they could use the Canadians for cover.

As the shells landed, the dried-out brush and shrubs around the camp was set ablaze and the whole rocky ridge they occu-

pied went up in flames and black smoke. Steve Atkins was in awe
of the blasted heath around him. In Sector West it had been the
devastation of the buildings that had stunned him. Here it was
the land itself. The bombed-out towns were "sort of World War
II rural Germany . . . But when we moved down to Sector South,
the one thing that struck my mind was moonscape. Like it
wasn't even on the planet. It was like an entirely different planet
altogether. The earth was scorched . . . And of course nothing
was alive in a lot of the places we were at."

Mike Spellen was among the most experienced in the company, but those days in the mountains pushed him to his limits.
He worried about the young reservists. "I would never say I pan-
icked," Spellen admits. "But I remember, after the shelling, I
always took a few moments for myself, I'd walk off somewhere
and—you know—kind of thank Christ no one got hurt."

Spellen nonetheless recalls moments of pure joy about the
smallest of things, the kind of bliss that is only possible when
everything around you is completely bleak. For instance, they
were able to contract a local man to bring them fresh bread each
morning. Spellen would dig into one of those hot loaves and
walk up to sit in the bright sunshine on the rocks by himself,
looking out over the azure blue of the Adriatic. "That was my
space I guess. I would sit there with a cup of coffee and a good
big hunk of warm bread and open a can of French rations. I had
sardines and mushrooms—mushroom-coloured sardines . . . it
was like eating steak . . . I don't think I've eaten sardines since."

The soldiers of Delta Company discovered a deep cistern of
water next to the school. It was strictly forbidden to use it, since
the probability of contamination was high. But Spellen remembers the soldiers frolicking in the deep pool as though they were
just ordinary young men in the prime of their lives, out on a
summer lark. He should have ordered them out, but he didn't.
He enjoyed the innocence of their play.

At such times, Spellen would marvel at the soldiers'
resilience. He would see fear in their eyes when shells fell near
them, but they'd be laughing and kibbitzing the next moment.

The inherent faith in one's immortality that is the hallmark of youth had been mightily reinforced during the intense pre-training as a necessary preparation for combat. Solidarity and camaraderie can overcome adversity and danger, Spellen believed. With that, he hoped they would be able to face down even the most threatening foe.

***

In the second week of August, the French command told Drew to bring his platoons back over the mountains to French battalion headquarters in Gracac. On their arrival, Delta Company learned of the first death among the ranks of the Second Battalion of the Princess Patricias.

Johnny Béchard was only twenty-four, and one of the most popular young corporals in Delta Company, perhaps in the whole battalion. He had managed to get his UN leave back to Winnipeg just before the move to the Krajina, so that he could be home for the birth of his first child. He had timed it perfectly, and was able to hold his baby daughter Jannessa before having to return to Daruvar.

Béchard was keen to meet up with the rest of his company in Sector South. He tossed his rucksack onto the back of the truck that was about to depart Camp Polom for his new home-away-from-home. At that moment the truck rolled back, pinning him against another vehicle and crushing him to death. It was the first fatality for Calvin's battle group and it had a devastating effect on everyone. "The psyche of a battalion is very much that everybody who goes should come home. I don't want to dwell on this very much but it's a point of pride. You will hear units saying, 'Yeah, we brought everyone home.' And when suddenly you are not going to bring everyone home, it affects people."

Dr. Brett remembers the speech Calvin gave to the troops following Béchard's death. Clearly, Calvin intended to offer comfort, but the doctor thought he had the opposite effect. "I don't want to pick on the good colonel but this was one of the most demoralizing speeches I have ever heard in my life. He was trying to do the right thing but the words didn't come out right." Brett says Calvin's chief message was to soldier on. "They were basically told to get on with it. Don't think about it." The doctor believed that Calvin's response to the death of Corporal Béchard was consistent with his reaction to a number of other alarming developments. In sworn testimony at later inquiries into the Croatia mission, Brett said that Calvin seemed more concerned with the optics of "not bringing everybody home alive," than with the actual death—a harsh judgment indeed.

Mike Brown had known Béchard in Winnipeg and had provided spiritual counsel for his wife, Amy, when she converted to Roman Catholicism in order to marry him. Brown's own fiancée, Cate Vesey, attended the little instruction sessions as well, and the two couples became friends. On the Sunday before the Patricias departed, Brown says he had seen Amy at the back of the church after service, crying, "Mike, promise me you'll make sure John comes home for this baby," she pleaded, and he agreed. Now Amy was a widow.

Brown gave the euology for Béchard, laying the corporal's hat on his poncho in the middle of a field in the Lika Highlands, and lighting some candles. He told the soldiers that they should feel no shame if they cried. "And then Calvin came along and told them to buck up and get on with the job. I was so mad at that man. . . . He was out to save the UN mission and I wanted him to save the men under his command." Brown began to challenge Calvin's authority and his decisions at every turn. Calvin claimed he was acting out of duty.

Within days of Béchard's death, the Erdut Agreement fell apart. There would be no deal, and it seemed that everything the soldiers had been doing to prepare for the agreement had been futile. But General Cot believed the Canadians had made important progress with local Serbs and Croats just by demonstrating that they were not going to run away when they were fired on. The general had been to-ing and fro-ing about whether the Canadian battalion should stay in the Krajina permanently;

now he decided that the French would move to another area of responsibility, presumably where they had no history with the local people, and the entire Canadian battalion, including those still in Sector West, would regroup and take over a newly fortified Sector South.

Delta Company would return to Calvin's command and the Canadians would be put in charge of the Maslenica Bridge, the Zemunik airport near Zadar and an altogether new region for the Canadians, the Medak Pocket.

* * *

Major Drew's first order of business under Calvin's command was to return to Maslenica, and once again show the Serbs and Croats that Canadian peacekeepers were in charge, with or without the Erdut Agreement. But this time they were ordered to be even more aggressive. "The UN was really worried about the Maslenica Bridge," recalls Calvin. "It was the flashpoint of Sector South, and the UN wanted to know who owned it." The lookout Drew had established up in the Velebit Mountains was the best post in the whole region from which to watch the bridge. They could see if the Croats were resupplying, which would be a major indication that they might be planning an attack. And after the collapse of the Erdut talks, the UN began to suspect that the Croats were indeed planning another offensive.

The school was once again Delta Company's headquarters. On their first day back they were treated to a horrendous artillery barrage from the Croats. Drew briefly pulled back to a safer area but was determined to stand their ground, a determination he says Calvin supported.

To abandon the post under shellfire would have been a contradiction of everything Calvin believed about soldiering and peacekeeping: "If you're going to be a credible peacekeeper, you have to share the risks of the indigenous people in the area. The Serbs weren't running away because they were being shelled." Calvin concluded the Patricias would improve their reputation as soldiers if they also came under fire: "If you're going to gain credibility with people, if the UN is going to be effective, you can't turn tail and run every time you get stuck." Mike Brown says Drew would never have challenged a decision from his commander. "There was no such thing as the word 'no' in Danny Drew's vocabulary," says Brown. "If you gave him a knife and some rice, he would go to war if he were asked to do it." Drew was the kind of stuff that great Canadian soldiers are made of, says Brown, from Vimy Ridge to Kap'yong, and Calvin knew it. "That's why Jim Calvin loved the man," says Brown. "He knew he could tell Dan Drew to stand twelve guys on their heads and look over a mountain and he would do it." Brown didn't have a problem with the "can do" principle. "But it was a peacekeeping mission for God's sake. We were not at war!" Calvin agreed that they were not "at war" but they were *in* a war and they had a job to do. Calvin was determined they were going to do it. Drew decided they would build a huge bunker around the school, reinforce it with as much sandbagging as the rock-strewn landscape would allow, and then just sit tight and damn the torpedoes.

As the soldiers began their work, the heat was intense. Two collapsed from heatstroke and had to be rehydrated intravenously. The temperature had soared to the high forties, and it was difficult to reach the outpost with supplies of drinking water.

What alarmed many of the soldiers was the peculiar colour of the soil they were using to fill the sandbags. "It was red," recalls Steve Atkins, who says he was still trying to rinse it out of his clothes months later. It was a shade of such intensity that some of the soldiers wondered what was in it. The stuff saturated their clothing and seemed to make them short of breath. Still, in the hard rock of the Velebit Mountains, there was very little loose dirt and the red earth was all they could find.

Many of the soldiers had been to Prince Edward Island, where the earth is rust-red, but no one recalled ever seeing soil of such an unnatural colour. "The dirt was very fine and it would seep through your clothes and into your pores," recalls Byrne. They mostly worked at night when the shelling stopped and it was cooler, and then they would "spend all day trying to get this red stuff off of you."

Was it contaminated? It came from a nearby landfill, and God only knew what had been dumped there. "Some of it came from the pit, some of it came from the mine tailings," says Warrant Officer Matt Stopford. "Some of it came from a factory. But we built the bunker and we lived there." The idea that the wall protecting them from certain death might be made of something harmful was too much to compute. For Stopford, whatever it was, it was better than the alternative.

They were shelled continuously as they built the bunker. No one doubted that they were the target of the attacks: every time they sent radio communications back to Camp Bedrock to say they were under siege, the Croat artillery got more accurate. The heat and the black smoke were overwhelming. Each artillery blast sent more clouds of the sinister red dust into the air.

Mike Spellen will never get over those days. "I mean, you could see the look in their eyes when you looked down at them in the bunker . . . you look at each other and never say anything. Your eyes told it all." The artillery barrages were sustained and went on for hours. Though a peacekeeping mission allows soldiers to return fire when they are fired upon, the company was still not equipped to fight back. They had no artillery. When a round landed within three feet of the bunker, knocking them out of their cots, some of the soldiers began to question the sanity of the mission. Calvin was determined they would hold their position, no matter what.

"According to the CO [Calvin], it was necessary to establish this observation post at all costs," says Chris Byrne. "However, at no time did we as soldiers train to dodge artillery bullets without being able to call up a fire mission, which is what you do when you train for war. We had no artillery backup. We were a UN contingent." Drew made their orders more than clear: they would hold that ridge or die trying. But he would do everything possible to make sure they didn't die.

Byrne was particularly furious at Calvin one night when the colonel came up to visit. "He arrived at about two in the morning.

We were working hard and we were just putting the finishing touches on the bunker. The reason for his visit was that he wanted to feel what it was like to be shelled." It was a sincere gesture on the part of Calvin who was concerned that morale was breaking down and wanted to encourage the company. But Byrne says the gesture was ham-fisted: Calvin left in the morning, before the predictable daily barrage actually began, and according to Byrne he radioed back that he wished he could be there. Byrne couldn't share the sentiment. "We were there. We didn't want to be there. Trust me."

Kelly Brett also found the Maslenica Bridge operation alarming. "I was worried for the safety of some of the people in [Delta] Company. If the guy running the show is the guy putting these guys at risk, the private is not going to say, 'Hey, I'm not doing that.' The private just does it because that is what he is trained to do." Brett says when he complained to Calvin, Calvin would tell him, "Shut up, doc. Soldier on. Get out of my office."

Miraculously, no one was killed. To Spellen, their luck was unbelievable. "We didn't just have a horseshoe up the ass we had the whole friggin' horse and that horse was a Clydesdale."

Bob Sparks was the man with whom Mike Brown shared the chaplaincy responsibilities for the Patricias' Second Battalion. Sparks was alarmed one day when he saw Brown return from a visit to the infamous bunker. "He saw all the red dust on my uniform," recalls Brown, and asked Brown where he had been. Brown described the site near Obravac where the soldiers were gathering the only loose dirt available with which to build the towering bunker. Sparks has a post-graduate degree in chemistry and asked a lot of questions about the abandoned factory near where the soldiers were digging the red dirt.

The next day, Sparks paid a visit to Obravac and found that the sandbag source was directly beside an aluminum smelter. The soldiers were probably being exposed to a toxic chemical called bauxite, Sparks concluded. He buried some unexposed film in the dirt there, an old trick he had been told could determine if the soil was radioactive as well since the film would chemically react. Sparks ultimately concluded the soil wasn't radioactive but he was alarmed about other residues. He contacted a scientist friend in British Columbia to find out what the implications of bauxite exposure might be. Sparks subsequently warned Kelly Brett that the soldiers could develop skin blisters or, even worse, lung damage.

Brown remembers that Brett and Sparks went to talk to Calvin about the red dirt, but the colonel was already planning to call down the Maslenica lookout.

The Croats had managed a few direct hits on the bunker and a corner of the structure collapsed, causing the soldiers to choke on the clouds of red dust that billowed out of the sandbags. At last, Calvin determined that they had made their point and called the company down from the observation post. Drew and Spellen understood that Calvin was trying to establish credibility but they could also see what it was doing to the soldiers. It wasn't so much the artillery barrages that affected them, it was the feeling of helplessness. They were trained to fight but, lacking the capability for combat, they could only cower in the bunker, feeling impotent.

* * *

While Dan Drew and Delta Company dodged artillery up in the Velebit Mountains, Calvin had to figure out how he was going to get all of his battle group into the new area and find adequate places for them to bunk down. First he had to gather up the forces he already had scattered all over Sector South and move the headquarters about fifty kilometres north of Knin, back through the Velebit Mountains and into an old Yugoslav National Army base called Sveti Rok.

General Cot believed that Calvin's soldiers had had an impact and he wanted to keep the pressure up. There was a looming suspicion in international circles that the Croats were growing weary of diplomacy and were planning an attack. The Canadians would be the only line of defence for UNPROFOR.

Calvin tried going through diplomatic channels to get the Croats to stop shelling his peacekeepers. He protested to the UN headquarters in Zagreb, and they sent a sharp message to the senior leadership of the Tudjman government. Calvin thought this move might have an effect because, he says, "The Croats were very, very sensitive about their relationship with the UN." It did get results.

The head of the army in Zagreb ordered General Ante Gotovina, the commander of troops in the region, to meet with Calvin and prove to him they were not deliberately targeting the Canadians. Gotovina pulled out an aerial photograph which, Calvin says, "showed every inch of ground—the whole position, you know, all around the beachfront area, all up where the school was—where Danny [Drew] was." The Croat commander made a great display of his evidence, trying to convince Calvin that it was only the Serbs who were firing. Calvin knew it wasn't true, but during Gotovina's presentation, he was distracted by something else. The photos revealed some artillery pieces that Calvin knew had only been installed in recent weeks. How did the Croats have up-to-date satellite pictures of the area around the Canadians when Calvin didn't have any? Only the United States had the capability and the Americans hadn't shared any such photographs with the UN or the peacekeepers on the ground.

Gotovina may have suddenly realized what Calvin was thinking because he quickly put the photos away. There had been rumours in the UN senior command that the United States was providing covert military assistance to the Croats. Calvin's officers recently had reported seeing Croats in brand new uniforms—uniforms that looked American. Calvin also heard that the Germans were providing heavy equipment to the Croats: "We'd heard rumours that the Germans had been floating tanks down the Danube, you know, and getting them into Croatia to rearm Croatians with T-72s [tanks] from East Germany, so they looked like Soviet equipment.

The Clinton administration was appalled by the Croat–Muslim war in Bosnia and President Clinton's ambassador to Croatia, Peter Galbraith, warned Tudjman to cease the campaign or the United States would withdraw its support for Croatia. In late summer of 1993, the U.S. was just beginning to get unilaterally involved in the Balkans and Clinton wanted more involvement in Croatia.

Clinton and his administration believed that Croatia was entitled to the return of its legal territory now held by the Serbs. They had openly signalled to Tudjman that if diplomatic measures failed to achieve the objective, the U.S. would support a military solution. The Americans had concluded that Milosevic was the villain in the Balkan narrative and they were trying to help Tudjman defeat the enemy. The U.S. needed clear white hats and black hats, but Tudjman kept muddying the waters.

Croatian public opinion was also dead set against the campaign in Bosnia. The Croats of Herzegovina were considered backward peasants by the people of Zagreb, who suspected that the government of the breakaway "republic" was nothing but a mafia. Car theft was rampant in Zagreb throughout the war, and many Croats believed it was their gangster hillbilly brothers from Herzegovina who were responsible: some members of the new Herceg-Bosna administration had mysteriously become overnight millionaires. The Croatian public wanted Tudjman and Susak to get the Krajina and Slavonia back into Croatian hands; they weren't interested in any other military adventures.

General Janko Bobetko, the old Partisan fighter who had traded in his Communist credentials for nationalist ones, was the biggest advocate of breaking international agreements and launching a full-scale attack on the Republic of Serbian Krajina. Bobetko wrote in *All My Battles*, "Whoever holds Velebit holds half of Croatia. If one loses Velebit, Croatia is cut in two."

Susak had made many friends in the Clinton administration, and he was also the main point man for the U.S. and Croatia's other friend, Germany, who regarded Susak as a man they could do business with. Ambassador Galbraith said they all knew Susak was "up to his eyeballs" in smuggled weapons, but they believed his goals were honourable ones—provided he stopped the dirty little war in Bosnia.

Susak never lost sight of his ambitions for Greater Croatia, even as he publicly proclaimed his readiness to do so. Susak and the rest of the inner circle—Bobetko and Tudjman—were preparing for the big one, a massive operation to take back all of the Krajina. But no one, least of all their American supporters, was sure that they had the strength and the military machine to pull it off. Bobetko argued that, in the meantime, they had to take some key strategic places. The most important was the Medak Pocket.

CHAPTER SIX

A CALL TO ARMS

. . . the two sides had picked the best ground. They were there for a reason. They have dug in their trenches there because they are the best piece of tactical ground. That in between is commonly known as the killing zone. And that is where we had to move our soldiers in to.

—Colonel Jim Calvin,
Board of Inquiry into Potential Exposure of
Canadian Forces to a Contaminated Enviroment, 1999

THE VILLAGE OF MEDAK is nestled in a deep fold of green pasture at the southern end of what's called the Lika Fields, in the highlands of the Velebit Mountains. The town is identical to every other town in Lika, consisting of little more than a few houses, a café and a store. During the war, Medak became the headquarters of the Lika Corps of the Republic of Serbian Krajina, but that did little to boost its population since the corps was mostly made up of local farmers.

Medak is connected, through a maze-like series of back roads and cattle paths, to a network of other villages and hamlets, all hidden out of the sight of travellers. This is exactly as the Krajina warriors of the past centuries wanted it: their homes were invisible and secret. An estimated four thousand people had lived in the region before the war, although an accurate estimate was impossible after the "population exchanges" (the euphemism for forcing one ethnic group out of their homes and replacing it with a different one) of 1991.

The farm villages around Medak appear out of the landscape suddenly: first a few rickety wooden fences peek out of the shrubbery, then some farm buildings come into view, followed by an old stone house built to withstand almost anything, except modern explosives.

Jim Calvin's soldiers, who moved into these highland fields in late August, were not the first Canadians to be there on military business. On April 21, 1943, three Canadians of Croatian origin parachuted into Lika, landing near Brinje, a village fifty kilometres north of Medak, at the opposite end of Lika Fields. The soldiers were intelligence agents carrying out an Allied operation code-named "Fungus"; they had flown to Croatia from Cairo. Petar Erdeljac, Pavle Pavlovic and Aleksander Simic entered what was then the Partisans' heartland, to make the first Allied intelligence contact with Tito's fighting force. The contact, and the subsequent alliance with Tito's brigades, established the Partisans once and for all as the prime liberation movement in Yugoslavia, and tipped the balance of power into Tito's hands.

Gospic is the capital of the Lika region, and it was the home of a Yugoslav National Army garrison long before the war of independence. When the Krajina Serbs seemed to be winning in the fall of 1991, the Croats responded by launching a campaign of terror in Gospic, systematically rounding up the town's Serb intellectuals—doctors, judges, professors—and murdering them.

In all, 120 people were put to death in Gospic, a massacre that included Croats who disagreed with the state's anti-Serbian policies. It was one of the worst examples of ethnic cleansing in Croatia, a crime made all the more heinous since the Serbs who were killed were those who had chosen to stay in Croatia instead of crossing the border and joining the Republic of Serbian Krajina only kilometres away. The JNA unit in Gospic became trapped in its barracks, and a full-fledged battle erupted between Croat and Serb forces. The Croats won: they took the JNA soldiers prisoner and killed their commander.

The defeat of the JNA in Gospic halted the relentless progress of Serbian territorial expansion. The self-styled Serbian republic had been swallowing up more and more land, but Gospic became the end of the road: the Serbs would not make it all the way west to the Adriatic, as the Knin rebels had dreamed. But the massacre in Gospic also established the twofold objective of the Tudjman government: to take back the land that rightfully belonged to the Croatian state, and at the same time, to eliminate the Serbian population that had lived in Lika for eight hundred years.

But the Serbian forces didn't retreat very far. The front line was redrawn just southeast of the Gospic city limits. The biggest irritant was a bulge, or pocket, pushing forward from the front line and held by the Serbian Lika Corps—Medak Pocket.

From Medak, the Serbs continued to rain artillery fire down on Gospic, whose citizens practically lived in their basement shelters. The local Croatian commanders were frustrated with the diplomatic dance Tudjman was playing on the world stage. They wanted to seize Medak and to force all the Serbs out of Croatia.

The Canadian peacekeepers were dropped into the middle of this tense division, no doubt finding the same polarized situation that the Croatian-Canadians dropped into the region in the Second World War had found, exactly fifty years earlier.

***

The Sector South headquarters was in Gracac. But Jim Calvin based his operation in the town of Kijero, well south of Medak but close to the vast area covered by his battalion. Delta Company was still up in the Velebit Mountains near the Maslenica Bridge, several hours' drive to the north. Though they had abandoned the bunker and come down to a presumably safer place, they were shelled again for four straight days in August.

It was around this time that Mike Brown and Kelly Brett first heard about a possible plot to poison the leadership of Delta

Company. Brown says he got wind of it from the medic, Steve Atkins, and then was told by the soldiers who claimed to be involved. "There were people within Delta Company trying to poison the command structure of Delta Company, namely Dan Drew, Mike Spellen and Matt Stopford," Brown says. He was certain the soldiers meant it.

What the soldiers confessed to the padre would fit the classic Oxford definition of the word "mutiny": when soldiers plot against their leaders because they feel they are being subjected to excessive hardship or unrealizable orders. Brown learned from his sources, whose names he will not disclose, that men were putting substances such as Visine in Matt Stopford's coffee, digging graves for their commanders and "carrying an extra bullet," an old military expression for preparing to take out one of your own. Brett and Brown took the mutiny up with Jim Calvin.

Brown had become a Cassandra-like presence within the command of the Patricias—trying to alert Calvin to the dangers lurking both within and outside the battalion. Brown says he told Calvin about the poisoning attempts, though Calvin says he has no recollection of the conversation. Brown says he went further, speculating as to why there was a spirit of mutiny within the ranks. He told the colonel that his troops had lost their sense of purpose. They no longer understood what it was their commanders wanted them to accomplish.

No military operation can be successful if the soldiers do not have a clear, single-minded sense of the objective, Brown maintains. A peacekeeping mission, lightly armed and spread out over hundreds of kilometres, should not have to stand up to armies. A peacekeeping mission should not have soldiers so afraid for their lives that they contemplated harming or even attempting to harm their superiors. Brown says he raised his voice when he told his commanding officer, "Sir, if we don't leave now, we will regret this for the rest of our lives." Brown wanted a complete pull-out for the mission.

Brown was right, but so was Calvin. Peacekeeping missions are not supposed to be violent exercises, but Calvin had come to understand that this wasn't peacekeeping anymore. Calvin remembers that the padre warned him frequently about pushing the soldiers too far and he says he listened to these warnings. But he had a job to do. He had orders to pull his whole battalion together for a possibly dangerous final assignment and he didn't even have a place to bunk half of them. Alpha Company, under the direction of Major Craig King, was on the move from Sector West to Sector South. Major Tony Kaduck and Bravo Company were even farther to the south in Miranje, near Zadar. The battalion was spread out over 2,500 square kilometres.

Bryan Bailey moved Charlie Company into the ruins of Sveti Rok and took up the task of protecting the villages around Medak. The complex of buildings had once been a JNA ammunition storage facility; now it was home to the Patricias. Medak Pocket was actually not part of the UN Protected Area of Sector South, but was in a Pink Zone. Bailey made contact with the local Serbian commanders, and tried, futilely, to meet with the Croatian commanders in Gospic. The only liaison he could manage was radio communication with the UN military observer there who was trying to monitor the Croatians' military activities.

But he knew the country and its players much better than most of the Canadian peacekeepers. Bailey's curiosity about history was broad. He always had a book with him, and in September he was reading *Monty: The Making of a General* in his spare time—which there wasn't much of, since he also wrote to his wife almost daily.

Bailey had been on the previous rotation and had come on the second mission, he says, when Jim Calvin offered him the chance to command a rifle company for the Second Battalion and be back in the field once again, which he loved. Soldiers who go on back-to-back missions tend to be those without a lot of domestic responsibilities, but Bailey had two small children at home, including a one-year-old he hadn't seen for six months. After he got back to Croatia, he learned that he and his wife had another child on the way. The strain was considerable, but the opportunity was too attractive to pass up.

His unit was well trained now, and he knew they could face down just about anything, but they were tired and had only one thing on their minds that September: "We were looking forward to getting back to Canada. We were all looking to rejoin our families. We all felt like we'd been through a grinder." The last thing they needed was trouble.

Within days of arriving, Bailey decided to go for a little tour of the Lika Fields and surrounding highlands. He knew that the village of Medak, on the main highway halfway between Sveti Rok and Gospic, was the last major Serbian stronghold in the region of hamlets and subsistence farms and if something was going to start up, Medak would likely be the place.

The countryside appeared peaceful, but Lika Fields was laced with secret military installations and combat communications centres run out of farmhouses. Everyone in the villages was responsible for Lika's defence. With a Serbian commander as a guide, Bailey drove the entire highlands.

The Serbs' Ninth Brigade was about two thousand strong, but only half the soldiers were on duty at any given time. Bailey noted they were all local people, farmers from the area ranging in age from twenty to fifty, wearing a mishmash of military uniform pieces. They were domobrans, the traditional backbone of regional defence. Now they were acting for the Serbian Republic. What Bailey noticed most of all was how dispirited they were. The two-year standoff had left them depleted.

The most important intelligence he took away from his reconnaissance mission was that the Serbs didn't seem to be planning anything. He wished he could be as confident about the Croats' intentions.

* * *

On the very day that Bailey was touring Lika, General Bobetko, head of Croatia's armed forces, was secretly devising his plan for the Medak operation with the local commanders. As Bailey combed the Serb side for clues, and the rest of the Canadian battle group settled in to the Lika area, the Croats were already well advanced in their preparations.

The Croat forces would attack Medak Pocket with three different forces. General Mirko Norac would lead the charge with tanks and artillery. Norac was as cunning as they come; he would be charged later for the Gospic massacre. General Mladen Markac—who had spent the past year in the Velebit Mountains strategizing this very offensive—would lead his special police. Markac was a founder and commander of the notorious Croatian special police units, the advance troops of ethnic cleansing. The local Croat domobrans would finish things off. Bobetko could not have had more motivated forces than these. They had been trying to take back Medak Pocket for two years and in just a few days, they would get their chance.

* * *

In late August, Tyrone Green and the platoon under his command were ordered to take over from the French in the village of Medak as the forward party in the region. They found an appropriate house, where the usual amount of garbage and destruction had to be cleaned out, and quickly got to know the town. These final weeks of violence were wearing everyone down—even Green, who had taken time off university to come on the mission. In Medak House, as they called it, they believed they could at least enjoy a degree of independence from company headquarters in Sveti Rok for this last stretch.

Medak was home to the Serbian military headquarters for the region. The Croatian military headquarters was fifteen kilometres up the road in Gospic. The paved road in between was the front line, and it was now the responsibility of Green's platoon. All other roads in the area were dirt, which meant a high probability of land mines. Despite the feeling of freedom, their situation was extremely precarious—they were cohabiting with one side of the conflict. Everyone knew the Croats weren't going to like that, and it was no picnic with the Serbs either.

Corporal Glen Peters from Halifax spent his first day filling sandbags to better protect Medak House from attack. The French had left their fortifications behind but their white plastic sacks were falling apart with age. Peters and the others dumped them out and loaded the sand into sturdier green bags from Canada. Peters's mom had sent him over a giant box of Kraft Dinner that a grocery-store neighbour had donated, and he was planning to feast on that at supper. Peters realized he could probably drain the pot of macaroni through one of the discarded white plastic sacks if he punched a few more holes into it. With a little ingenuity, life was more than bearable.

Medak House was a buzz of activity. The soldiers of Nine Platoon found local people to do laundry and help translate; village women would bring them bread. "There was a degree of loyalty to the people by then," says Green. "We'd adopted a whole bunch of children who came in each day to play volleyball with the soldiers. You know, we had dogs, we had cats." Out on patrols, people served them the little cups of thick strong coffee characteristic of the region and no one was above a little slivovitz party in the front yard. The local plum brandy is offered at all social encounters in the Balkans and the Canadians were often amazed at how much they could penetrate language barriers and come to a full understanding when a bit of the home-brew crossed their lips.

Morale in Nine Platoon rose. Green and his soldiers were actually enjoying themselves. It wouldn't last long.

***

The Croatian Army attacked Medak in the early hours of September 9, rousing both the Serbs and the Canadians from their beds. Tyrone Green's artillery report to Bryan Bailey on the morning of September 9 was the first news of a large-scale incursion. Mortar shells fell like rain all day at Medak House, but it was only the most severe of the hot spots the Croats were shelling all through Sector South and its vast expanse of Pink Zone. Nine

Platoon recorded that five hundred rounds fell around the town of Medak on the first day of the battle. They had a little notebook and tried to enter the time of each impact, but admit they missed some. Calvin gave orders to start reinforcing the defences of Medak House. As the United Nations peacekeepers in Medak, they had to hold this ground.

Bailey's troops were caught between two belligerents trying to kill each other but they were not the direct target of either, at least at this stage of the battle. There's almost nothing an infantry soldier can do about indirect fire, Bailey says. "There's no direct enemy you can focus on and return your fire back to, which is a great stress reliever. If a soldier's got an opportunity to do that, they take full advantage of it and it's a wonderful way to deal with stress in a situation. [Not being able to fire back] just continues to bottle up in people and gradually eats away at them." Their fighting instincts were roused, and what they wanted was to respond as soldiers. But who would they fight? To what end? And with what equipment?

* * *

High in the observation post Rob Dearing's section were desperately trying to figure out what was going on. Eight Platoon had built an impressive two-part bunker on the mountainside about three kilometres outside of Sveti Rok.

They had been there about a week when the Medak operation started. The radio was normally just a constant chatter of scratchy sounds and crackling voices. No one who didn't have to really paid much attention to it. But on the ninth of September it became the object of intense fascination. Charlie Company was under attack.

Rob Deans was hanging on every word. He had friends in Medak House, and he urgently wanted to know what was happening. But there was more to his interest. "To this point we had been this omnipotent entity that would move fairly freely. There was always hiccups, and people who didn't want you to be in certain places, and we had to negotiate through them. But there was some sort of . . . invulnerability to us. Now it was like, whoa, this is something serious."

Deans could hear the voices from Medak House describing their danger, then there was the voice of Colonel Calvin trying to get the Croats to move the mortar launchers away from the UNPROFOR installations and Major Bailey calling in situation reports. Deans could hear those inside the house trying to guide Bailey and Calvin as shells rained around them. It was real-time, real-life drama, and no war movie could have captured a group of people so intensely as that scratchy field radio with its tiny speaker.

While Deans worried about Medak House, Medak House worried about the townspeople, especially when an old woman they knew was brought to their compound. She was covered in the plaster from her ceiling, which had come down under a shell: one soldier picked a piece of shrapnel out of her hair. The medic tried to fix some wounds on her head, but she was mostly suffering from shock. Her house no longer existed.

During lulls in the shelling, the platoon ventured out in the armoured vehicles to find out what was happening, and to rescue local people from their destroyed houses. Even when it wasn't wise to be out on the road, Green would let them go because they were going stir-crazy inside. On their patrols they met wounded Serb soldiers in retreat, who told them which towns and villages were falling as the Croat ground troops moved in. The soldiers realized they were hearing about the defeat of hamlets where just days before they had enjoyed the sight of farmers preparing for the fall harvest and had longed for the tranquillity of their own well-ordered homes. Feeling the intensity of the time and place, and perhaps longing for ordinary human society, in the few days they'd been there the soldiers had become more attached to the people of the area than they had realized.

By the end of the first day of the renewed conflict, Green was in no doubt that the Croat tanks were just around the corner. They had actually fired some rounds right down the road toward the Serb brigade headquarters. He sent out tank hunting teams whose job it was to confront and actually stop the Croat advance. Sergeant Rudy Bajema was probably the most insouciant soldier in Nine Platoon, but even he admits he was unnerved when he was ordered to go out and fight tanks. He was relieved when Serb reinforcements got to Medak in time to stop the assault before the Canadians had to try. But that only freed him up for another task.

The Canadian battalion was stuck on the Serbian side of the front line. No matter how well situated Dearing's lookout tower was, the United Nations Forces did not have eyes and ears on the front line of the Medak operation. Reports of the Croatian offensive were flashing up the long chain of communication to London, where the Contact Group worked, and to the UN Secretariat in New York City. Zagreb was feeling the heat. The international community descended on Tudjman, demanding a halt to the offensive, but Tudjman insisted the Croats were acting only in self-defence.

The negotiators in Zagreb needed better intelligence as to what the Croats and Serbs were up to. Calvin got orders from UN headquarters to establish an observation post to determine who was doing what, where and when. The UN also wanted to know about incidents of ethnic cleansing or war crimes committed in the area; they needed detailed, accurate documentation to pass to the newly constituted war crimes tribunal in The Hague.

Bailey had scoped out the perfect location for such a lookout only the week before—a place where one could see all the way to Medak from Gospic. The first order of business on September 10 was for a section led by Rudy Bajema to climb to that high point, where they would become the eyes and ears of Medak for the world. Bajema actually questioned his own sanity as he led his nine-man section out of Medak the next morning and headed up the mountainside to the new observation post. He was another person on his second rotation, coming up on twelve months in Croatia, and he hoped to be heading home soon. Having survived this long, he was determined he wasn't going to die now.

From the new vantage point, Bajema and his men could see everything: it was the fireworks show of a lifetime. They saw a MiG jet take out a tank as the Croat air force got involved; they saw the villages being pounded; they saw fires blazing and smoke rising as the Croats forced people from their homes.

The UN military observers had provided Bajema and his section with high-quality Swedish binoculars; they already had a night vision thermal viewer. The valley below became a twenty-four-hour movie. It would have been exciting, except that Bajema knew only too well what was transpiring in those villages. He had been around long enough to identify the signs of ethnic cleansing.

The Croats had taken swift advantage of the weakness of the Serbian Army in the area: there had been no heavy fighting in a year and the professional Serbian fighters were in other parts of the country, leaving Medak in the hands of the Domobrans. But within a day, Serbian reinforcements were rolling in. Bajema was amazed to see a battalion of Serb soldiers arrive on school buses, in convoy with trucks, armoured personnel carriers, tanks and a very impressive array of artillery pieces. At one point, Bajema and the others saw a train roll in behind Serb lines on the still-functioning track from Knin: the front car had a tank barrel and rocket launchers mounted on its roof. Flatcars followed, carrying tanks, and then at the end another weaponized car offered more protection.

With all this new firepower brought to bear on Medak, there wasn't much more that either side could do. Both Croats and Serbs were locked in position on a hard front line. The Serbian villages trapped inside the Croatian pincers were ablaze and there was obviously a military clean-up operation in progress, the nature of which UN observers could only guess.

As the hours crept by and the Canadians could only sit and watch, their fear gradually gave way to anger and frustration. A sense of impotence swept the entire company. They were trained, ready and very motivated soldiers, but they were compelled to sit on the sidelines while an army rolled over the territory they were supposed to be protecting. Those were their orders: they weren't to do anything except in self-defence.

***

This was the most intense fighting in Croatia since the January 22 offensive that almost ended the UNPROFOR mission. But it was even worse. Battles and firefights erupted all over the country. Serbs attacked an oil refinery south of Zagreb, hitting the target with twenty shells; Croatian warplanes bombed Serb positions; Serbs shelled the Croat stronghold of Karlovac. Civilians bore the brunt of all these assaults, setting off more streams of displaced people.

Like a frenzy in a madhouse, the call to arms in Croatia caused a brutal chain reaction. Over the border, the Bosnians were inspired to new heights of aggression—as though the conflict there needed any more fuel on the fire. The entire Balkan region had become unstable and the UNPROFOR mission was teetering on the brink of collapse. The international community appeared powerless to stop this spiral down into war. World leaders had failed to make any progress in two years of diplomatic dithering and now their weak-kneed interventions were close to irrelevant. John Arch MacInnis in Zagreb was alarmed but not surprised to watch the mission coming down around their ears. As he saw it, a political solution seemed beyond the reach of the negotiators.

In Zagreb, Thorvald Stoltenberg, special representative of the UN Secretary General and the civilian head of the mission, negotiated furiously with Tudjman while his military counterpart, Jean Cot, tried unsuccessfully to meet with the even more defiant Janko Bobetko. MacInnis was handed the most difficult of all the Croats to deal with, Gojko Susak. The diplomatic Cape Bretoner found Susak to be brash, cocky and intransigent. They met in Susak's cavernous defence ministry office in St. Mark's Square, where the church outside speaks of the irrepressible national dream. MacInnis and Susak, who had both lived in

Ottawa, discussed the situation in English but sometimes, MacInnis says, it was more like shouting.

Tudjman agreed to stop the bombardment, even unilaterally, but he would not comply with the most pressing request: that the Croats withdraw from the villages of Medak Pocket and return to their pre–September 9 positions. That would not be possible, he declared, unless the Serbs cooperated.

But the Serb general, Mile Novakovic, would only reaffirm the message he had earlier sent to Bobetko: that the Serbs would continue to attack Croat targets all over the country until the Croatian army withdrew from Medak. By Saturday morning, forty-eight hours into the conflict, the belligerents had exchanged six thousand artillery and rocket shells in Sector South alone, most of them falling on or near the Canadians and the civilians they were there to protect.

General Bobetko could not have been more pleased with himself. He boasted the operation had smashed the Serbian brigade in the region and broken the choke hold of the Chetniks on Lika. He insisted that Serb civilians—old men, women and children—had been allowed to go freely, while Serb soldiers had willingly surrendered to the Croats' highly disciplined army. Bobetko's ministry issued press releases stating that Serb soldiers were being executed by their own officers as a warning to those who might consider fleeing or surrendering.

In *All My Battles*, Bobetko claims Jean Cot was arrogant and confrontational in their encounters. Cot was enraged, according to Bobetko, only because he and the other internationals had underestimated the strength of the Croats. "Judging by Cot's reaction," Bobetko writes, "one cannot make any other conclusion, except that they were horribly surprised by the speed and efficiency of the Croatian army." His self-congratulation was shared by his hard-line cabinet colleagues, including Susak. All of them were disappointed when Tudjman started to bend under international coercion: "There was pressure on the president, on me personally, to stop the operation," writes Bobetko. "We could have continued on to Gracac, we could have liquidated Medak."

Eventually, Tudjman did order the ceasefire, but refused to reverse the gains of the Medak operation. The American ambassador's influence on Tudjman was great, but the Croats weren't convinced that the United States would or could support them; the Americans had promised a military solution, but only after diplomatic efforts were exhausted. Galbraith didn't think they were. Tudjman's hard-liners did.

As the political process bumped along, the Canadians began to take casualties. At the junction of a road just north of Sveti Rok, three soldiers were driving a load of supplies up to Medak on the Saturday morning when their vehicle was hit by artillery or a heavy mortar shell. They were driving an old clunker of a truck that had taken as much abuse from bad roads as from the curses of soldiers who could hardly get it up a hill. A large piece of shrapnel pierced the soft cab and and lodged itself into Corporal Fred Taylor's ankle, and Bombardier Troy MacPherson, a reservist out of Halifax, took a faceful of windshield glass after it shattered under the shrapnel. This was what Kelly Brett feared the most—pulling shrapnel out of people without the proper facilities. The French had left behind a surgical team the Patricias could use but Dr. Brett knew he wasn't set up for much of this. Then there was a problem with evacuation: the roads were mined, the entire sector was under shellfire and helicopter movement was controlled by Zagreb.

Bryan Bailey recorded in his own notes that he was relieved, and surprised, that the three weren't killed. Later in the day another of his soldiers was hit by shrapnel, which cut a tendon in his thumb while he tried to wash some pots and pans in a little ablutions tent outside Medak House.

The scene before Bailey was surreal, with former Warsaw Pact equipment and vehicles moving around as though it were decades ago. There were heavy artillery pieces, which the diaspora Croats had purchased on the black markets of Poland and the former Czechoslovakia. The bullets and shells were compliments of Croats in Canada, the United States and Australia. Susak was a master arms dealer and, despite an embargo against selling

Croatia weapons, he had amassed a giant arsenal. Bailey had no idea where it had come from: only that it was impressive.

The mission took on its most surreal quality the following morning when the regiment's colonel-in-chief, Patricia Edwina Victoria, the Countess Mountbatten of Burma, arrived in Sector South to present the soldiers with their UN peacekeeping medals. Since this was the end of the peacekeeping tour, it was considered the appropriate time to bestow honours on the battle group. Few moments could have illustrated more vividly the absurdity of the mission. Here was a dignified recognition of the efforts of peacekeepers who far from keeping any peace were smack dab in the middle of a war zone, where entire villages were being removed from the face of the earth only a few kilometres from the parade grounds. Strangely, the enemies seemed to cooperate that morning; the Countess was able to supervise the little ceremony and award the citations in relative peace—as though everything was simply a show that could stop and start at will. Things were so calm that the Canadians even took the sixty-nine-year-old princess to Medak House, where she presented Nine Platoon with their awards.

***

Major Craig King and his Alpha Company also arrived in the Medak Pocket that weekend. They were the last of Calvin's battle group to make the journey down from Sector West. King had turned over his responsibilities in Pacrac to a battalion of Argentinians who had proven themselves very capable of the job. Because their tour was coming to a close, King had been obliged to leave the armour and vehicles they had been using in Sector West for the next rotation. He had moved his men down to Sveti Rok in buses, one of which they had had to borrow from the French, bringing little more than their helmets and their kit.

It's said that a person can get accustomed to anything. The soldiers who had been in Sector South for weeks had somehow adjusted to the reality of the shelling going on all around them to the point that they almost seemed not to notice it. But to King, it was all new, and it seemed as if everything they had accomplished had completely unravelled. The heavy weapons and ammunition that had been locked away in weapons caches had been reclaimed and were being used with impunity all around him. Not only was there all-out war between Serbs and Croats, but it was apparently open season on UN peacekeepers.

King went to the operations officer to see if he could get some protection for Alpha Company. But everything the battalion possessed was in use by soldiers in the thick of combat. The fact that there wasn't enough armour to go around was understandable for peacekeeping, but unforgivable in the situation the Canadians now found themselves in. Despite King's concerns, the Alpha Company soldiers continued on to their new home, a not-yet-occupied part of the compound at Camp Kananaskis (the name the Canadians had given to Sveti Rok). The soldiers found filth and debris everywhere. "The place stunk of defecation," says King. But he didn't have much time to think about these problems. Within hours he and the others had a whole new set of emergencies to jangle their nerves.

* * *

Zagreb had been spared much of the horror of the war up to now. Perhaps its citizens would have put more pressure on their leaders to find a solution if they had been forced to hide in basements and go without food or electricity, like their Croatian compatriots in the countryside. But life in the capital was still civilized: one could walk the streets freely and get a decent cappuccino in the afternoon and a passable Wiener schnitzel for dinner.

The city was, of course, chock-full of displaced people, many of whom were keeping a vigil at the UN headquarters for news of missing loved ones, but people still went about their business apparently unconcerned. Flashes of artillery fire could be seen at night—at a distance—but eventually that had become routine.

And so it came as a severe shock when Serb retaliation for the attack on Medak suddenly hit close to home: the Zagreb suburb of Lucko was struck with a land-to-land missile known as a FROG 7, which comes with a warhead weighing 500 kilograms. The Zagreb population was terrified, not least since Croatian TV stated—falsely—that the Krajina Serbs were loading their warheads with poison gas. Other northern Croatian cities were also shelled, and over the weekend the media broadcast a warning of "general threat." This emergency finally brought the Croat leadership to the table in earnest.

Tudjman called a meeting of the Council for Defence and National Security the following day, September 12, to discuss the implications of the Medak situation and consider how it could be resolved. He had received a steady stream of high-ranking diplomats through his office warning him of consequences if the Croatians did not withdraw. According to people at the defence council meeting, the pressure was principally coming from the American ambassador, Peter Galbraith, a key ally of Tudjman's and the man he would depend upon, overtly and covertly, for the big battle they were planning in the future. The UN had received the dispatches from Rudy Bajema and the members of Nine Platoon up in the hills, detailing the destruction of the villages.

Tudjman would have been a farcical figure if he hadn't been so dangerously unpredictable. He emulated Tito right down to the sparkling white commander-in-chief uniform he sported during public appearances. He had an almost mythical status in Croatia; the public ignored or forgave Tudjman his taste for expensive champagne and caviar and his use of Tito's former villa near Zagreb.

At the defence council meeting on September 12, everyone in the room could see that Tudjman was agitated. He seemed furious at Bobetko, blaming him for letting himself be manipulated into the Medak operation by his army chief. Following Tudjman's death some years later, secret documents came to light. They are very revealing of what the Croatian president actually knew on September 12 about what was going on in Medak: much more than he let on at the time. In his dealings with the outside world he claimed to have been shocked by the events, but in fact he had ordered the attack. Tudjman had many of his key meetings recorded for posterity: the regime that succeeded him leaked transcripts of those tapes to the press. They give a very complete picture of the political machinations behind the scenes. Most of the cabinet didn't know they were being recorded, and Tudjman didn't care. The record of the September 12 meeting is astonishing.

"I admit that I made a mistake in allowing the Lika operation," Tudjman announced to the defence council, though only after he has called the Medak Pocket operation a military success. As of that day, the Serb forces had suffered two hundred military casualties while the Croatian Army counted twenty dead and forty wounded. Tudjman's ticklish problem, it seems, was simply a matter of appearances. He had been negotiating a comprehensive ceasefire agreement with the Serbs through the offices of the international community and at the same time launching an assault on Medak. One would think this conflict was obvious, but in the meeting, Tudjman suggests that the difficulty with it has only now occurred to him. "I have to admit," says Tudjman, "I am partly responsible for allowing the Gospic operation. When General Bobetko approached me with the proposal I was swayed by [Serb] provocations." Tudjman goes on to say that three Croatian special police had been killed in Velebit recently, and one of them had his ear cut off. There was also an attack on Pacrac that Tudjman counts as a major provocation and, he says, these acts were enough to compel them to strike Medak. Then, having presented his justifications for the attack, Tudjman blames Bobetko for failing to make it appear to have been a defensive move. "Didn't I say that after the operation it should be made known that they attacked first?" demands Tudjman.

Instead, Bobetko had issued a statement that Tudjman describes as "catastrophic" for the cause. "You said, 'They have been provoking us for two years so we have decided to take

action.'" Clearly, it was a premeditated attack. "And what especially bothers me is that fighter planes were used, without my
knowledge, and that leaves no doubt about our intentions. When
[your side is the first to use] fighter planes, it means war, which
is the opposite of what was being talked about."

Tudjman's preoccupation was with optics: his words show no
concern for what is happening on the ground, only for what the
world will do when it finds out. He is clearly aware that the operation includes ethnic cleansing, as he mentions that it was part of
previous incidents. He says the world is starting to get the impression that Croatia wants to impose a kind of "final solution" on its
Serb population. "This [impression is gaining credence] because
we cannot hide [the] information that in western Slavonia, some
thirty Serb villages disappeared from the face of the earth, and now
these three, four Serb villages [in Medak Pocket] were eradicated."

Tudjman worries out loud how he will be able to build a
modern state with normal world relations when everyone knows
they destroyed villages and murdered their Serb minority. It
seems that the problem lies not with the act of ethnic cleansing:
it lies with the world's knowledge of it. If the pesky peacekeepers
and military observers could just be kept in the dark about these
things, then Croatia could win the war, keep its reputation
intact, then join the league of nations as a respected member.

Throughout the council meeting, defence minister Susak
has nothing to say; to this day his role in the Medak operation is
ambiguous. One of the other ministers suggests that perhaps the
timing isn't right for the final solution. The director of Croatian
TV, Tudjman's propagandist, Franjo Greguric, who one can
assume doesn't realize the session is being recorded, reassures
Tudjman he has nothing to apologize for in Medak Pocket. "It
was something that had to be done." The prime minister, Nikica
Valentic, agrees and adds that he knows the character of the
Serbs in the Krajina. "We will never be able to resolve our differences with Serbs in Croatia diplomatically. When the time is
right, we will have to resolve them another way." Tudjman
responds: "Yes, I know." The Serbs in Croatia depend on

Belgrade for everything, he says, and if the international community would make good on its promise to cut off the supply of arms from Serbia, they would solve the problem of Serbs in Croatia. Once that was done, "the remaining 10 or 20 percent will leave and that will solve that," Tudjman says. Valentic complains that this will take too long, but Tudjman says they must prepare the ground better politically and militarily before they can pull off their plan.

Valentic suggests that in the meantime they do a little PR by rounding up the refugees from Citluk, Divoselo and Pocitelj who are being held in some kind of a camp, and putting them into more posh surroundings. "And then show all that on air. You know, a little makeup, a little wash and so on." Tudjman agrees this is an excellent idea.

After this meeting, he entered into negotiations with the UN over the withdrawal of his forces to the pre–September 9 border. Something he had no intention of doing quickly, or willingly.

* * *

Rumours that UNPROFOR would soon get orders to intervene spread through the various Canadian camps and installations like wildfire. From the bunkers of Rod Dearing and Rob Deans, where everyone was glued to the radio for news, to the lookout post of Rudy Bajema, where the troops watched, forbidden to help, as the villages burned, to the Medak House of Tyrone Green where they darted out between shell strikes to find out who was still alive, to the vile bunkhouses where Craig King had only just installed his dispirited and weary soldiers—every one of them was excited by the information that they were to act instead of cowering. It gave them all a charge of adrenaline, testosterone and anxiety—exactly the chemistry that soldiers have experienced just before action since warfare began.

General Cot had moved the Canadians into Sector South, and specifically up to the Lika area, for exactly this reason. Medak was a flashpoint, and he wanted a gung-ho group of UN soldiers in the region, not his listless French conscripts. He couldn't ask for a more gung-ho commander that Jim Calvin.

The UN in New York had instructed the UNPROFOR headquarters in Zagreb that it was not to intervene to stop the fighting, or even the ethnic cleansing, unless there was a ceasefire and withdrawal agreement signed by both Serbs and Croats. The Serbs readily agreed, but "someone had to sign for the Croats before Calvin could go," recalls MacInnis.

The UN's proposed agreement was composed on the laptop computer of the chief of operations for UNPROFOR, a Canadian colonel from St-Jerome, Quebec, Michel Maisonneuve. He had been posted to the mission as the deputy to MacInnis and it was his job to make sure the deal was signed and carried out. Maisonneuve is an indefatigable French Canadian with a bristling brush cut and a trim moustache. If MacInnis was the diplomat and Jean Cot the man of action, Maisonneuve was something in between, trying to smooth the way for an agreement but also willing to be aggressive, even pushy.

On Monday, September 13, Maisonneuve worked until after midnight trying to finesse the language in order to get the Croats to sign. On Tuesday morning, he and Jean Cot headed over to Bobetko's office at the defence ministry in Zagreb where they unsuccessfully attempted to persuade the Croat general to sign the withdrawl agreement as written. Cot wanted the Croats to start leaving Medak Pocket the following morning, but Tuesday dragged by, and their plans were thwarted. Colonel Calvin received a rough sketch of what the Canadians would be expected to do if the UN in Zagreb could get both Serbs and Croats to agree. The overall plan, at least, was clear: UN forces would enter the fray from the Serbian side and literally replace the Serbian front line. Then more peacekeepers would pass through the first group and take over the Croatian front line. They would wedge themselves between the two belligerents and then push the Serbs and Croats back, so that neither side would be in control of Medak Pocket. UNPROFOR would not just be at the front line, it would be the front line.

Calvin wondered how he would implement this optimistic and ambitious operation. Soldiers at both observation posts, Dearing's and Bajema's, heard gunfire in the night. It sounded as if the Serbs were attempting to retake the town of Licki Citluk. There was no artillery, only machine-gun and rifle fire, indicating the enemies were fighting at very close range. The idea of wedging oneself in the middle of that kind of firefight was alarming.

* * *

On Tuesday, September 14, as Michel Maisonneuve and Jean Cot were locking horns with Janko Bobetko, Jim Calvin was in Gracac with other senior members of UNPROFOR working out the details of what the peacekeepers would do the very instant the signatures were on the agreement. Time was of the essence; the Patricias in the field were reporting back to headquarters what they could see of the ethnic cleansing operation. In phase one, the UN operation, Charlie Company and a company of French soldiers would replace the Serbs in their front-line position. Phase two would open a crossing point over the main road in Medak Pocket, where an anti-armour platoon would stand watch. In phase three, Delta Company, along with another French company would cross over to the Croat side and occupy the Croatian front line. And in phase four the Canadians would "ensure" that the Croats withdrew to their pre–September 9 position and UNPROFOR would begin patrolling duties in their new area of responsibility. Calvin's own addition to the plan was the sweep team—soldiers assigned to look for survivors. The peacekeepers had been listening to the explosions and gunfire inside Medak Pocket for five days now. Calvin believed there was reason for the UN civilian police to investigate and headquarters agreed.

Late Tuesday afternoon, Calvin called in his company commanders to issue orders. The two companies of French soldiers who would be joining the Canadians for this swift and direct operation had not yet arrived. One of them was on its way from

Sector North, two hundred kilometres away. The other was travelling from Bihac Pocket, a battle-scarred hot spot on the Bosnian side, about 250 kilometres away over rough and hostile terrain. The two French units knew almost nothing about the Canadians, and Calvin as little about them, but he had to make them an integral part of his battle group as soon as they showed up. There would be no time for him to take their measure, but he was relieved to learn the soldiers would be regular army units and not conscripts. In fact, Calvin was about to take command of some of the best soldiers Europe has to offer.

Bailey had the first appointment with Calvin to discuss Medak plans. Since Medak had been Bailey's area of operation and he was the only Patricia to have really scoped it, Calvin needed to know exactly where the front line was located. Bailey gave the details as he knew them from his own tour of the region from his observation posts and finally from what he could actually see and hear of the fighting, which was now at close range.

Calvin then told Bailey about phase one: he was to take his company and the French company through Serb lines, order them to withdraw and take over their positions. Bailey couldn't believe what he was hearing. "Because at that point in time, the cooperation that I was getting from the Serbian brigade was abysmal. It was extremely poor," recalls Bailey. Not only would it be impossibly difficult to interpose his soldiers among the Serbs, there was also the reaction that would be forthcoming from the Croats if he should successfully breach the line—he wasn't even going to think about that. Bailey's relationship with the local Serb forces was downright brotherly compared to the level of cooperation he was getting from Croats. But Calvin insisted Bailey go right over to the Serbian brigade headquarters that evening and have a little schmooze with them.

Bailey headed out as ordered into a night of cold, driving rain. The Serb in charge, as belligerent as ever, told Bailey to come back at eight o'clock the next morning. Bailey responded immediately that he would be there at seven, "because he always used to play these little power games and that's the way things got negotiated." When Bailey got back to the office he was told his wife had managed to get a phone call through while he was gone, and he had missed it. Deeply concerned about the plan, but even more angry that he had missed the call, he sat down to write her a letter. It was the last time for another week.

The UN wanted to have everything in place the moment they had the much needed signatures. During the long night of the fourteenth, UN forces were on the move. The French made their arduous journey down from Bosnia and northern Croatia; Delta Company had to come down across the Velebit Mountains from the post near the Maslenica Bridge, while the anti-armour platoon of Bravo Company, who were to protect the road, had to come from the refugee-packed towns of Bruska and Rodaluce, in the far south of Calvin's area of the sector.

Rod Dearing had been hankering to get off the mountain and do something ever since he heard the first whistling shell streak over his head on September 9. So he was happy when he got the order. They hauled out their C6 machine guns and, hefting backpacks the size of refrigerators, slipped and slid down the mountain on the wet mud. In Medak, they were told to start getting their armoured vehicles ready because their orders were to head out into the combat zone and separate the belligerent forces. Dearing recalls, "We were like, Whoa, this should be good—how are we going to do that?"

Rob Deans remembers the order coming over the radio. They were to get down to Medak as quickly as possible. "We had everything—tents, digging tools, defensive stores, pickets, tripods, barbed wire, the GPMG [general purpose machine gun], with all the ammunition to the tune of 1600 rounds. We had the nodler [the night vision thermal viewer]. And it all had to be humped down the mountain." Deans didn't complain—he was actually going to get into some action.

* * *

Franjo Tudjman's defence ministry was stalling for time, and the UN knew it. Michel Maisonneuve and his team in Zagreb worked all Tuesday night, trying to come up with an arrangement the Croats couldn't refuse. On Wednesday morning, he was told by the Croatian ministry of defence that they would get their signature from General Petar Stipetic. No one in the UN knew anything about Stipetic, except that he was in charge of Zagreb, not Medak. Since there was no fighting in Zagreb, no one had ever dealt with him. "They told me he was a nice man and that I'd like him," MacInnis says he was informed by the Croats. "What I found was a man who would put Machiavelli to shame."

Stipetic is a tall, gangling, chain-smoking general, who had learned to keep on Tudjman's good side. But he was disliked by the hard-liners in the defence department, who weren't sure he shared their territorial ambitions. Stipetic has a permanent ironic smile on his face, as if he is perpetually enjoying a private joke. He may have seemed like a Machiavelli to MacInnis, but in interviews much later, Stipetic claims he was being coerced into doing something he knew was only going to bring him grief.

Tudjman was meeting resistance from the army, from Bobetko down to the officers in Gospic, and required someone to kick-start the withdrawal before he took any more heat from the international community. He told Bobetko to get the process moving by ordering Stipetic to sign the agreement. Bobetko called Stipetic into his Zagreb office early on Wednesday, September 15. Several international representatives listened intently as Bobetko informed his fellow general that he was to sign the agreement on the withdrawal of troops from Medak Pocket.

Stipetic knew that Tudjman wanted this task done, but he wondered why Bobetko didn't sign the document himself. As Stipetic recalls the conversation, "General Bobetko tells me, 'General, I would not sign that.' To which I replied, 'I am a soldier, you are my superior and I'm executing your order and that of the Supreme Commander.'" Stipetic was cornered. He knew the order came from Tudjman, and he had to sign. But he also knew Bobetko would give him no support if he did sign.

The agreement consisted of nine clear sentences that had taken forty-eight hours to write. Stipetic reluctantly put his signature on the document, and then headed down to Gospic. He had been instructed to force the Gospic commanders to comply. He knew they would not, and that he would get no help on the ground.

But MacInnis and Maisonneuve had what they needed—the key to launching a UN intervention. With the precious Croatian signature in hand the Canadian contingent could get to work, even though it was far from clear if anyone had really agreed to anything.

* * *

Bailey woke very early on the morning of the fifteenth of September and was told that the big operation would start at noon. Bailey hadn't realized it was going to happen so quickly, but a few minutes later he was on the road, heading to meet the Serb commander. He had absolutely no expectation of success, but to his surprise, he was greeted by a warmly smiling colonel and a receptive Serb brigade. That morning, some members of the high command in the Serbian Lika Corps had turned up in Medak and brought the local contingent up to date on what the UN was planning, namely, that the Croats had finally agreed to go back to their previous positions. Nothing could have made the Serb commander happier. Whether Bailey liked it or not, UNPROFOR was about to become the Serbs' reinforcement. By eight that morning the Serbs were ready to take Bailey and his platoon commanders on a little tour of the region.

Meanwhile, an extremely significant visitor had helicoptered in to see Jim Calvin—the United Nations force commander. General Cot need not have come in person; he could safely have assumed that his orders had been received by Calvin and that the forces on the ground would execute the plan. But so much was riding on this initiative, not least his own reputation, that Cot was determined to do everything he could to ensure its success. The

UN was afraid the peacekeeping operation in Croatia was going down. Cot was not going to let that happen on his watch. Jim Calvin was the last chance for UNPROFOR and Cot. But the force commander also had something very important to tell Calvin.

The two men talked for three hours. They sorted out the rules of engagement. As they were bound by the parameters of a Chapter 6 mission, no one could fire unless fired upon, and the peacekeepers could return only equal fire. The point was to strictly avoid any armed conflict unless it was forced on them.

A force commander had a fair bit of latitude to change the rules—if he was willing to take the risk—and Cot was clearly willing to enter uncharted territory to save the mission. By reputation he was a gruff, uncompromising officer, and not terribly concerned with diplomatic niceties. Cot knew that Calvin would need the widest possible latitude if they were to have any hope of success. He had been impressed when Calvin had transported four hundred men from one sector to another over hostile territory in just over a day. He knew that Calvin's soldiers had aggressively moved up the front line at Maslenica and had not flinched under fire when the September 9 offensive began. He also knew that Calvin's battalion was the only one besides the French that was fully mechanized (every company had their own armoured vehicles). The highest mark of Cot's confidence in Calvin was that he was placing his own son under Calvin's command; he was a captain in charge of the French company that was coming down from Bosnia.

Up to this point, the anti-armour platoons had not been permitted to fire without the authorization of Calvin himself. "Going up against tanks, I said I would have to loosen that," Calvin recalls of his private chat with General Cot. "I said, We won't fire first, but if a tank shoots at one of my anti-armour weapons, I want the non-commissioned officer to be able to return fire in order to protect himself, and to knock out the tank without asking me if he can. The general and I agreed on that."

Cot then gave Calvin two further pieces of information, the

second of which was shocking and highly significant. "He said one, how important it was that we have a successful implementation because the UN had not had any successful implementations up until this time. And second, he did not believe the Croatian high command had told the soldiers in the front line that they would have to withdraw."

Calvin was taken aback. It was bad enough to have to push your way through enemy lines and place yourself between hostile forces when everyone involved was fully aware that you were going to be a gate-crasher and had agreed to pull back. It was certainly a different order of business to do so when only one side was actually prepared to cooperate. At the highest level, both sides had agreed to step back. The agreement signed by Stipetic clearly stated that the ceasefire would begin at noon, September 15, and the Croats agreed "not to hinder the implementation of this agreement." But now Calvin was learning that at the level of commanders on the ground, he wasn't going to get much cooperation.

Calvin didn't blink. The heaviest piece of equipment he had was the TOWS, which could take out a tank at 3,750 metres. In that department, the Canadian Forces for once hadn't scrimped. The battalion had eight of the systems and Calvin was fully prepared to use them. The French company would impose itself on the north end of the pocket; Major Bailey would be in charge of the southwest where the fighting was still intense.

But Calvin also didn't blink about something else: this was clearly a change of mission, with considerably more potential for violence. On whose authority was this new assignment approved? What latitude did Calvin have to agree to something that probably should have been reviewed in Ottawa? Calvin says his tour was not like later missions, when DND headquarters would have used its bureaucratic screwdriver to tinker in the middle of overseas operations. He believed that John Arch MacInnis was on-side, but even so, it's not certain that Calvin was free to accept Cot's orders without Ottawa's direct aproval. It was definitely within his authority to refuse them if he thought following through would place his soldiers in danger. Both Cot and Calvin were in a grey area, and neither hesitated.

* * *

Throughout the morning, while Cot met with Calvin, Bailey and his entourage were on the Serb side of the Medak Pocket, setting up the launching stages for each of his three platoons. When they arrived at the position that Bailey was assigning to Eight Platoon, a fierce firefight between the Serbs and the Croats had just abated. Bailey could only guess at the intensity of what had just happened by the look of fear in the Serb soldiers' eyes and the fact that they were actually still cowering behind the lines.

As soon as the Serb commander explained to his men what UNPROFOR would be doing, everyone was as relieved as though the cavalry was arriving. The local battalion commander broke open a bottle of slivovitz. Moments before, everyone had been in a state of tense concentration: now they jovially toasted each other's success and health with the potent plum brandy.

Captain Dave McKillop was the Eight Platoon commander. This was to be his home for the next hours, or possibly days. Bailey told McKillop to try to get his platoon in as close to the Croats as he could, bearing in mind that both sides were jittery. With his Serb escort and a little slivovitz fortitude, Bailey continued up the Serb line looking for a strategic position for Tyrone Green's Nine Platoon. In what they thought was the middle of the Serb line, Green and Bailey walked together for about a kilometre into a chilling no man's land without any kind of reaction from either side. Bailey chose a place that he thought was suitable for Nine Platoon to begin, then left Green to gather his thoughts, and his men, for the incursion into the front line.

Seven Platoon was led by a newly minted second lieutenant, Shawn Moran, who had only arrived in Croatia the week before, replacing a homebound officer. Bailey was concerned about his level of experience and so he found what he thought was a nice safe approach through which the platoon could reach the most southern end of Charlie Company's positions. With everything in place, Bailey had to leave the rest up to the soldiers.

* * *

Tyrone Green returned to Medak House and quickly mobilized his force. They were all revved up and ready to push into their position when Green heard from his commanders that they were stalled again. By early afternoon, word had come down that they should approach their positions with caution. Green doesn't recall the exact warning—their radio communications were monitored by both sides and so UN messages were always coded and cryptic. But he understood that it wasn't certain that all the Croats had agreed to the plan.

Green was concerned that waiting might actually put the men and women of his platoon in danger: "As it got into the mid- to late afternoon, there were two things I wanted to avoid at all costs. One was to be stuck on the Serb lines once it became dark, and second was to have to move into no man's land when it was dark. And I knew I was going to have to move out eventually and I really wanted to move out while it was light."

Bryan Bailey was always receptive to suggestions from his subordinates and he decided to give Green the go-ahead. Nine Platoon began to breach the Serbian lines, immediately coming under fire from the Croatian side, which was only about a hundred metres away. "Initially we thought, oh, maybe they're thinking this is a Serb attack, even though we have fairly prominent vehicles." The white APCs have large and conspicuous blue United Nations markings on all sides, but Green decided to give the Croats the benefit of the doubt: "We thought, well, let's raise the flag. On the end of each antenna we have UN flags, so we popped those up. Then we started receiving machine-gun fire." The platoon had one last idea: Medak House had a giant UN flag the size of a bedsheet and they pulled that out into the open. "And then we started receiving anti-aircraft fire in a direct roll."

The new rules of engagement—and even the old ones—would have permitted Nine Platoon to shoot back, and Green's warrant officer, William Johnson, remembers that they did exchange some small-arms fire with the Croats. But Green decided they should pull back and reassess the situation. The UN military observers (UNMOs) were the only ones who had contact with both sides, Serb and Croat. In a furious exchange of radio calls back and forth, the UNMOs tried to get the message to the Croats to hold their fire.

The danger, Green realized, was that Croats would think they were practically embedded with the Serbs, and so he determined that they should break out ahead of Serb lines as quickly as possible. Green crawled out into the field close to where the Serbs were, then rolled onto his back to look behind him at his platoon tucked in behind the trees. He called to Rudy Bajema to have someone fire two warning shots toward the Croats. "I rolled back over to observe my front and basically the whole tree line behind me opened up—you know, everyone took it upon themselves to ensure that warning shots were fired." Lying out in the field between enemy lines, with an eruption of warning gunfire going off behind him like an explosion, Green suddenly found the situation funny. He started to laugh, partly from nerves but also from a sense of release. They had been taking indirect fire for days, huddled in Medak House or in their APCs, and had been directly attacked by the Croats. This was the first opportunity to respond and it felt good.

Green looked to his left and realized the Serbs had just deserted the crazy Canadians. Nine Platoon was on its own. He decided they should push on.

Moving slowly forward in the armoured vehicles, they advanced ten metres at a time. They took fire each time they advanced, but less and less as they progressed through the field. Perhaps the Croats realized the peacekeepers weren't going to give up. The Canadians were up against dismounted soldiers manning heavy weapons, but Green noticed one tank on the Croat line that was pointed his way. He asked Bailey if he could actually employ his

TOWs. Without waiting to hear back, Green told the master corporal to move the anti-tank vehicle out from behind the tree line, so the Croats could see it. "As soon as they saw the missile launcher breach the tree line, we saw the tank immediately go off and lower its barrel and a few minutes later, back up and get the hell out of there." Whether the Croats had any knowledge of the ceasefire agreement or any idea at all of what the Canadians were up to, Green to this day has no idea. He just knows Nine Platoon eventually snuggled right up to the front line, where they wanted to be, and the firing stopped altogether. The Serb forces behind them had already melted away. Mission accomplished.

It would not be so easy for Eight Platoon.

***

Rod Dearing had been on the go since three in the morning, rounding up his section and getting them to Sveti Rok. Rob Deans, Dearing's second-in-command, told the men to bring as little with them as possible: a change of socks, some rain gear, but no rucksacks. There was excitement in the air but Deans got his first sense of what was ahead for them when the platoon's warrant officer started to hand out the ammunition.

Crates of grenades were pulled out of storage: "'Distribute these to your section, that's your ammunition,'" Deans says he was told. "'Here's some extra rifle ammunition.' Clunk, clunk, clunk. He's pushing all this extra ammunition at us. I look over and see our anti-tank weapon, the 84-millimetre Carl Gustav, anti-tank rocket launcher that each section has. They're normally kept in a pack board with a canvas cover, but the cover's off, the 84 is coming out and being bungeed inside the track vehicle." Then came the light anti-tank weapons and more ammunition. Finally, the soldiers were told to get their helmets on, for the first time that Deans could remember: "And everyone is trying them on because they're all community stored and so we had to find the right ones. So we got that sorted out and thought, Boy, do we look silly. What are we about to get ourselves into?"

Deans had one final, excruciating task: to choose two of the men to stay behind and guard their gear. Two names were drawn and Deans had to be the messenger of the bad news. Nobody wanted to be left behind when a real soldier adventure was beginning. "I remember a lot of daggers coming my way when I said what I said to them. And I remember them just sort of turning and walking away."

Dearing recalls the spectacle of the white-painted armoured vehicles all rolling in the same direction; he saw people he hadn't seen for many days—his colleagues from Seven Platoon, the soldiers of Delta Company who had been up at Maslenica for what had seemed like an eternity, and the French who were just arriving from the north and from Bosnia. They were all moving in a cavalcade of armoured vehicles.

They were told to tuck in around Medak on the Serbian side of the fighting. Dearing found a good place for his section in a farmer's field as the sun came up on a warm September morning. "I thought, it's nice and quiet, maybe nothing's going to happen, maybe the ceasefire is working. So I told the boys— we hadn't eaten all night—'Brew up, make breakfast, have coffee and I'll go down to the platoon headquarters wagon to see what's going on.'"

Dearing met up with Dave McKillop, his platoon commander, who was grappling with the hasty orders he had just received from Bailey and was also trying to take stock of just how risky this operation was going to be. McKillop told Dearing his section was to take the lead and so would have to leave immediately. Dearing remembers the moment with some amusement. It was like being given directions to someone's hard-to-find house. "So he reads me off the orders. 'You got to go to this grid and you're going to see a tank squadron in this intersection,'" McKillop explained. " 'It's a crazy intersection so make sure you stay on the main road. Go through it, there's a Serb position here, get a guide, go through the minefield, punch through and the

Croats will see you, and then you'll be in between them.' Oh . . . Okay! Got it. So I run back to tell the others," says Dearing. No one had had any inkling that they would be moving so quickly, and not a single cup of coffee had yet materialized. Now they were informed they were on their way.

As soon as everything was stored, Dearing gave the nod to move. He pulled out onto the road and watched as the other vehicles did the same, rolling out behind him in formation. "So you picture all these wagons, all my mates standing out there giving me the high five and stuff," Dearing remembers. "We've got all our weapons on, the machine-gunner's got the heavy kit on and we're driving real slow. I was feeling pretty wired for sure."

As they motored along, Dearing's vehicles pushed the speed and they rumbled up the main road at 45 km/h until they arrived at the intersection. Buildings all around were on fire, and Dearing warned the driver to stay on the hard-packed road for fear of land mines. Right on cue, a Serb guide flagged down the APC—Dearing was amazed to hear him speaking English. The guide climbed onto the front of the carrier and directed them off the track, and across a field and right into a deserted farm complex where at least one of the buildings was still on fire. The farm was on the outskirts of the village of Pocitelje, also known as Sitnik, and right on the front line. The Croats had attacked this village just the day before.

Dearing and McKillop walked into the little knot of houses to take stock. They were right on the front line, on the Serbian side. McKillop wasn't sure how quickly they should move in, but Dearing decided, "Fuck it, sir. We've got to get on with this." Dearing directed the vehicles up beside a barn. "Parked there. The sun is shining. Could hear the odd shot going off, nothing serious. Turning out to be not a bad day at all."

Deans was shocked when they turned off the road and into the open field. If the ammunition and the helmets hadn't convinced him that everything had changed, this certainly did. He could see the Serb soldiers crouched at their front line, and there was the look and feel of fear all around. The threat of land mines was a constant in Croatia and his platoon had never rolled onto open ground before. As it turns out, they should still have been on their guard. Dearing learned there had been a little misunderstanding—the Serb guide's English was perhaps not what it appeared to be, and the platoon had actually stopped just short of a mine necklace, a ribbon of deadly explosives laid across the road to stop the Croat advance.

Dearing's was already the most forward of the three sections in Eight Platoon but he was supposed to be even farther out, ahead of the Serb line. A dead cow in the middle of the field, recently killed, was a pretty good sign of where the mines were: the cow's head had been blown off when it had either stepped on the mine, or stopped to have a little lick on the lethal contraption, as livestock in mine-infested countries have an unfortunate habit of doing. Then Dearing noted several tilt-rod anti-tank mines sticking up out of the ground. This was as far as they could go. But it meant they were as uncomfortably snug as one could be with the Serb fighters and that was only going to cause trouble.

The day had begun at 3 A.M. and it was now high noon. Dearing got the engineers to come up to his positions and bulldoze the top layer of hard soil so that the troops could start to dig deep trenches for themselves. The other two sections of Dave McKillop's platoon dug shell scrapes as well, while McKillop plotted where they might go for cover in the event of a mortar attack.

In the distance, Dearing could see a platoon of Croats standing under a tree. Through the binoculars, he noticed that one of the men was an officer who was clearly giving orders. "Great," thought Dearing. "they're getting the ceasefire instructions." His men fired up the cook stoves and prepared for what they thought—or hoped—would be a a straightforward job of babysitting a ceasefire line.

They had entered the farm with the Serb guide on board— helmet on and rifle cocked. Serb tanks were dug in all around and everywhere Serb soldiers were milling around cautiously with their weapons. Deans was handed a shovel and told to start digging trenches, something Charlie Company had never done since they arrived. Dearing began to scout for the most strategic high point to put a general-purpose machine gun. No one actually said the rules had changed. No one had to.

Between the bulldozer and the three sections working their picks and shovels, the platoon was able to dig itself down relatively well. Deans was constantly reminded of the stories of Second World War vets who would describe exactly this situation, and claim that the berms and trenches were all that saved them. Deans was hoping the theory wouldn't be tested here. Dearing put his GPMG in the top floor of the barn and sent a series of rotations in to man it. He ordered the men to build a bunker in the basement of the farmhouse ruins that could be used as a refuge in the event of mortar attacks.

While the platoon dug itself in, the Serbs and Croats continued with sporadic shooting, as if the peacekeepers and the cease-fire agreement were just a movie going on elsewhere. Dave McKillop tried to get the Serbs to stop: he warned them that they would only draw fire to the peacekeepers. It didn't seem to matter to them. And so it took a moment for the Canadians to fully realize that they had actually become the target.

McKillop was issuing orders to his three section commanders when the first bullets whizzed by the blue-helmeted heads of the peacekeepers. "It started out, pop-pop-pop," recalls Dearing who was standing with McKillop. "As soon as I heard that, I started running back to the section and I'm whistling through this courtyard." Deans saw Dearing streak by and go to ground just in front of the armoured vehicle. As though in a dream, he watched Dearing put his rifle up on his shoulder and fire toward the Croat side. Whatever the wording of the official command was when they were told to fire back, Dearing couldn't recall. The other soldiers remember it was something on the order of "Kill them. Get them." They were under fire.

"This is it," Deans said to himself. This was what all the preparations were for. "What I remember the most is the crescendo of sound that went from zero to this amount of noise that I had never experienced before or since, which entirely fills your body, fills your head, fills your chest with the sounds of these rounds being fired at you."

Bill Ray and Guy Simmons dived for shelter in their shell scrapes and they all began to fire back. "Me and Simmons are shooting," remembers Dearing. "Changing magazines. I'm changing and Simmons is shooting. We're getting hammered by small arms and stuff. And I get dirt in my eyes and can't see. Oh, it's just a gong show!" At one point, Dearing looked over to see Bill Ray curled up in a fetal position in the trench. Bullets were bouncing off the back of the trench wall and Ray had to hold his legs up to prevent having his feet shot off. Simmons continued to shoot, even as he exposed himself to fire.

Deans was on the ground coping with a spray of blinding dirt in his eyes, but as second-in-command he knew his responsibility was to back up Dearing and that meant getting to the top of the barn where the machine gun was positioned. No one was firing from there and Deans was going to find out why. He signalled to Dearing that he was going up and Dearing nodded. Deans crawled along a woodpile, realizing that his hindquarters were directly exposed to incoming fire, then crawled through a hole in the barn wall and into the loft, where he found the entire area piled with furniture from the farmhouse. It was an obstacle course of chairs and tables, which he clambered over until he got to a clear space where his foot went through the floorboards and he found himself stuck up to his crotch in rotted wood. He climbed out only to strike his head on a beam and knock the blue helmet down around his eyes.

Deans was feeling pretty foolish when he finally got to the machine-gun position. They had laid a door flat on the floor for the gunner to lie on and Deans flopped himself down on the door in front of the gun but landed smack dab on the doorknob. "Thankfully the adrenaline numbed all the pain."

Just then, the Croats ratcheted up the attack, shooting 20-millimetre cannon rounds at the Canadians. Dearing watched the gunfire walk across the courtyard, spitting up little puffs of dust, and striking their APC. The Croatian cannon shot up the farm-house where one of his men was making a bunker in the base-ment, it pinged off the APC and then hit the roof of the barn where Dearing had installed his machine gun and observation post. "So now I'm looking at it, going, 'I just killed those guys,' 'cause I just sited the observation post in the barn."

But Scott Leblanc, Archie Hamilton and Rob Deans in the barn tower were unhurt. Leblanc, a gunner, knew they could do very little except sit out the firestorm: the machine-gun fire was coming from very close, but he couldn't see anything except Dearing down below with his rifle on his shoulder, shooting. LeBlanc also wasn't sure if the rules had changed. What was he allowed to do in self-defence? After his initial fear subsided, Leblanc just said a prayer that he could do his best here, and that "no one was going to die in this godforsaken hellhole."

Deans realized Leblanc was right: even up in the barn, they couldn't see where the Croat shots were coming from. Dearing signalled to the men to fire but Deans and the others remem-bered the rules of engagement—don't shoot unless you have a target. The only way to spot anything would have been to survey the hedgerow with the binoculars. The afternoon sun was streaming into the barn and Deans realized the light would gleam off binoculars and would make them an instant target. He was feeling guilty for not backing up Dearing, his section leader and good buddy, but he honestly didn't know what he could do. Later he would realize that between their hesitation and Leblanc's prayers they had managed to do just the right thing. Had they fired, the Croats would have made the peacekeepers in the barn an easy target.

Dearing's section was taking the brunt of the attack but all of Eight Platoon was under fire. Tony Spiess, Dean's best friend from the Seaforth Highlanders, was an energetic corporal from Vancouver. Spiess had been to Cyprus and thought he knew what the business of peacekeeping was all about; he had signed up for this mission because he couldn't bear it if Deans went on such an adventure without him. He had rolled up into another part of the field about a hundred metres away and had found his section, alarmingly close to the Serb front line.

As the sun burned off the remains of the morning mist, Spiess noted that he had been issued armour-piercing ammunition for the 20-millimetre machine gun he was manning on top of the APC. "We were loaded down with all this stuff," recalls Spiess. "And then there was the smell in the area, the fires and the rotting flesh of animals and you know, humans and stuff. That I remember. I'll never forget."

Spiess had been watching the shooting match between the Serbs and Croats when all of a sudden the first bullets whipped past the heads of his own section. Spiess at first didn't notice that the trajectory of the firefight had shifted. He was standing on the carrier when he saw a fellow peacekeeper with his rifle on his shoulder. "And I asked, 'What are you doing, man? You're going to draw some fire!' And he goes, 'We're being fucking shot at.' And that's when it kicked in." Spiess got behind the mounted gun as the air around him split open with noise. "It was deafening. I can't explain it to you. And then we got the order to fire back. I'm beside the carrier and behind the gun. And I opened up and we just started knocking some guys down in the hedgerow that was in front of us, about two hundred metres away."

Spiess remembers shooting, while the man behind him—who was to give him cover—shot in the same direction. Spiess felt his colleague's rounds come dangerously close to his own head just as the Croats opened up with the cannon fire. Spiess turned to yell at the other soldier: "Don't fucking shoot me, man," and as he did, he noticed the wall behind them was disintegrating from the impact of Croat fire. Spiess watched with alarm as the Serbs, with whom they were so tightly located, began to drop. "I just knew guys were going to die that day," Spiess says. "And now I just didn't want it to be us." As the hail of gunfire continued, Dave McKillop had to chainsaw his way through the door of a building in order to take cover. McKillop had wanted to avoid damaging any property, but he decided staying alive took precedence over respectful conduct.

As suddenly as the deafening hailstorm of bullets had started, it stopped. The body-filling, head-splitting noise ended and the silence was screamingly loud. It had lasted for about twenty minutes, and it had caught the Canadian soldiers completely off guard. It was the first firefight of its kind for Canadian forces in decades and Dearing determined that the Canadians had lost.

Dearing immediately ordered Deans to make the rounds and determine if everyone in his section had survived the attack. Deans asked each man if he was okay and how much ammunition he had used. It was a standard practice that Deans had remembered from his training, but then he recalled a story he had heard from an old war veteran, who had discovered that soldiers don't always know when they've been wounded. He started to grab each man and shake him. But only one person in Deans's unit didn't seem quite right—the driver, Bill Ray, who had curled up in the trench to avoid the bullets. Deans couldn't see any injuries, but Ray was acting strange. "He was breathing heavily and focused on his gun. And my God, his magazines were laid out on the parapet ready to go, and the thing that struck me most was he had his bayonet on the end of his rifle." Deans had a strong sensation that Bill Ray wasn't all there but he didn't know quite what to do. "So I told him, 'Nice bayonet, Ray.' And he said, 'Thanks.'"

Dean's next thought was for Spiess. He dashed over to the other section's position a hundred metres away. Spiess was doing the same thing—looking for Deans. "My major concern was that I had to find Deaner, right? Best friend. And it was probably the longest moment in my life looking for Robbie. When I actually saw him it was just like, thank fuck you're all right, man." The two men had done everything together, as fire team partners with the Seaforths, and in training. "I didn't want to be the one to come home and tell his parents," Spiess says.

In fact, everyone had survived unscathed, to the enormous relief of Gord Parker, the platoon's medic. Parker had tried to work up as close to the battle as possible in order to help, but as he did so he got farther away from his ambulance. He was surprised to find Dearing quite calm and composed. "'How ya doing, doc?' he said to me. 'Welcome to our hovel.'"

No one was quite sure if the firing had stopped for good and Parker was torn between being on the front line with Dearing and being back with his ambulance. He decided to stay with the vehicle. He planned to crawl back up if he had to take care of wounded soldiers. But all the time he was wondering, "How am I going to get people out of here if the bubble bursts?"

***

Colonel Calvin had told Bailey to have his company on the road by nine and the platoons in their positions by 1200 hours. Through the moxie of the men and the relationships Bailey was building with the Serb commanders, he was actually able to pull this off. When he reported his success to Calvin at 1300, Calvin was surprised and alarmed. He hadn't expected them to be so quick and told Bailey for the first time that the Croats hadn't signed the agreement yet. Calvin asked Bailey if his company couldn't just ease off on their deployment for a bit.

Now it was Bailey's turn to be surprised. What could he tell the men? They had nearly got themselves killed getting into their positions. He could hardly instruct them all to pull back and sit on their hands again, not now, when they were so close to the ethnic cleansing they could smell it. But what if the fire they were taking was because they had pushed in prematurely? Bailey decided not to tell Calvin or his platoon commanders. He needn't have fretted that he was ahead of schedule; when the Croats did get the orders they didn't change their behaviour toward the peacekeepers one iota. Indeed, the attacks on the Canadians became more intense.

***

Dearing had saved the lives of the soldiers in his section. Without the trenches, bunkers and sandbag walls he established the instant they went into the area, a number of his men would undoubtedly have been shot. But he also knew he had made some major mistakes. He immediately ordered the men to take the C6 machine gun down from the attic of the barn. He called in the engineers to scrape out another trench and put his C6 machine gun well into that hole while he fortified the armoured personnel carrier with a berm of dirt.

Dearing then called his men together for what can only be called a kind of locker room pep talk. He told them he didn't know what had just happened or what would happen next. There was a ceasefire but obviously no one was honouring it. But, he said, they had dug in to their positions and they knew how to scrap, if that's what the Croats wanted. "It's their problem that we are going to win," he said. It wasn't that Dearing wanted a fight with the Croats, "But it was a question of, look, if you're going to mess with us you're messing with the wrong people."

Deans remembers that everyone was hanging on Dearing's every word and they all felt this enormous burst of confidence sweep through them. The rules of engagement had changed, and they were fighting men now. They had lost the first battle, but they weren't going to lose another.

Eight Platoon fought four more firefights, some lasting only minutes, others lasting well over an hour. The Croat fire coming from behind the hedgerow included rocket-propelled grenades, small arms, machine guns and anti-armour weapons.

The Canadians fought back with their machine guns and rifles while the French—who were well back of the front line—used their own 20-millimetre cannon. Each attack followed the same pattern: the Croats would move in to the hedgerow, 150 metres away, and concentrate their fire on Dearing's position, and sometimes open up on the rest of the platoon. The French company under the command of Captain Fontaine were tucked in farther to the east. They weren't exposed to much of the fighting until the end. In the final battle, early the following morning, the French too were compelled to fire back.

The Patricias' counter-fire became more intense as the night wore on. Each of Dearing's soldiers took a turn manning the C6 machine gun, and by nine or ten o'clock that night Dearing himself was on the trigger. When the Croats began to shoot, Dearing returned fire with one very long and sustained burst. He shot into the hedgerow continuously until the other side stopped. He has a distinct memory of one of his hits. "I'm looking right over the barrel and the guy is right in front of me—bang, bang, the muzzle flashes—so I just hold down the trigger for about five tracers and that was the end of him."

After each successful encounter with the Croats, Dearing says, they would run around and find the others in the section—hugging each other, high on adrenaline. It was a kind of lethal sports match—the stakes couldn't be higher or the sense of accomplishment more profound. They had no idea why the Croats were firing on them, but they were not going to give up. Quite the opposite.

Dearing told his section they should take turns trying to get some sleep in between the attacks since they had been up since 3 A.M., but it was impossible. "I personally didn't want to miss anything," says Scott Leblanc. The adrenaline kept them alert, and they were all amazed at how much of their training had kicked in. The Serbs came to warn the Canadians that after dark no one should wander around outside the farmyard, because the Serbs were prepared to shoot to kill anything that moved. So much for the ceasefire.

Rob Deans was alarmed when the warrant officer took some Serb soldiers up to the attic of the barn to have a look at the scene through the Canadian night vision equipment. Showing off their toys was something they had done in the past in order to create some instant friendships with local soldiers, but this was no longer a peacekeeping operation. Deans and the others were never exactly sure what all the rules were now that they were actually engaged in combat.

Gord Parker wasn't sure what the rules were for him, either. He was tuned to his radio waiting for word that someone was injured, and he knew that if he was shot going to the rescue he probably wouldn't know which side had done it. He had received the same warning from the Serbs not to move around, so he and his assistant stayed tight in their armoured carrier. Parker had a red cross on the side of the vehicle but also a gun mounted on top, a curious contradiction that the medics had complained about. They thought it made their medical vehicles into targets. But that night he was glad he had the gun.

Parker realized at one point that he was being fired on and he could see the muzzle flashes of the Croat guns in the hedges. He decided since he had to bear the consequences of having a .50 calibre machine gun on his ambulance he might as well use it. He opened fire, shooting directly into the muzzle flashes. By dawn he had gone through an entire belt of ammunition. Despite being a medic, he felt a sense of satisfaction.

* * *

September 15 was a bad day for Petar Stipetic. He'd headed down to Gospic after being coerced to sign the withdrawal agreement. Bobetko had sent him to order General Mirko Norac back to Zagreb for further consultations, but Norac flatly refused, giving Stipetic a succinct message for Tudjman: "Fuck all the Croatian generals with Franjo Tudjman at the top. The only general for me is General Maks Luburic." Luburic was the Ustashe military hero who ran the Jacovac concentration camp during the Second World War and whose Otpor organization was thriving under the leadership of the Croatian-Canadian Marin Sopta.

Norac had spent two years plotting the Medak operation and he was delighted with his success. He had no intention of withdrawing. After hearing Norac's answer, Stipetic thought it might be a good idea to go out into the field and try to determine if Norac had any support among the other commanders, "but I was prevented from doing so with a message that, if I went in the field, I would be eliminated." Indeed, the Croatian soldiers on the ground were shooting at any of their own commanders who ordered them to pull out. It was truly a mess.

In Zagreb, Bobetko was explaining to the UN representatives that the UNPROFOR plan to which his political master had agreed was seriously flawed. The document proposed that the Croats would start to withdraw from Medak Pocket at 1400 on September 15, and be completely gone by 1900. Withdrawal was possible, claimed Bobetko, but only if it was gradual, extending over a number of days or even weeks. The Croats would have to bring fresh forces into the area, because the soldiers who had won the battle would refuse to give up what they had won. The new ones would not have the same emotional investment in Medak. Bobetko argued that the withdrawal operation was trying to move too fast, while Jean Cot argued it was not fast enough.

As Charlie Company engaged in all-out combat with the Croatian Army, Colonel Calvin was told to report for a meeting in Gospic. This was a very new development since the Canadian Forces had been unable to make direct contact with the commanders in Gospic except through the UNMOs. Negotiations were only at the most senior level in Zagreb. Calvin welcomed the chance, but how was he supposed to get there?

Calvin decided they could drive down the road until they had gone far enough to be met, on foot, by the UNMOs from the Croatian side. Then they could walk across the front line with the military observers and get picked up on the other side. All of this would take place as night fell. Calvin had thought he would go alone, but his regimental sergeant major, Mike McCarthy, announced that he was going with the colonel whether Calvin liked it or not.

In Sveti Rok, Major Dan Drew had just set up camp with his soldiers. Having found a bottle of Bordeaux left over from their cohabitation with the French, he was planning to drink it as he dined on ration-pack hamburger. Calvin called and told him dinner would have to wait. Delta Company was going to have to cross over to the Croatian side of the front line if they ever got to phase two of their operation, and Calvin decided Drew should come with him so he would know what it looked like. Mike Spellen also joined them, as did an UNMO who had Motorola radio contact with the Croats.

"So we began about 1900 hours or so, the long walk, as we called it, across no man's land," says Drew. The journey was eventless except for the jangling of their nerves as the UNMOs accompanied them to Gospic. It was the first time Calvin had been at the Croatian headquarters since they had arrived in the area.

Gospic is a dreary town and the meeting took place in a soot-covered government building in the central square. Michel Maisonneuve had made the same journey as Stipetic had, with the same feelings of trepidation. Maisonneuve was the sole representative of the UNPROFOR headquarters and he regretted that he had not brought an entourage. His negotiating team consisted of himself, a Danish UNMO named Neilson, and Jim Calvin.

The Croats marched in, a quarrelsome team of generals who filled the room with their military staff and their contempt for the UN. Stipetic was there, and Rahim Ademi, the general in charge of the Gospic region, a dumpling of a man not yet out of his twenties. Maisonneuve thought he was as arrogant as they come. The mystery for all the UN people was the quiet, bearded man in the corner, Admiral Davor Domazet. Maisonneuve had met him in Zagreb and knew he was extremely senior, but wasn't certain of his role. Domazet was in fact head of intelligence for the Croats and one of the most senior people in the Croatian military. To the Canadians his presence in Gospic that evening was puzzling.

Though the firefight between Eight Platoon and the Croats had started in the afternoon and was going on even as the meeting took place, Maisonneuve says neither the Croats nor Calvin mentioned it. Maisonneuve now regrets not having taken a few moments to talk to Calvin before they started the session, because it would have been useful to know how serious things were. In interviews, Calvin insists that he told Stipetic and the others at the Gospic meeting about the firefight and says he yelled at them to stop targeting his soldiers. No one at the meeting recalls Calvin's petition.

Maisonneuve waived the withdrawal agreement at Stipetic, and demanded the Croats withdraw. Stipetic argued they needed more time, and that the withdrawal could not really commence until the next day and it would take two additional days to complete. For Calvin, it was already taking too long. He told them he wanted his companies to cross over to the Croat side and take their positions by eight o'clock the next morning, which would already be twelve hours later than the agreement stipulated. The Croatian generals argued that they hadn't told all their soldiers yet, and that they needed till noon the following day. After much heated discussion, Calvin agreed to a noon deadline.

Spellen, Drew and McCarthy waited outside the dingy Gospic military headquarters building as Calvin negotiated, alarmed by the sound of explosions coming from the Medak area. When Calvin emerged at 10 P.M., exhausted, they drove back out to the no-man's-land crossing together.

At the meeting, the Croats had agreed to allow the Canadian battalion to establish a crossing site on the main road between Medak and Gospic, which they codenamed Maple Route. One of Dan Drew's APCs came up to meet them, and at midnight they finally opened the road between the Serb and the Croat side. Spellen and Drew spent the night in that position to make sure it wouldn't be shut down before the morning when the companies were ostensibly going to be allowed to cross.

A cold night mist fell on them as they watched the fires blazing in the distance. Spellen remembers he eventually fell asleep from sheer exhaustion. As the sun rose on the sixteenth of September and burned off the haze, he could see smoke pouring up out of what had been villages the night before. And he heard explosions that he thought were probably houses being blown up. Spellen says it was at that point that he realized why the Croats had wanted more time—to finish the ethnic cleansing. That wasn't quite true, as General Stipetic admitted much later, because by the morning of the sixteenth there was no one left alive in Medak Pocket to murder.

* * *

At the break of the day, while Spellen and Dan Drew watched over the road, Rod Dearing and his men faced their final and largest battle with the Croats. Dearing had spent part of the night tracking the Croats' moves and determining their exact positions with the nodler, a highly effective thermal observation device that picks up heat sources and projects them on to a screen. Dearing watched the ghost-like shapes of the Croatian soldiers as they moved around and figured out that he was fighting a platoon-sized force. There were a few small firefights during the night, which helped Dearing map the positions of the Croats a bit better. Come dawn, he swore he was going to finish this battle, and win.

The Patricias' new C7 rifles boasted a powerful scope that allowed the Canadians to look deep into the tree line at first light—a cold morning with a heavy mist. The Croats fired a few mortars at the peacekeepers, "but we had it all cased," Dearing says. The Canadians decided they would not stop shooting until the other side withdrew.

Reports vary as to the duration of the final firefight, but most concur that it lasted for more than an hour. Rob Deans had been given an arc of fire from the dead cow to the hedgerow and Scott Leblanc had an arc that spanned from the dead cow to the copse of trees. "We just worked our way back and forth," says Deans. "Scott Leblanc had his C9 machine gun and was firing on my left and I was starting on my right and we came together and went out, just back and forth like that." Leblanc is normally a restrained man who doesn't drink or smoke, but he was so overcome with zeal as he emptied his C9 into the hedgerow that his mates had to warn him to keep his head down. Neither Deans nor Leblanc has any idea how long this lasted: nor do they know if they killed or injured anyone. They do know they shot directly into the Croat muzzle blasts.

Bryan Bailey checked in with Eight Platoon in the early hours of the morning, just in time to witness the final battle between his soldiers and the Croats. They had been sending messages to him about the firefights all night and he had been sure they were exaggerating. If the reports were true, it would mean the Patricias were in combat with the Croats. Bailey thought the platoon was simply taking indirect fire because they were so tight to the Serb position. He didn't think so any more. Before leaving, the Croats dropped two more mortars on the Canadian position, just for good measure. Then they melted away. As the mist burned off, Dearing knew they had shut the Croats down. "It was dead silent. We couldn't see any more movement or even vehicles," he recalls.

Padre Brown arrived and was struck by the utter quiet. "There wasn't even birdsong," he says. Brown went to the forwardmost trench to see Dearing, the man everyone looked to for strength, and found him curiously pensive. "'I did that.' That's what he told me," says Brown. The padre looked in the direction in which Dearing was staring. He could see what he thought were several dead bodies. Dearing was telling the padre that he had killed the Croats. Brown was at a loss for words.

McKillop was finally able to persuade the Serbs to remove the mine necklace they had draped across the hard-pack road. Before the platoon had time to take stock of their post-combat state, they got the orders to advance. Gord Parker says they all hesitated, not sure how to react. "There were mines, there was the odd mortar round still exploding in the area. Then we could hear detonations in the villages behind us. Serious ones." But Bryan Bailey rolled up in his APC. "He said, 'Get moving forward!' and he just tore off down the road, right through the front line.

The platoon followed, finally emerging in front of the Serb line. Once through, they turned back toward the Serbs to ensure they didn't attempt to use this as an excuse to move up. It was the most difficult and tense twenty-four hours the men had ever experienced. After putting up with days of indirect fire and harassing snipers, the Canadians had done something. Well beyond the scope of peacekeeping—so far beyond that no one was certain how to report it all. But the soldiers of Eight Platoon knew one thing: it felt good.

* * *

Throughout the morning of the sixteenth, Colonel Maisonneuve continued to meet with the Croatian authorities in Gospic. With each encounter the withdrawal was modified a bit. Stipetic kept insisting that the withdrawal plan had to be spread out over more days. He could hardly have forced the Croats to move out any faster, given his status with the local commanders. Instead of an immediate occupation by UNPROFOR of both the Croat and Serb positions, Stipetic wanted the peacekeepers to enter incrementally, with the final time for withdrawal extended until last light on the following day.

Calvin was furious. Maisonneuve remembers him hollering on the radio that the Croats were killing people. Explosions shook the earth and Calvin wanted to get in to stop the fighting. When Maisonneuve confronted the Croats with this news, Stipetic told him they were only exploding old mines to make the area safe. He also warned Maisonneuve that if he pushed too hard, the agreement to withdraw would collapse. Calvin was determined to hold the Croats to their noon deadline, and accused Maisonneuve of being more interested in his agreement than in protecting human life and property. General Cot sent word Calvin was to follow the scheduled times as they were relayed to him but as far as Calvin was concerned, the agreements and their deadlines weren't worth a tinker's damn if they were all going to be rewritten in the next instant.

Calvin and his frustrated soldiers felt isolated. Press releases issued by UNPROFOR headquarters in Zagreb on September 16 indicate that the withdrawal had been postponed. The deputy

UNPROFOR commander, General MacInnis, also told the media that they had "no facts regarding human rights violations in the areas entered by the Croatian army on September 9 and 10." UNPROFOR press releases from Gospic on the same day refer to "a large degree of destruction" but the statements never mention who was responsible.

Major Bailey's Seven Platoon had successfully opened the southern crossing on the Maple Route despite nearly blowing themselves up in an anti-tank minefield. Bailey had instructed his new lieutenant to take a roundabout route into the area but he instead opted for a more direct course through a cornfield. A fortuitous call of nature on the part of one of the soldiers in the APC had saved them from a disaster. The soldier dismounted the carrier to relieve himself, and noticed the rod of a powerful anti-tank mine right at his feet. They sorted themselves out and managed to open the crossing. The north crossing was another matter.

Bryan Bailey rolled up the Maple Route to reach the northern crossing point before noon. He had half of Seven Platoon in APCs behind him and a deep sense of trepidation in his gut. Everything they had done up to now would have been pointless, a useless risk of their lives, if the Croats wouldn't allow them access to the other side. This was only phase two of the operation.

He drove past Jim Calvin and McCarthy, who were also waiting for twelve o'clock, and they all exchanged tense and knowing glances. Overnight, the Croats had established a substantial new defensive position on the road and had fortified their dragon's teeth (barricades that look like giant tacks) with a cluster of anti-tank mines. Bailey decided to aim his turret off to the side in the most non-threatening manner possible as he slowly rumbled toward their position.

Drew had been stationed on the road all night and he now ordered the rest of his Delta Company to roll up toward the checkpoint. The convoy stretched for about two kilometres.

No one was sure what the Croats knew of the ceasefire agreement or if they cared to honour it. This was shaping up to be the most tense standoff the Canadians would face. Shattering explosions came every fifteen minutes or so, powerful detonations that were coming from the not-so-distant villages. The air was clogged with the smoke of burning hay fields and houses. A platoon of Croats stood on the road and more were in fortified bunkers and trenches. At first it seemed they might be able to talk the Croats down. As Jim Calvin arrived at the standoff, a few of the engineers assessed the mine threat and declared that they could clear the devices away in about two minutes. When Calvin approved this plan, the Croats insisted they would do it themselves and obligingly began to push the dragon's teeth away as well. But then, suddenly, everything changed.

None of the peacekeepers had ever met Brigadier General Mesic, who now appeared out of nowhere. The Gospic regional commander, Brigadier General Ademi, was just as suddenly *not* around, and Mesic was clearly the man in charge of this roadblock. The new Croatian general was in a rage. The Croats had a number of powerful weapons, including anti-tank guns and recoilless rifles; Mesic now ordered them to uncover yet more weapons: three Sagger missile systems, on which they immediately began to conduct pre-fire checks. They aimed them all directly at the Canadians.

Jim Calvin, and all of his soldiers, believed the Croats were seriously prepared to fire on them—even at close range. The Canadian APCs were all on the hard road with anti-tank mines lining it on both sides. The Croats were dug into trenches and fortifications in front of them with a tank and missiles and with their weapons loaded and pointed at the Canadians. In a show of machismo, Calvin figured he better demonstrate to the Croats that he had large guns as well, and he ordered his men to lock their guns and TOWs onto Croat targets. If the Croats fire, he said, the Canadians were to fire back. One TOWs operator remembers the orders were "to destroy immediately the threat if the convoy was fired upon."

It was a lethal game of chicken. But there really was no other option. They couldn't go back and they couldn't go forward. The road had to open up one way or another. Calvin also knew that if one person pulled the trigger on either side, all hell would break loose.

"We're locked and loaded and trained on our targets of opportunity," remembers Steve Atkins, "and we basically have to check our arc of fire, make sure you're not going to hit anyone Canadian and that was the extent of it."

Sergeant Joe Wyseman of the anti-armour platoon had already been having a bad day before his unit arrived at this checkpoint. His detachment had rolled into a field the day before only to realize they were well ahead of the area that the engineers had cleared of mines, and probably in considerable danger. They had stayed put until the morning when engineers came to dig them out. His fellow detachment had rolled into another field and found that they were sitting on top of a mound of expended and unexpended ammunition, in addition to a fully usable 20-millimetre cannon. It didn't take long before a Serb unit arrived to tell them to clear out of their ammunition dump and pulled grenades out of their threadbare uniforms to emphasize their point. And now they were staring down the barrels of anti-tank guns, with Sagger missiles backing them up. Wyseman surveyed the scene through his binoculars and noticed that the Serbs also had three tanks pointed toward his section, only 1,500 metres away. As Wyseman noted in his subsequent report: "This was a Catch-22." Phil Tobicoe and his TOW carrier were at the southern crossing point on the Maple Route. He could see that the Croats had their tank gun turrets pointed in his direction, and he was ordered to pick out his own targets. Tobicoe instructed his men to try to take out as many tanks as possible, if the Croats opened fire. "But there were twelve tanks and we had only six missiles," he recalls. "My blood was pumping. There was a really good chance of being hit."

Tobicoe told his men that they would have to leave the carrier if it came to it. "No matter what, I told them, drop the ramp and grab the machine gun, and get out of the carrier." There were two options: fight or flee. Tobicoe decided they would fight.

But there was one other variable on the scene. By this time a horde of media had arrived, wanting to cover either a momentous withdrawal or what they suspected would be another disastrous UNPROFOR bungle; in either case, they wanted to report on the ethnic cleansing they had heard about in Zagreb. The media are always the weapon of last resort in the UN mission commander's arsenal and at this point Calvin was prepared to use them.

About two dozen reporters were crowding the back end of the convoy. Calvin told Dan Drew to bring them up to the site of the standoff—especially the Reuters television crew. Where bare-knuckled machismo was having no effect, Calvin suspected he might be able to shame the Croats with some public exposure. "You have to remember," says Calvin, "that the Croatian moral high ground was their international reputation. No one had ever pinned anything on them. They were the good guys."

Steve Atkins and the other soldiers couldn't believe their eyes when they saw the reporters tumble out of the vehicles. "That was hilarious," says Atkins. "Here we are in the middle of a standoff. We all thought we were going to die or kill somebody. And suddenly here are all these civvies. We went, what the hell?"

Calvin called an impromptu press conference in the middle of the road, with the minefields all around and General Mesic scowling in the background. The Canadian colonel's message was beamed via Reuters around the world: "Today we moved up the road at 1200 hours precisely and we found mines on the road and anti-tank roadblocks still blocking our path. The Croatians made a big show of moving the mines and the anti-tank barriers but now they are refusing to allow us passage . . ." Calvin's face in the video clip is tense and angry, and betrays only a whiff of fear and exhaustion. "At some stage you have to cut the bullshit and get on with the job. And all I've heard right now from the Croatian people at my level here is a bunch of half-baked excuses aimed at delaying us from getting on with the operation." It was Calvin's finest moment, and it temporarily redeemed him in the eyes of critics such as Brown and Brett. As a tactician, he shone.

The media conference did what the meetings in Gospic hadn't. With the cameras still rolling, the Croats quickly cleared away the mines, the dragon's teeth and the weapons, and waved the Canadians through. The incident had lasted for about ninety minutes. After seven and a half days of watching the Croat advance and even fighting Croat soldiers, the Canadians were finally going in to Medak Pocket. But the sense of victory was immediately shattered.

As they rolled past the Croat roadblock and into the villages, their worst suspicions were confirmed and then exceeded by the pungent smell of rotting flesh. Every barn and field was ablaze, every house smashed; dead livestock littered the sides of the road. But the most striking feature was the complete absence of civilians. Only Croat soldiers appeared on the side of the road, waiting to be picked up and transported out, carrying bags of loot they had stolen from the houses before they torched them. On both sides of the road, the Canadians saw the mean, angry sunburned faces of men in tattered uniforms, their weapons slung over their shoulders—their contempt for the peacekeepers in their blue helmets searingly apparent.

CHAPTER SEVEN

SCORCHED EARTH

I did not find any traces of animal or human life in several of the villages through which we passed today. The destruction is total, systematic and purposeful.

—General Jean Cot

THE SECOND BATTALION of the Princess Patricia's Canadian Light Infantry, along with two companies of French soldiers, inched their way into the Pocket. The earth still shook with the concussions of exploding shells, and the air was thick with acrid smoke from burning fields. Croatian soldiers were busy looting everything that could be carried off: furniture, tractors, cars, the roof shingles and windows from the houses and yes, even kitchen sinks. What they didn't take, they destroyed.

Craig King's sweep team pushed in, hard on the heels of Delta Company. His orders were to get into the Pocket as quickly as possible to prevent, or at least, limit the ongoing destruction of evidence that might prove useful to war crimes prosecutors in later years.

General Bobetko in Zagreb was still strenuously denying that the Medak attack was anything other than a purely military operation, and claiming that the only victims were lawful combatants. His soldiers, meanwhile, were busily getting rid of any evidence that might contradict his outrageous claim. The Canadians in the field were determined not to let them get away with it.

Delta Company and the French soldiers had passed through the lines set up by Charlie Company and now took their place on the opposite side. The two Canadian companies with their French troops now faced each other with Croats behind one and Serbs the other. Bryan Bailey wondered, only half jokingly, if the Canadians were in danger of shooting each other. Delta and Charlie Companies began to slowly push back, expanding the distance between the two armies.

The people on King's team came from various units; most of them had never worked together or with him. This was somewhat alarming, since there might be some gruesome moments ahead of them. King wondered if this thrown-together group could handle it.

The sweep team had potentially the most rewarding task of the whole operation—rescuing civilians. The UN High Commissioner for Refugees estimated the number of Serbs who potentially could be located and helped by King's team to be in the thousands, though no one was sure how many had fled, or how many had been there in the first place. A lot of the Serbs in Medak Pocket were from elsewhere: they had taken over houses and farms after they had been driven out of Croat-held areas. In many cases they were Serbs who had been installed in the region to secure the territory as part of the self-proclaimed Republic of Serbian Krajina. And there were, of course, the Serb families who had been in the region for generations. While it was almost certain the Serb soldiers had fled, many civilians might still be hiding in basements and barns. The sweep team's first job was to locate those people, give them medical attention, food and blankets, and then turn them over to the UNHCR.

Finding the living was one thing. It was the second task that King most worried about: locating the bodies of the dead and transporting them to a makeshift morgue. King was concerned that most of his personnel had no training in the proper handling of human remains. There were health issues to consider; the bodies could have been lying under the warm September sun for several days. And there were ethical issues as well; there is little official guidance on decorum for soldiers tasked with handling the remains of victims of torture and murder, on how to bring dignity, after death, to people subjected to violent indignities while they were alive.

While the UN was working out the withdrawal agreement with the Croats, King and his Alpha Company sergeant major, Ron Cameron, used the time to attempt some skill and sensitivity training. King was happy to have Cameron—someone he knew and trusted—helping with the task. At that point they were still expecting that most of the people they discovered would be alive, and so many of the training scenarios dealt with the proper way to approach and deal with civilians who were wounded or traumatized.

King had also devised macabre exercises. Some of the soldiers played dead while others practised bagging their bodies. "At first we used the normal body bags," recalls King. "But I think we either ran out or someone turned off the tap somewhere and we didn't get any more. So we had rolls of hessian, which is a hemp cloth. The soldiers would practise rolling the bodies . . . somebody would play dead and we would use him as a sort of living mannequin, if you will, to practise."

The third task was another unusual one for soldiers, but it would become routine over the coming years: they were directed to help gather and record evidence that might be useful in a future war crimes prosecution. The United Nations had recently passed a resolution to set up a war crimes tribunal for the Balkans, and although it was still months before the first of the court's many employees would meet in The Hague, there was already a commission of experts gathering evidence. Calvin wanted his sweep team to document what they found in Medak Pocket. No UNPROFOR unit had done this before, and so Calvin's work was establishing a prototype for investigations in the months and years to come.

King was given UN civilian police detachments to conduct these evidence-gathering operations. Among them was Constable Steve Marissink, an RCMP officer from Alberta, who had been raised in Guelph, Ontario. As an officer in the plainclothes unit back in Edmonton, he had seen his fair share of gruesome deaths and he had developed a sardonic sense of humour. He had been in the Balkans since June, doing routine patrols, and at last began to feel useful.

King also had Dr. Kelly Brett, two medical teams and the Roman Catholic padre Mike Brown. With his team in place—a cop, a chaplain, a doctor and a lot of young, inexperienced soldiers—King set off to confront the aftermath of ethnic cleansing.

Journalists travelled with the peacekeepers, and along with all his other duties, King was responsible for media relations. A Reuters television crew, the UN's press team and the Canadian Forces' own cameraman recorded the events of the coming days and the images are truly disturbing. In the video record, members of the sweep team walk the silent hills and valleys, calling to people, imploring them to come out of their hiding places. But there is no response. They pass burning houses and farm buildings, trashed cars and the bloated corpses of dead livestock.

As night fell, one of the French companies called King's team to report that they had found what appeared to be dead civilians. What once was a chicken coop was still smouldering. The only living creature, a chicken, pecked hopefully at the floor. The wooden door had been bolted from the outside. At least one of the two people they found inside had obviously tried to escape. The other was tied to a chair. Their bodies were so badly burned it was difficult to identify age and sex. But from the long hair that had survived the flames, and the remnants of their clothing, the team concluded that they were women.

Steve Marissink had the investigation of the chicken coop videotaped by the Canadian Forces cameraman, just as he had his crime investigations in Canada recorded for evidence. On the video, Marissink's six-foot frame fills the little room where the women spent their final hours. The Mountie collected forensic evidence, while Dr. Kelly Brett attempted a crude post-mortem.

No amount of playing dead and practising the recovery of bodies could have prepared the soldiers for the reality of loading corpses into body bags. The women's remains came apart as they were lifted—limbs and flesh baked in the oven-like conditions of the brick chicken coop fell away from torsos. The bodies were still so hot that the bags began to melt.

Warrant Officer Geoff Crossman poured bottled water on the smouldering body parts to cool them down enough to handle. Someone fetched a whiskbroom and a dustpan from a jeep to sweep up the last of the remains. A shaken soldier picked up what appeared to have been a woman's purse and placed it gently on top of a body bag. Crossman was swept by a revulsion that clings to his subconscious to this day. "The smell just killed me," Crossman remembers years later. "I still can't eat pork roast because of that smell."

The investigation of the chicken coop was performed in the headlights of vehicles and with a few flashlights. The bodies had become host to colonies of maggots, an indication that they had been dead for some time—as long as seventy-two hours— before they were set afire. The perpetrators had probably torched them just before they departed, presumably to conceal the evidence of what they, or their soldiers, had done.

It slowly dawned on the horrified Canadians that this was why the Croats had wanted time. This was what had been going on while they sat politely at the edge of town, waiting for negotiators to work out a ceasefire. The Croats were hiding the evidence.

The chicken coop was a scene from hell that, all by itself, would have been enough to affect the young soldiers for life. But they would encounter variations of the same scene, over and over again, in the coming days. "We ran into a group of Croatian soldiers," says King, "and I remember we were full of contempt for these people." As the peacekeeping convention of neutrality dissolved in the caustic acid of revulsion, the

Canadian soldiers actually became more effective even as they became less impartial. They worked tirelessly, hoping to find at least one survivor.

* * *

Craig King was also worried about land mines and booby traps. Luckily he had a detachment of experienced engineers who could search structurally damaged buildings and determine their safety before the soldiers entered. His people were also vulnerable to attack because they had no armoured vehicles; they had all been sent back to Canada. Most of his sweep team were travelling in soft-skinned vehicles—Ilitis jeeps for the soldiers and Toyota Land Cruiser for the UN civilian police.

The first night, they slept on the side of the road in their vehicles, under blazing lights to make sure everyone knew they were there. The engineers had the only armoured vehicle in the sweep team, but it broke down—as Canadian vehicles are wont to do—when the convoy entered the Pocket. Croatian soldiers, lingering there, opened fire on the engineers. King felt helpless: he had no way to rescue them. Eventually, the battalion's reconnaissance platoon came in with guns cocked and the Croats terminated what had obviously been an amusing bit of target practice.

At dawn, the team began the search again. Their first stop was to examine the body of an old woman who had been discovered the night before. She had been dragged, whether alive or dead wasn't clear, out into a field on a rope. Her left breast was slashed and fingers had been cut from her hand. Both legs were broken, presumably to prevent her flight. She had, finally, been shot in the head four times after what was clearly a torture session. In the days she had lain in the field, animals had started to eat her body.

They had to wrap the old woman in the hessian cloth, body fluids oozing through the hemp. She and the other recovered corpses were loaded into the back of a truck driven by a reservist named Corporal Grimmer. The soldiers, predictably, named his truck the Grim Reaper, as they routinely sluiced putrid fluids from its load-bed with bleach-laced water.

The most devastating circumstances seem to generate black humour, a natural coping mechanism for people struggling to suspend normal emotional responses to human suffering. Bryan Bailey named the sweep team Task Force Hamlet, in a reference, he says, to the famous graveyard scene in Shakespeare's play. Geoff Crossman called the unit the Ghost Busters and remembers they painted the lone surviving chicken from their first scene of atrocity a shade of UN blue, "so that no one would kill it." A horse, seemingly in perfect health, was the one creature left alive in an entire village. The soldiers named him Lucky. Dan Drew rode around on Lucky, playing cowboy, and trying to amuse the troops. Mike Brown remembers Drew's antics as the only moment of levity.

On the morning after the chicken coop investigation, Brown decided to put on the most optimistic face possible and busied himself with setting up a little reception centre for the survivors he had persuaded himself they would find. He made a pile of sandwiches and brewed some coffee, in order to provide a little comfort. As the day wore on, he gave the sandwiches away to the soldiers and then dumped the coffee. He rejoined the patrols who now realized they were searching for human remains, not survivors.

Brown was concerned about the effect corpse-hunting was having on the young soldiers. Whenever he heard that another body was discovered, he immediately went to the location. After a particularly gruesome encounter with some human remains, Brown asked why they didn't have proper body bags and was told that the regimental quartermaster had decided that the heavy rubber zippered sacks were too valuable. With the rank smell of decomposition all over him, Brown went to the quartermaster stores to demand body bags. He admits that perhaps he may have threatened the quartermaster with violence, but he successfully raided the shelves and walked off with a precious stash of proper bags.

After the initial shock, some of the more observant of the soldiers and the engineers began to notice the detailed planning that had gone into the ethnic cleansing. Since houses and buildings in the Balkans are generally made of stucco-covered bricks, they are hard to burn down. The destruction had been well-planned and executed.

From the observation posts, the Canadian soldiers had seen large numbers of Croatian military and police trucks, filled with lumber, moving in and out of the area over the past few days and the peacekeepers now realized that this was the combustible material the Croats needed to stoke the fires in the houses. Another means of destruction appeared to have been anti-tank mines, which had apparently been placed on the load-bearing walls of houses and buildings and then detonated.

An investigation of the destroyed buildings revealed that, in some cases, a timed fuse was used to blow out all the walls at the same time, causing the building to completely collapse on itself. Calvin was told that an estimated two hundred mines had been deployed in this fashion—undoubtedly, the source of the large explosions they could hear in the final days and even hours.

Why was it necessary to so completely demolish the houses? Was it to make sure that no one lived here again? But the Croats, themselves, would not be able to use the buildings. Was it to conceal evidence? What, or who, was buried under that rubble? The departing Croats poisoned wells and cisterns and took anything of value. No one would ever want to live here again.

Despite the efforts of the engineers, several of the soldiers had some very close calls with mines and booby traps as they attempted to investigate the bombed-out and burned-out structures. Almost every situation or incident report filed from the scene refers to a brush with an explosive device of some kind. But the mines were a bigger threat to the occasional civilian who tried to sneak home in the coming days to inspect the damage or to reclaim whatever had not been stolen. The area was off limits, but local people knew all the tiny goat trails and footpaths. Perhaps they had particular knowledge of the hidden perils, as it was often the job of civilians or members of the home guard to lay the anti-personnel devices.

Among the most intriguing and perhaps significant discoveries of the sweep were foreign food packages and bottles among the litter left behind. A number of Serb refugees recalled hearing other languages spoken among the Croat forces. One that was unmistakable was German. It's possible that the foreign soldiers were mercenaries. Reports would emerge later that Dutch mercenaries fought among the Croats in the Pocket. A Delta Company patrol found remnants of American rations in the hills, which offered some support to the persistent rumours that the United States was operating covertly in Medak Pocket and that the CIA was providing logistical support to Croat soldiers.

As the days progressed, UNPROFOR continued to encounter hostile Croat forces in the region. Calvin allowed for the possibility that some of them were unaware of the withdrawal order, but others just seemed unwilling to stop fighting. On one occasion, two Patricias on patrol in an Ilitis jeep came face to face with a heavily armed Croatian fighting patrol. The two Canadians, in a moment of moxie or madness, cocked their weapons and shouted, "Halt! Throw down your weapons." To their surprise, the Croats actually stopped in their tracks and stared at them just long enough for the Canadians to radio for help. A platoon of French soldiers arrived quickly in their APCs. They surrounded the Croats, disarmed them, trussed them up and shipped them out of the UN Protected Area. The weapons they seized were high quality and German-made. The operations officer, Major Shane Brennan, examined the seized weaponry back at headquarters and was amazed that it was practically brand new. Defence Minister Susak had been busy.

The Canadians eventually gave the Croats their weapons back, though Brennan says he kept a couple of the grenades. Such was the level of fear that Brennan admits he carried a grenade in his pocket when he went to meetings with the Croatian officers, "just as a precaution. If things were going to go wrong I'd have something to influence destiny."

The two French companies under Calvin's control seemed determined to prove that France did contribute something more to the UNPROFOR mission than good wine. Jean Cot's son patrolled aggressively and his soldiers had their own death-defying encounters. A French section came face to face with two T-55 tanks on a sideroad. The Croats warned the French that they would force their way past if necessary but the peacekeepers wouldn't budge. Michel Maisonneuve and a group from UN headquarters went to investigate the standoff and found that Croat General Rahem Ademi, himself, was part of it. With his gun slung loosely over his shoulder he waved a map—with UN orders scrawled on it—at the peacekeepers, claiming that they were in violation of the agreement and that the Croats were allowed to cross into the area the French were guarding. Maisonneuve looked more closely at the Croatian map and noticed that it appeared to have been crudely doctored. Someone from the Patricias produced a copy of the same document with entirely different markings; the fastidious Canadians had actually plasticized their copy. Maisonneuve brandished the Canadian map in a duel of documents. Ademi gestured wildly, yelled at his men and then ordered his tanks to pull out, Maisonneuve and his team whooping and hollering for joy. It was rare to catch the Croats so flat-footed.

Calvin had vastly underestimated the extent of the task of looking for bodies and recording evidence from more than a dozen villages and hamlets. He originally assumed that this would be principally a humanitarian rescue mission but what he had before him was a massive crime scene. King's fifty-person team was quickly overwhelmed by the clean-up and investigation required, so Calvin deployed the other units to help.

But it was King's people who would get the call to investigate, and their police who conducted the forensic work. They found Serbian soldiers who had clearly been executed, as well as older men and women, tortured, killed and then mutilated. None of the victims seemed to have been killed in any action that could be described as combat. The severed fingers, the

non-lethal knife wounds, the torn clothing, the burned flesh bog-
gled the minds of the young Canadians. What would motivate
people to behave with such sadism?

King remembers one body—a man, probably in his sixties—
lying face down and quivering as if he was still alive, because of
the maggots that had infested his corpse. When they turned him
over, the man had no face. A reporter with the team walked a
few paces away from the group and vomited. King watched in
amazement as the RCMP constable, Steve Marissink, meticu-
lously counted the bullet holes. There were twenty-four. How
many bullets in the back and in the head—shot at close range—
does it take to kill a sixty-year-old man?

* * *

Steve Marissink knew what he was doing. As a homicide investi-
gator, he had a lot of interesting work at home, but he had come
to Croatia with an old-fashioned desire to do something good for
humanity. He could sum up his pre-deployment training in
forensics with a few handy phrases. If you didn't drop it, don't
pick it up. If it's not paved, don't walk on it. He was also told he
didn't need combat orientation because he wasn't going into a
war zone. But on his first day on the job in Croatia, he watched
the Serbian forces mobilize thousands of men and send them
out to the front line. Marissink knew that a war zone was exactly
what he'd landed in.

He had spent his first month in Sector East, cohabiting with
the Russian contingent. He was just getting used to the primitive
conditions—bad food, cold-water showers and Serb snipers who
thought it was amusing to shoot at the civilian police when they
went jogging—when he was moved to Knin to be the investigations officer for all of Sector South. That's when the job got
interesting.

Marissink had been with the sweep team when it entered the
Pocket late in the afternoon on the sixteenth. His sharp eye had
picked out something that appears in no other reports: in the

distance, he saw a section of young, fit, well-rested Croatian soldiers, wearing impossibly clean uniforms. They had assault rifles of a kind that police use when they are facing lethal force, not the AK47s carried by the weary departing regular army soldiers and domobrans. They drove dark blue vehicles. Marissink suspected this was the dreaded "special police" unit led by Marcac. The Croat squad seemed unintimidated by the UN presence and indifferent to its activities. The Mountie wondered what role they had been playing in all of this destruction; perhaps they had just come in now at the end, for a specific task. He had recently heard single gunshots in the distance. Now, putting two and two together, he suspected they were the sounds of executions.

Marissink secretly photographed the men in dark uniforms. He figured the picture might be of interest in a future investigation, but he didn't get much time to think about it because his specialty, homicide investigation, was urgently required.

The Canadian soldiers were aghast at the corpses, but Marissink showed them what to look for and taught them how to get past their initial horror. "I don't mean to be flippant," says Marissink. "But I guess by this time in my career I had become or I was more or less immune to death. I view death as work. Dead is dead. Nothing we can do about it."

He was able to pass on some forensic tips to the soldiers but they acquired none of his "immunity" to death, which Marissink couldn't understand. "I was surprised that even though we train our soldiers to take lives, they had very little, if any, experience with death."

Marissink and Kelly Brett became a grim little team. The two men quickly worked out a routine. The doctor would perform a rudimentary examination of the bodies and Marissink would document anything of potential value to a prosecution. By the second or third day they had developed so much shorthand in their communication that they could perform an on-site investigation of a corpse in about twenty minutes.

The circumstances were far from perfect. But it was a big improvement over the investigations at most massacre scenes in the Balkans in these early days. The war crimes scenes elsewhere were mass graves, or in many cases the bodies had been moved many times in order to conceal them. In Medak Pocket, the evidence was still fresh and uncorrupted. The two men estimated that some of the victims were recently executed; they mentioned one in particular, a man who had a single bullet hole through his eye. They found a number of people executed in this way.

Marissink was concerned for Brett. "He was overwhelmed," recalls Marissink. "He would tell me, 'Steve, I'm a physician, not a fucking pathologist!'" Marissink had seen autopsies many times and told Brett what to do. Brett was the only doctor in the area, and he also had responsiblity for the Canadian soldiers themselves. He needed help, but there was no one to provide it.

On one occasion, Croatian soldiers sent a message to Delta Company that they should search a bit higher up in the hills. Marissink set out to investigate, with Dan Drew as his guide. As they trekked up the steep incline, they heard an intense but brief firefight close by: further evidence that the Medak Pocket operation was continuing past the agreement to cease hostilities.

They found two Serbian soldiers partially covered by leaves, both shot in the head. Marissink couldn't figure out why the boots of one of the bodies had been removed and left by the body, until he realized that the laces had been taken. He could at least understand the usefulness of laces, but what he couldn't fathom was what use anyone could have for what was removed from the other body, the man's ear. Judging by the lack of blood, Marissink estimated that the trophy had been severed after the body was cold. Delta Company found two more bodies high in the hills, but in both of these cases it appeared that the men had been killed in combat.

Brett worked out of a makeshift morgue in the town of Medak, where he continued his post-mortems as best he could. They had no X-ray machines to determine with precision what bones had been broken or how many bullets were embedded in the corpses. They had no way to properly clean the bodies to see what other smaller horrors might have been inflicted on the victims. But Brett persisted, though he gagged as maggots crawled out of the bullet holes he tried to count.

Even in hell, the small banalities of bureaucracy seem to survive. Or perhaps hell is the home of petty functionaries. Midway through the clean-up, Geoff Crossman was called in by the regimental quartermaster, who even after his confrontation with Mike Brown was concerned about the number of expensive body bags going out the door. "The RQ told me that the cost was $530-odd for each body bag, and that was unacceptable . . ." recalls Crossman. The RQ instructed Crossman to retrieve the expensive body bags already used.

Corporal Grimmer was Crossman's driver. The two men headed out on a dark night in search of Dr. Brett. They found him, not surprisingly, at the morgue. "And we went to the doc who was working in candlelight and wearing those little white gloves and he was in maggots up to here and we said, I said, 'I need those body bags.' And he looked at me with one of those weird looks."

Grimmer started to gather up the slime-streaked rubber containers. Crossman studied the doctor's frozen expression of astonishment with a growing uneasiness. At last he could only shrug. "I said, 'Don't shoot the messenger.'"

It was a scene of such absurdity that the writers of the darkly comic *M*A*S*H* could hardly have invented it. Crossman and Grimmer drove, in silence, back to the regimental quartermaster's storeroom, struggling not to think about what might be crawling around inside the used body bags. They unceremoniously dumped their pestilent cargo in front of the quartermaster's door.

* * *

For Brett and Marissink and the other soldiers, the most disturbing murder scene they found was that of an old woman who, it was determined, had been blind. The killers tried to hide her body in a marsh.

Mike Spellen was among the members of Delta Company who had been reassigned to the sweep team. Spellen had thought there was something unusual about a wheelbarrow in the middle of a swamp. And sure enough, in about thirty centimetres of water and muck he discovered the corpse. Marissink noted in his report that the woman was fully dressed and had a long, rabbit's-fur coat beneath her body. She had been shot at least six times, four times in the back. Inexplicably, someone had erected a small cross with wooden branches, a gesture of piety and respect that no one could reconcile with the brutality. She had a handbag full of papers. The murder was not the most gruesome but the victim was probably the most vulnerable of all the soldiers saw.

Something about violence and death fascinates the living. Studies confirm that soldiers, in particular, can become almost indecently enthralled with victims of brutality. There are many theories to explain it, but when Steve Marissink and Craig King discovered the phenomenon in their midst, they were appalled. They found that many of the soldiers were photographing corpses. While Marissink had few qualms about examining dead bodies, he found this souvenir-taking to be tasteless and disrespectful. There were official photographs of the crime scenes—1,200 of them were eventually handed over to war crimes investigators—but the personal photos served no forensic purpose. Some individuals offered plausible reasons for the practice. Mike Spellen, for example, said that he wanted pictures "so that no son of a bitch could come along and say it never happened." And maybe the soldiers suspected, correctly as it turned out, that when they got home no one was going to believe what they had experienced at Medak Pocket. The soldiers were overwhelmed with the unreality of the environment and the photos were an attempt to make it real. But King was not convinced; he asked Calvin to outlaw snapshots at the crime scenes.

There were three other officers of the UN civilian police with Marissink, two Norwegians and a Swede. They had the right to leave if they wanted to, and all three of them exercised that option on the second day. Marissink thinks they'd been frightened by suggestions that the Croats might attack. The UN sent in replacements to work with Marissink on the following day, but they too were gone by nightfall. Marissink stayed at it. "I felt up to that time . . . I had been underemployed. We were waving flags and driving around and not doing an awful lot of what we had been trained to do." Now he was.

By day three, they had found and examined a total of sixteen bodies. Craig King's sweep team set up a base from which troops could be dispatched when they got the call about another corpse. There were fewer and fewer volunteers and many tried to avoid having to go out at all. Mike Brown was going out on every call to be with the soldiers when they encountered the horror, and now he looked exhausted. Each discovery was traumatic, but what was becoming more disturbing was that there were so few of them. Had so many people been able to flee?

The soldiers had noticed scores of rubber gloves strewn over the ground in a few places and suspected that bodies had been dragged away and hidden. And there was the alarming possibility that somewhere nearby, perhaps right underfoot, was a hastily created mass grave.

Near a spot where soldiers found a number of surgical gloves, at the edge of one village, there were signs of recent excavation. When one soldier kicked what he thought was an old boot out of the way—and found that it still had a foot inside it—they called in the sweep team, which brought a backhoe that was part of the French contingent's equipment. As they dug, the team found more surgical gloves soiled with blood, but only one corpse—the one belonging to the foot. The soldiers had braced themselves for the possiblity of an even greater carnage. But they were not prepared for the news that would reach them next. News that struck with more immediate force than the scenes of brutality around them: the death of one of their own.

* * *

On September 18, Jim Decoste, a captain with the Second Battalion, was in a truck driving between Medak and Gracac. Rounding a narrow and dangerous bend in the road, the truck collided head-on with an oncoming vehicle. Captain Rick Turner, who had also been at the scene of John Béchard's death, suffered a broken jaw and arm but was in stable condition. The driver was Corporal Stacey Bouck, a twenty-three-year-old reservist from the Royal Regina Rifles. The steering wheel had been pushed deeply into her chest. She received emergency treatment at the scene from Serbian medics, then was taken to hospital in serious condition. But she survived. Jim Decoste did not.

Lieutenant David Gosse remembers when they heard the news of Decoste's death. "Everybody was tense, dealing with highly stressful situations, under fire, living in the mud, eating hard rations, not knowing what was going to happen next, in the middle of Serb and Croat forces." Decoste's death was a wake-up call for soldiers who had been sleepwalking through this nightmare. "Everybody stops and it's like, 'No, I don't want to be here. That is it,'" recalls Gosse.

The sweep team members, for whom the morgue was routine, were shaken to see the body of a man in a Canadian uniform laid out on one of the makeshift tables. The possibility of casualties hangs over any peacekeeping assignment, and soldiers function by not thinking about it. The smell of death was literally all around them, but the impact of Decoste's death was profound. "If you had to reach into the unit and pick one person that everyone knew and respected," says Calvin, "it was Captain Jim Decoste. And then he died."

Craig King admits that he wept that night. Decoste had been his warrant officer when he worked in intelligence for the Second Battalion in Germany. Decoste had got him through his first few rough years in the Patricias and King had counted him as a close friend. He was a man with a magnetic personality, who would "whip his signallers and infantry guys into shape and win all the competitions . . . a guy with everything ahead of him, and now he was killed."

After six months of stress and a final baptism of fire, the Second Battalion had achieved the singularity of purpose it had lacked at the beginning. Decoste's death was a massive blow to morale. Steve Marissink remembers watching the chill pass through the battalion, affecting everyone, including himself. "It caused an enormous amount of psychological trauma to everybody . . . There was a lot of belief that it is one thing for the locals to kill each other, but it certainly wasn't worth a Canadian life." True or not, the soldiers' feeling that a Canadian life was somehow of greater value than the lives of the Croatian dead was perhaps the only way that they could survive their ordeal.

Mike Brown and Kelly Brett warned Calvin that the soldiers were near the breaking point, and that he should get out among the troops to try to raise morale. Even Calvin's kindest supporters cannot claim that comradeship and morale-boosting were his strongest qualities. Calvin says he did respond to the warnings: he dispatched officers with the message that the soldiers should regard themselves as heroes. But few can remember getting much encouragement from the commander.

Just before Decoste's death, the Canadians learned that they would not be going home on schedule. The next rotation of Operation Harmony was delayed and the Second Battalion would have to stay in theatre for an additional two weeks. The commander of the first battalion of the Royale 22e Regiment had come to the same conclusion that Calvin had reached nine months earlier: the operation in Croatia was not Cyprus, the preparation phase needed rethinking and he would delay the deployment of the Van Doos. The news was devastating. Depression and a sense of vulnerability had grown exponentially with the death of Jim Decoste.

On September 19, a bleak, overcast day, the Canadian chief of defence staff, Admiral John Rogers Anderson, paid a visit to the soldiers in Medak. He was perhaps happy to have a break from the home front, where he was struggling with the fallout from the Somalia incident (the details of which Anderson and the senior brass were desperately trying to keep secret). But

Anderson's visit meant little to the soldiers, who were feeling more and more estranged from their larger military family as they became more deeply involved in a horror story they suspected most Canadians knew, and cared, nothing about.

The men of the sweep team remember Anderson's visit on that grey day. They remember that Anderson and his entourage of VIPs drove past them without slowing down to inquire about their work, let alone offer moral support. Geoff Crossman remembers how angry they were: "Here we were doing stuff that is totally out of our realm and [the brass] didn't even stop to say thanks. We didn't even get a pat on the back and that's what the troops wanted. In the leadership role they kind of blew it there."

Craig King had tried to rally them just that morning, telling them how important their work was and promising that they would one day help hold the Croats to account for what they had done. The head of the Canadian military didn't seem to notice. Crossman says the soldiers were almost ready to mutiny. The issue was principally hygiene. "We were living in a tent," he says. "We were full of body juice, dead body juice everywhere. Smell! No one would come near our little group." They had minimal protective gear—bright yellow rubber kitchen gloves and surgical masks. Many of the soldiers used their own rain gear to keep the mess off their uniforms, knowing there was no way to clean them. Crossman says he approached King to ask about showers, but was told that Calvin's orders were that they were not to leave the area. Movement was dangerous and the colonel was trying to keep it to a minimum.

Finally, at eight o'clock on the night of the nineteenth, the sweep team was relieved of its duties. The mortar platoon that had been the core of the Grim Reaper detachment was sent back to Sveti Rok for showers and a hot meal. King remembers the sheer release. "There were these bottles of French wine around and Bob Glint and I . . . I think we had a bottle apiece." Crossman says of coming back to Sveti Rok that they arrived at a place without lights and had to fire up the generators in the dark.

They had been told that they would be able to trade in their combat gear at the end of the job, since they would never be able to get the smell out of their clothes, but the quartermaster balked. Crossman says they eventually got fresh fatigues "only because I threatened violence if they didn't give me some new combats."

What was breaking morale perhaps more than anything was the complete absence of survivors. The UNHCR had told them to expect perhaps thousands of people in the area, all in need of aid and rescue. The Canadian sweep team found sixteen bodies and other investigating teams found more. The Croats eventually turned over the corpses of dozens of Serb soldiers but it didn't come anywhere near the numbers that even the Canadians had seen in the area before the attack on the ninth of September. The peacekeepers were deeply affected by a sense of personal and collective failure, an overwhelming feeling of impotence. They had failed to stop the attack. They had stood by, listening to the gunfire and explosions, suspecting that ethnic cleansing was going on. Rudy Bajema had told the world what was happening, but the Canadians had done only what they were told to do: stand by, and wait for orders. And now they were seeing the consequences. If only they had come in quickly, guns blazing, saving people, doing what real soldiers are supposed to do.

For the first hours and days, Mike Spellen says they believed that clusters of civilians would gradually emerge, wide-eyed and trembling, from basements and the forest and fall into the arms of those who had come to liberate them. But not a single person did. "Almost all the soldiers were mad, frustrated, angry," says Spellen. Delta Company troops were supposed to seek survivors one grid at a time, and kept expanding the number of grids, hoping against hope that they would be rewarded. Lucky, the horse, became a depressing mascot. The less fortunate animals lay bloated in the fields. The soldiers were ordered to burn them to remove the possibility of disease. The smell of scorched flesh spread like a sickening smog.

For Craig King, the morale breakdown was more intellectual but no less devastating. King was able to rationalize a lot of what he encountered, but slowly he became profoundly disillusioned. "Being a humanities student in university and believing that the divine spark was in every one of us, I think you come to the realization that sometimes it's quite absent." King couldn't comprehend the level of cruelty—man's inhumanity to man—that he encountered in Croatia. But it was mostly the feeling of failure he couldn't shake: "We had an expectation . . . that we were going to help these people. We were going to bring out survivors. We were going to feed them, clothe them. We were going to reunite families. . . . But there was no one. What happened to them?"

Dan Drew was one of the few to see anything positive in the operation: it was a first for UNPROFOR in the region to have taken any kind of forceful action at all. "We reacted much quicker than . . . than . . . well, we were the only ones to react." Dangerous Dan Drew, as some soldiers called him, could be a bit of a wild card, prone to awkward attempts to buoy the spirits of his soldiers. Alcohol abuse had been a growing problem in the battalion, particularly in Drew's Delta Company, since the dreadful days of the bunker construction. Calvin's policy was that the soldiers and their commanders should judge for themselves when and what to drink. In the final weeks of the rotation, by many accounts, they were drinking a lot.

Alcohol consumption was highest at the company "smokers" as their parties were called. Sometimes fights broke out—one of such intensity that a man was almost killed. The Canadians drank cases of French wine and gallons of German and Croatian beer from Zagreb. Some platoons enforced their own "dry" policies in order to avoid the excesses, but they were the exception.

The disciplinary breakdown hit its nadir on a drunken night in Camp Kananaskis when Dan Drew emptied his pistol into the air as a salute to the reservists in his company, who, he declared, were the unsung heroes of the battalion.

"We had just spent nine months together," Drew remembers. "They were like my own kids." The shooting, and his subsequent expletive-drenched tribute to the soldiers, was an alcohol-induced but heartfelt attempt at compensation for the lack of cheerleading from their higher-ups. The soldiers wildly cheered Dangerous Dan. But shooting off his pistol rattled already high-strung nerves in the camp and sent many skittish soldiers scrambling for safety. The fallout of that gesture would haunt Drew for the next ten years of his career. Using a gun for entertainment purposes was not only forbidden, it was illegal, and Drew realized the gravity of what he did. "It didn't seem like a big deal at the time," he says. "But judgment gets skewed." Surrounded by weapons, war and corpses, Drew says, he found it hard to imagine propriety, let alone enforce it. "What monsters had we seen?" he says, describing the carnage in Medak. In the morning, he went to see Colonel Calvin, in effect to turn himself in.

Calvin's "field justice" was heavy: Drew was stripped of his command and made administration company commander. It was perhaps the only way Calvin could send the message that breaches of discipline would not be tolerated.

Calvin, himself, admits to a growing sense of isolation on the mission. He had been compelled to make snap decisions, which had threatened the lives of his soldiers, with no precedent to guide him or senior leader to consult. Ottawa had almost no contact with Operation Harmony. General Cot had pushed hard and General MacInnis in Zagreb trusted Calvin to act as he thought necessary. But often the orders were vague and the resources to accomplish the task non-existent. Mike Brown praises Calvin for the logistics of the Medak operation, which Brown says was brilliantly executed. But he believes Calvin is personally responsible for the breakdown in morale. He says Calvin just did not know how to lead people.

Calvin certainly had a lot to prove when he went to Croatia. He had been handed a battalion made up of nearly seventy different units and he had made it into a cohesive whole. Had he pushed them too far? Calvin says any commander would have done the same thing and that he had no choice. Because of his orders or because of his personality? Calvin says he can't distinguish which of the two compulsions was the determining factor. Even Dan Drew won't say he went too far. They had gone into every situation with their chins out and the soldiers had faced down more than most peacekeepers. "If it hadn't been for Calvin in the lead," says Drew, "we never would have gone into Medak."

Discipline did break down, but Craig King was amazed that it wasn't worse: "By the time we arrived in the Pocket the acts had already occurred so it was a matter of discipline then not to take your personal revenge as a soldier. It was testament to our soldiers that the situation didn't deteriorate further."

Concerns about discipline were overshadowed only by a more pressing concern: early signs of some serious mental health problems. The most obvious casualty was Bombardier Bill Ray. Rob Deans of Charlie Company's Eight Platoon had thought Ray was "not all there" the afternoon of the firefight with Croatian forces, having seen him with fixed bayonet and a faraway look in his eyes. Afterward, he was paranoid, moody and couldn't sleep. Dearing sent him back to Camp Kananaskis in Sveti Rok, where he was put on static guard duty. But the assignmentt also gave him access to the seemingly limitless supply of French wine.

An officer with the reconnaissance platoon, passing through the gates one night, observed with some surprise that there seemed to be nobody on guard duty. Suddenly the corporal appeared and lunged at the officer with his rifle and fixed bayonet, demanding documentation and ID, something not normally required of a Canadian soldier in uniform. The officer ordered Ray to disarm and found that his C7 had a round of ammunition in the chamber and it was on repeat. A medical officer later diagnosed the corporal with combat stress.

After that, Calvin finally heeded the warnings of Padre Brown and Dr. Brett. The men and women needed help. Calvin had provided some peer counselling instruction for the section commanders when they were still in Winnipeg and they had trained fifty soldiers in stress debriefing, but it was clearly not enough and he called Ottawa for reinforcements. Ottawa dispatched a critical incident stress debriefing (CISD) team, one member of which, after a brief tour of Medak's horrors, threw up. "[This] didn't instill a lot of credibility in her," says Bryan Bailey. A male officer was no more credible when he suggested that he knew exactly what the soldiers were going through. Matt Stopford was appalled by the "experts." By then he knew that a lot of people were going home damaged or depressed, himself included, and that these debriefers were incapable of doing anything to help. The female stress debriefer set up her clinic in the camp kitchen, and waited for the soldiers to come and "share." "The guys just wanted to kill her," says Stopford. "They wanted to chew her up, spit her out and leave." Mike Spellen eventually evicted the team from the kitchen, declaring the area restricted to soldiers looking for their lunch. Kelly Brett had thought sending in a team was a good idea, but realized it was causing the soldiers to bottle up even more. What was of even greater concern to the doctor and Padre Brown was the disquieting realization that these soldiers were about to take a lot of rage, disappointment and loathing home with them; no good could come of that.

**

John Arch MacInnis was one of the many senior members of the UN mission to come for a personal look at the scene in Medak. MacInnis subsequently wrote a harshly worded report of what he learned of the Croat operation, calling it the result of a "scorched earth policy" and concluding that "the destruction which I have witnessed . . . could only have been achieved through the execution of a systematic and well-orchestrated plan." It was all the UN soldiers could do, MacInnes wrote, to keep from retaliating against the Croats. "It would have been extremely unhealthy for any Croatian soldier or commander to be seen not to be complying with UNPROFOR demands," he wrote.

In UN terms MacInnis's report was uncharacteristically damning. His superiors not only agreed with his assessment but seconded it, in what would be the most critical UN condemnation of the Croats since the UNPROFOR mission began. The deputy chief of the mission, Cedric Thornberry, toured the region after MacInnis and he told the UN that he "had never seen anything like it. There's nothing larger than a good-sized brick left [of the villages]."

While MacInnis was in the region, Calvin took him out to the field where Charlie Company's Eight Platoon had fought the Croats for fifteen hours. MacInnis and Calvin concurred that, given the description of the fighting, the Canadians must have inflicted casualties among the Croats, and were puzzled as to why the Canadians did not suffer any. MacInnis theorizes that the Croatian soldiers were mostly domobrans with little training. They would normally shoot and then go to ground while the other side retaliated. The Canadians had dug trenches and were able to shoot while being shot at, giving them a tactical advantage.

What MacInnis can't explain is why there is no UN or Croatian report of the incident—not even an official complaint from Calvin—on file at the UN. MacInnis says he only heard of the firefight when he arrived in Medak Pocket and admits there was no discussion of it in Zagreb where they were following events in Medak very closely.

Jim Calvin can't explain why there are no reports filed from the field in the immediate aftermath of the extraordinary events of the fifteenth and sixteenth of September. Bryan Bailey made note in his own company report that the platoon came under fire and it responded in kind. But there is nothing reflecting the scope of the event. In Dearing's section alone, the soldiers had fired hundreds of rounds each from their rifles and they had used several belts of ammunition—a hundred rounds to the belt—on their C6 machine gun.

The battalion's war diary, marked "secret" and acquired after an access to information request, says of September 15, 1993, only that "There has been slight resistance to increased presence of UN pers [sic] but nothing significant. The major problem is the clearing of land mines to allow our subunits to deploy."

The operations officer, Shane Brennan, doesn't think it surprising that there is so little written record. He says they had no time to file reports at the time and they had no reason to ask Dearing and the others to make written records. "The Canadian Forces don't have much of a writing tradition," says Brennan. And yet other, less significant events in Medak Pocket have a number of first-person after-action documents from those involved. There are a dozen reports from the Second Battalion on such matters as land mines, booby traps and ambushes—many of them carefully hand-written or laboriously printed by the soldiers who experienced them. There are no such entries in the annals of the DND from Charlie Company. But Shane Brennan says no one asked anyone to write a report after the firefight. Bailey solicited several first-hand accounts from his soldiers later, when he wrote recommendations for some men to receive medals and citations. But Bailey says he and his troops were too worn out to document the firefight in its entirety. Padre Mike Brown says he filed his own report of the Medak operation upon request from Calvin. He says he was told that his, and all other such reports, were to be folded into the final after-action document submitted by Calvin at the end of the mission. Many significant moments from the tour don't have much written about them.

MacInnis says the Croats never mentioned the event to him or spoke of any casualties and he was content to allow the matter to slip into obscurity.

* * *

International outrage over the ethnic cleansing in Medak Pocket eventually registered in Zagreb. Tudjman quickly moved toward damage control. His trusted defence minister, Gojko Susak—who had to know what was happening in Medak—ordered a "full investigation" into the events. Within days, he suspended General Rahim Ademi and Major Mile Kosovic. It was well known in Croat circles that Ademi had been quite deliberately kept out of the loop during the planning of the Medak operation, but Croat military intelligence reports indicate that Ademi had dutifully followed orders to "clean" the Pocket of bodies and evidence when the operation was over. If, as Tudjman claimed, no crimes were committed, why was the clean-up order given and why was General Ademi suspended? Even as the Croatian leadership tried to cover its tracks, their efforts raised more troubling questions.

The Croatian government's public relations office issued a statement saying that only Serb military personnel had been killed: "civilians living in three quoted hamlets [Divoselo, Citluk and Pocitelj] were in the service of Serbian paramilitary forces." There was "no intentional killing of Serbian civilians either during the Croatian army action or during its pullout" and "any possibility of planned or commanded systematic destruction of houses and hamlets in the Medak Pocket can be vigorously rejected." Two of the five women who were found dead, the government claimed, were killed in combat operations in which they were participants. Three others—who had been shot at close range—had been killed "while guiding groups of terrorists who were trying to escape." Presumably, these "guerrilla fighters" included Bosiljka Bjegovic, the seventy-four-year-old blind woman found by the Canadian soldiers in the swamp, shot in the back and clinging to her purse and fur coat; the two women, aged eighty-six and sixty-seven, who had been locked in the chicken coop and set on fire; and another dead woman who had been considered mentally challenged.

To their advantage, the Croats were able to cite propaganda broadcasts over Serbian television that seemed to lend a tiny bit of credibility to their claims. One Belgrade "news" item, broadcast weeks earlier, showed an old Serbian woman with her arm draped over a machine gun, declaring that she was prepared to use the weapon against attacking Croats. It's not clear if the geriatric defender was from Medak Pocket or another location, since Serbian media claimed that grannies throughout the Krajina were rising up in defence of the putative homeland. But the Croats pointed to these reports as proof that old women were indeed lawful combatants and they issued a statement that one of the dead women was the well-known "Baka" (Grandma) Danica who, "although getting on in years had fired shots from a machine gun."

There was, undoubtedly, a thin line between the role of combatant and civilian throughout the Balkan conflicts, and in Medak Pocket there were certainly wires and communications equipment indicating that civilian houses were part of the Serbian homeland defence in Medak. Domobrans generally lived at home and wore a mix of military and civilian attire. In addition, there were eyewitnesses to an incident in Medak when an elderly woman blew herself up with a grenade in the presence of Croat soldiers.

All of this tended to somewhat muddy the waters for war crimes prosecutors. But the acts of cruelty inflicted on the deceased and the efforts to conceal the bodies point to a more sinister reality. UN reports indicate that at least a hundred civilians and soldiers *hors de combat* were killed in the Medak operation, and more than 160 homes utterly destroyed between the ninth and the seventeenth of September. UNPROFOR press releases describing the events of Medak as criminal came under heavy criticism from the Croatian government, who accused the peacekeepers of losing their impartiality. That was a charge that few soldiers would have contested.

But the Croatian government's indignation over being accused of crimes is undermined—once again—by Franjo Tudjman's propensity to record his working moments for posterity. The Council for Defence and National Security met again on September 19, and, once again, the session was recorded and the tape later found its way to the news media and the public.

In this meeting, Tudjman was in a rage over the steady stream of news from SKY and CNN broadcasters. He tells his ministers "UNPROFOR people and others tell us that we did not leave the cleanest clearance behind when we retreated," he laments. General Bobetko admits that "UNPROFOR entered a little bit too fast." The Canadian soldiers may have seen more than they were supposed to.

Bobetko then reassures the meeting that the area "was cleansed, absolutely." But admitted he wasn't entirely confident that the UN peacekeepers would find no evidence. The Serbs had collected a number of bodies before King's sweep team had arrived and Bobetko boasts that they managed to turn over to the enemy fifty-two "usable" Serbian bodies including those of the five elderly women that the Croats claimed were actually warriors. Since the final UN report indicates that at least a hundred people were killed in the region, the statement suggests that the rest of the bodies were so mangled and mutilated as to be not "usable"—for propaganda purposes, presumably. The sixteen bodies found by King's sweep team were obviously not the corpses the Croats hoped the world would see. Bobetko worried out loud at the meeting about the possibility that fifty or sixty bodies were still in the forest where it was too difficult to retrieve them. The Croats must have hoped it would be too difficult for UNPROFOR as well.

It's clear from the two recorded meetings of the Croatian defence council that Tudjman was unhappy with Bobetko's handling of the operation, even though the Croats blamed Rahim Ademi for it. Michel Maisonneuve didn't know whether to laugh at Ademi or pity him. "Ademi was a chubby little wild man," says Maisonneuve. "He looked barely in control. The kind of guy who would walk around with his weapon cocked. Unprofessional." Although he found Ademi to be a nasty piece of work, Maisonneuve was also not sure how much power he had.

Nowhere in the meetings or in further statements is there any mention of perhaps the most dangerous and important player in all of this: Davor Domazet, the highest-ranking member of Croatia's intelligence service at the time and the right-hand man to Janko Bobetko. Domazet sat in all the meetings in Gospic with UNPROFOR and Jim Calvin, although Calvin doesn't remember him. Michel Maisonneuve does.

He recalls the bearded Domazet as a dark and sinister presence who sat calmly while the negotiators ranted and railed. He appeared quietly confident that his will and that of his masters would be executed, and that blame would always be pointed elsewhere.

* * *

At the time of the negotiations, Colonel Calvin thought that the agreement to withdraw to the pre–September 9 positions was a fairly straightforward proposition. But he soon discovered that nothing is easy when it comes to managing territory in the Balkans. The Croats insisted that the pre–September 9 line went considerably deeper into the Medak region than UNPROFOR or the Serbs thought it did.

Shane Brennan remembers meetings between all parties— Serbs, Croats, UNPROFOR UN military observers and UN civilian police—that became so heated that people were screaming at each other. As the commander of Headquarters Company, Major Brennan attended these negotiating sessions with Calvin. (These were the sessions to which he brought his trophy grenade in case he had to "influence destiny.") They would lay maps out on the floor, and then both sides would scribble furiously on them to indicate who owned what. Brennan could always assess just how stressed out Calvin was getting by watching the prominent vein in the middle of the colonel's forehead begin to throb. "I would look over to see how big that vein was getting and I would make a mental assessment as to how long this meeting was going to go on."

Brennan suspected that the Croats were emotional, in part, because of news his interpreters at headquarters had translated from local radio reports. UNPROFOR soldiers were said to have killed as many as twenty-seven Croatian soldiers during the Charlie Company battle in the Pocket. The Croat leadership flatly denied that there ever was a firefight with UN troops. The Croatian senior command did release a number for deaths among their soldiers from the Medak operation—the number was twenty-seven—but the victims, they insisted, had been killed by the Serbs.

Bryan Bailey went out to take a close look at the hedgerow where he was told the Croats might have been killed, but he found not a trace of evidence that there had even been a battle on the other side. The bodies that Mike Brown was sure he saw were long gone.

***

October was probably just about the right time for the Second Battalion to get out of Medak, and out of Croatia altogether. The Van Doos, under the command of Colonel Mark Lessard, were finally in place and the Patricias were more than ready to go home. Calvin and the company commanders tried to prepare the young reservists for what would come next, something they knew they would find incomprehensible and even shocking. Within twenty-four hours of their return, their companies would be broken up. They would no longer be together. In most cases, they would probably never see each other again.

The soldiers were on overtime and the bureaucrats were determined to move them back to Winnipeg and out again as quickly as possible, lest they incur more costs. Everyone was exhausted, nervous and agitated. "When I first went over there, I went out without ammunition," recalls Dr. Kelly Brett. "By the time I left, I had my pistol under my pillow when I slept and I took a C7 with about five magazines of ammo with me everywhere I went." Croatia had been an ordeal that changed every person in the battle group, hardened soldiers and weekend warriors alike.

In the final days, the United Nations heaped praise on them. The special representative to the Secretary-General—the most senior civilian in the international force in the former Yugoslavia—wrote a glowing letter of recognition and thanks, commending the Patricias to Boutros Boutros-Ghali in New York

City. UNPROFOR Headquarters wrote that the soldiers should return home "in the knowledge that you have saved many lives, enhanced the credibility of the United Nations, helped greatly to create the conditions for peace that must someday come, and above all, you have been a credit to the military profession, your regiment, your army and your country. No one could have done more." The letter suggests that the Medak Pocket will one day be added to other great moments for the Patricias such as Ypres and Kap'yong. Finally, General Jean Cot awarded the soldiers a special United Nations citation that no other contingent had yet received. It was a heady conclusion for the young soldiers. Cot then took the officers to dinner in Zagreb and picked up the tab. It wasn't just the mission that had been saved by the Canadians, it was also the French general's reputation.

The Canadians tried to shake the dust of Medak Pocket from their feet, and its ghosts from their weary minds, as they boarded a plane for home.

CHAPTER EIGHT

WITCH HUNTS AND PAPER SHREDDERS

I had been in charge of 2,500 square kilometres and the lives of nearly nine hundred people, and I came back to a world where they would question whether your collar was straight.

—Colonel Jim Calvin

WHEN THE SECOND BATTALION of the Princess Patricias returned from Croatia in the fall of 1993, they were coming home to a country gripped by scandal and a military consumed with paranoia, secrecy and subterfuge.

A barren desert on the Horn of Africa had been the setting for a tragedy that touched every soldier of every regiment in the country. The image of a gagged, beaten and murdered Somali teenager named Shidane Arone was becoming a symbol of the Canadian army's tarnished reputation in peacekeeping as bureaucrats and defence careerists tried to distance themselves from both Somalia and the efforts of some to suppress the story of what happened there.

Somalia had a devastating impact on Canada's military. A long tradition of command responsibility was reversed as leaders blamed subordinates who passed on the blame to lower ranks. The buck-passing destroyed morale and pride for a decade. The Somali affair claimed countless casualties, not least among them soldiers of the Second Battalion of the Princess Patricia's Canadian Light Infantry, men and women who had never gone anywhere near Somalia.

Journalists savoured each tiny revelation of DND foibles and the farcical attempts to hide dirt under the well-worn rugs of headquarters. Major-General Jean Boyle, whose job was to control the release of information on Somalia, made it his mission to locate potentially incriminating documents before anyone else did. Nothing mattered more to the Department of National Defence than protecting bureaucrats, the brass and the politicians from embarrassing revelations.

It was to this charged atmosphere that the exhausted soldiers returned when they landed in Winnipeg during the first days and nights of October 1993. Kim Campbell, the minister of defence when they left, was now a desperate, embattled prime minister who was in the process of leading her party into its grave. The Department of National Defence was preoccupied with the first of six courts-martial for criminal acts in Somalia. The prosecutions were to begin on October 18—exactly a week before Canadians were to go to the polls. The last thing anyone in Ottawa wanted was another military controversy.

That a Canadian battalion was returning from a mission during which they might have actually killed another country's soldiers was, to the scandal-shy DND headquarters, a political land mine. No one went near it.

There was a daily media frenzy over even the tiniest detail of the incident in Somalia, but only minimal coverage of the return of the Second Battalion. Nobody asked the questions that might have unlocked the story of what happened in Medak Pocket.

While the Canadian Airborne had come to grief in the sands of Somalia, the Second Battalion had, they were told, saved the UN mission in Croatia, almost single-handedly. Its soldiers had seen the first Canadian combat since the Korean War. They had laid the basis for a war crimes investigation of the atrocities they had documented in Medak Pocket. But for the public, distracted by the unseemly spectacle at the DND, the significance of Croatia would be overlooked for almost a decade.

***

In the past, soldiers who completed overseas campaigns had time to adjust, sometimes long periods of time. Months passed before the soldiers of the First and Second World Wars were back with their families. Even in the aftermath of fighting in the Korean War, the camaraderie and *esprit de corps* continued on the return trip. But in the penny-pinching 1990s, when people could be flown home in hours, units broke up and dispersed within days of the end of a mission.

It was a logistical challenge to ship the soldiers, who came from so many different units, all home expeditiously. The reservists in particular had to be moved in and out as quickly as possible, because they were getting overtime pay. "When a reservist arrived in Winnipeg," recalls Warrant Officer Dave DesBarres of Charlie Company's Eight Platoon, "you'd walk by someone who filled out a medical questionnaire stating that you had your ten toes and ten fingers and your head was on top of your body, then you turned in your personal weapon and a day or two later you found yourself in an airport in Halifax, St. John's, Newfoundland, Vancouver." One day the soldier was in the midst of a battle or a minefield, coping with fetid corpses, and the next he was standing in his living room surrounded by family, and wondering how a single species on a single planet could accommodate such extremes of experience.

"My reservists went straight from hell back into the normal world," says Dan Drew. "They went from 150 miles an hour to zero in a heartbeat . . . And they were scattered to the four winds."

Corporal Hugh Tull and his fellow Seaforth Highlanders were overwhelmed when they arrived back in Winnipeg. On the first night everyone was confined to base. Tull remembers a rebellion as they found a way to ignore orders and head to town. There was a nip of frost in the night air and an endless array of diversions before them in the city. Tull had been picking up corpses a week earlier and now he was getting inebriated as quickly as physically possible along with his buddies.

"It was insane, the amount of drinking people were doing," he recalls. "The next day we had to be at parade at eight o'clock in the morning. I rolled up in a cab with a couple of other people from another company that I had never spent any time with." Parade was in an airport hangar where the usual diesel fumes were overwhelmed by the reek of alcohol from the men. Literally propping each other up, they heard the news that they would be departing within forty-eight hours—their flights home were already booked. "This is your flight time. Be there for it, okay? See you later. Have a nice life," recalls Tull.

Tony Spiess carried on to Vancouver with the other Seaforth Highlanders and found himself rattled and edgy: "I just wanted to get the fuck out of the airport. I didn't want to be around it. Got in the car. Started driving home and I was like, holy, you know, things have changed, a lot of things have changed. Look at this place. The whole world has changed and . . . nothing had changed, it was me." Spiess had a nagging feeling that he was missing something. He didn't feel all there. He finally realized what was absent was his gun.

Craig King remembers sitting in his living room watching TV—pictures of Boris Yeltsin standing on a tank outside the Moscow White House—when he suddenly realized how surreal it all was. The world was celebrating the end of the Cold War and cheering for the "peace dividend"; but what he and his fellow Canadian soldiers had just confronted was the continuing horrible fallout from Cold War politics.

Phil Tobicoe was thrilled with the reception that the regiment's wives and families laid on for them at the airport in Winnipeg, where they had a little Rendezvous Café set-up. "My God, when we arrived in Winnipeg, we felt like something. There were ribbons on trees, signs greeted us, a hall, people . . . loved us and shook our hand."

But it didn't last. Tobicoe had to continue on to Calgary where he and the other soldiers found only a box of doughnuts and a coffee urn to welcome them. There was no one to talk to about what they had experienced. The living nightmare they had walked through just days before, the feelings of anger and bewilderment: that was all smothered.

The soldiers had two weeks off, just long enough to do their laundry and banking and then re-enter the daily grind. The Medak Pocket was over. Forget it. Move on.

Jim Calvin sat down to write his final report to the United Nations and a formal After Action Report for the Department of National Defence, which he filed three weeks after everyone was home. He tried to tell the whole story, how they had managed to disarm both armies in Sector West and the Medak operation—how they had negotiated their way into the no man's land between the Croats and Serbs; how they had entered the Pocket to find only dead people; how they had gathered up the corpses and collected the evidence of crimes.

Calvin carefully phrased what he had heard about possible casualties. "Numerous firefights occurred, some lasting up to ninety minutes between Croatians [sic] and CANBAT [Canadian Battalion] 1 troops over the following 15 hour period," reads Calvin's report. "It is not confirmed if Croatian soldiers were injured, however the Croatian media reported twenty-seven soldiers killed or wounded during this operation." The phrase "this operation" presumably refers to the engagement with Charlie Company's Eight Platoon, but in an otherwise blunt report the wording is uncharacteristically vague.

This wasn't the first time the DND heard about casualties. Shane Brennan had sent a brief and cryptic situation report to Ottawa on the day he had heard the potential casualty figure from the Croatian translator. At the time, Brennan had feared there might be some retaliation and he had thought it very important to notify the Canadian DND in Ottawa.

Brennan had often been surprised by how little interest Ottawa seemed to have had in their mission. Over the months, he would sometimes pick up the satellite phone and test it to make sure it was working, so perplexed he was by the lack of communications from home base. When he filed the sitrep—that Canadians might have been responsible for more than two dozen Croatian deaths—Brennan braced himself for some alarmed response. It never came.

Calvin and Brennan didn't know that the Defence Department was in the grips of a different kind of hysteria until they returned home. But why did no one respond to them at the time? Although a number of Brennan's situation reports from the field turned up as a result of access to information requests, the one describing twenty-seven dead Croat soldiers seems not to have survived. Calvin couldn't confirm the deaths for his report and wasn't about to start digging around for more details. The headline "Canadian Soldiers Kill Twenty-Seven Croats" was to be avoided at all costs. Perhaps there was a time when it could have been explained in heroic terms. But not now. The media were out for DND blood. Even a good war story would blow up in their faces.

Calvin's report disappeared into the files. A part of it was released several years later, but the full After Action Report only became available, after much insistence, during the writing of this book.

* * *

It's possible that the DND would have been just as inattentive to the veterans of Medak Pocket even if there had been no Somalia scandal. There were numerous warning signs; peacekeeping missions had changed fundamentally in the 1990s and the new circumstances were taking an unexpected toll on the Canadian Forces, mainly the army.

But Ottawa didn't have time to think about the new environment. Canada was under pressure to satisfy the United Nations' insatiable appetite for Canadian troops. There were more UN peacekeeping missions in the first half of the 1990s than there had been in the previous four decades. Canada served on almost every one. Burnout became a major problem for regiments across the country with soldiers taking on back-to-back assignments. Marriage failure and domestic breakdowns in the army became common.

When Corporal Paul Delmore didn't report for work at the Kap'yong barracks in Winnipeg on the morning of Monday, September 13, no one picked up on it as a sign of distress—but someone should have. Delmore had served in the Patricias unit that preceded Calvin's. Compared to the Medak mission his tour had been uneventful, but even so the level of violence was overwhelming for many soldiers who hadn't anticipated the chaos and hostility of the Balkan conflict.

Delmore had told his mother that he hated serving in Croatia. He was shocked that people spat at the peacekeepers and displayed a visceral hatred. He adopted stray cats and dogs in Sector West and looked after them to relieve the atmosphere of hostility and, perhaps, to get some small sign of appreciation. His mother sent him a care package of pet treats for his "admirers."

On the Sunday night, September 12, the twenty-six-year-old, alone in his Winnipeg apartment, put on his full dress uniform and shot himself. Margaret Delmore told reporters her only son was a casualty of the Balkans. In the suicide note he left for her he wrote: "Fuck Croatia."

Soldiers of the Second Battalion, returning just after Delmore's funeral, couldn't make any sense of his death. But there was something ominous about his suicide. Had he seen the beast that they had seen? And if this is what it did to him, what morbid plan might it have in store for them?

Those who knew the corporal remembered him as easygoing and something of a clown. How could he have flipped so quickly? As the years went on and Croatia claimed more victims among the peacekeepers who had served there, the Delmore suicide would be seen by some as an early warning signal.

* * *

In her book *An Intimate History of Killing,* Joanna Bourke argues that soldiers in combat must have their actions recognized and validated by their societies if they are to find moral legitimacy.

A soldier is trained to kill, which is a highly anti-social act. But in a military context, killing is sanctioned by the state and ostensibly performed for the protection of innocent people. If societies fail to acknowledge and indeed celebrate the efforts of soldiers who are acting in their defence, soldiers may be traumatized by their apparently anti-social actions.

Whatever application this may have to the peace-enforcement exercise in Medak Pocket, the passive, or perhaps active, decision of the DND and the mass media to bury or ignore the story had a profoundly troubling effect on the soldiers who had served there. The firefight experienced by the Canadian peacekeepers was not a battle—or at least not in the terms with which people are most familiar. The common understanding of "battle" corresponds to imagery from the Great Wars, with massive divisions of soldiers mobilizing over hundreds of square kilometres. Medak Pocket was obviously not on this scale. Instead, it was a perfect example of the kinds of war fighting in the 1990s: skirmishes fought bitterly by platoon-sized forces. This is what the Canadians had encountered. It was not classic war and it was certainly not UN peacekeeping.

Peacekeeping in the 1990s changed because the world's power balance was fundamentally reordered. The peacekeepers who went on the missions of the nineties, to Bosnia, Croatia, Kosovo, Rwanda, found themselves in the middle of fighting. This was a new phenomenon. The rules were no longer clear, and sometimes they were non-existent. The necessity of violence in peacekeeping was becoming a reality, for which Canadian soldiers were ill prepared and, perhaps more to the point, inadequately armed. The Patricias had stood up to an attack; most peacekeepers had not.

The public was still stuck in the past. Peacepkeeping was thought of as a largely benevolent activity that involved helping people and supporting their communities. Assuming that Canadian politicians and defence bureaucrats understood that this was no longer the case, it's clear that there was a profound reluctance to share the news with the public.

A monument to peacekeeping in downtown Ottawa features three vigilant figures in military uniform, clearly doing nothing but observing. They have radios and binoculars but carry no weapons. The installation is called "The Reconciliation," and it undoubtedly sums up what most citizens think peacekeeping is all about. The business of peacekeeping is passive observation, according to the official literature that accompanies the monument: "keeping the peace to allow time for reconciliation to take place."

Jim Calvin wrote a series of recommendations in his final report, warning future commanders how much things had changed: "Soldiers must be prepared to use force to support the political aim. In this case, it meant moving into positions under fire, digging in and responding to fire in kind."

The truth—that Canadian soldiers now had to use their weapons, not just to make peace but to defend themselves against attack—might have had political consequences the authorities were unwilling to confront. The Medak operation illustrated this new reality as nothing before it ever had, and the Medak operation, therefore, had to be erased from the official record.

There would be some internal recognition of what individual soldiers had accomplished. Tyrone Green and Scott Leblanc were cited for their bravery; Rod Dearing was decorated in honour of his leadership during the firefight of September 15. Warrant Officer Johnson also got a medal, for rescuing a French soldier from a minefield one rainy night. Eighteen months after they returned home, Jim Calvin received the Meritorious Service Cross. There were a number of citations and memos to file for soldiers who had performed exceptional work. The Second Battalion, as a whole, received one of only three unit commendations awarded by the United Nations during UNPROFOR's history.

What they wanted, and what the DND refused, was recognition for their collective effort. That lapse was profoundly hurtful and short-sighted. A careful study of what happened at

Medak could have made possible important refinements in the entire institution of peacekeeping. It might have affected, for the better, the outcome of many vital missions in the decade that followed, when UN peacekeepers from many countries faced similar hostility with tragic results. The official failure to face the aftermath of Medak head-on was a huge loss, both on a geopolitical and a personal scale.

For Rob Deans, who had stood up to a barrage of shooting and experienced moments of religious insight in the attic of a barn in Croatia, the return home seemed more unreal than the war. The young reservists had bank accounts fattened by their unused paycheques, and most of those without families managed to burn through the money quickly. Deans bought a car in Winnipeg and drove it home with a buddy from Medak. They were high on the thrill of what they had just lived through, but the larger truth, that their efforts were probably meaningless, slowly dawned during the long drive. "You might as well have been hanging around at the corner store for all the people around you cared. They had no idea that we were there. Or perhaps not a care. It just wasn't part of the consciousness of the country," Deans says.

Rod Dearing had the same experience. He came back buzzing with the adrenaline of his accomplishments, and justifiably proud of having led a section of mostly reservists through the first combat of its kind since the Korean War. But Dearing was greeted with disbelief. "I would tell people about it and they would say, 'No way. If that had happened we would have seen it on TV.' So I just don't talk about it much."

Sergeant Chris Byrne, who had helped with the investigation of the crime scenes in Medak Pocket, and had lost his friend Jim Decoste in the final weeks of their deployment, found his first problem back home was sleep. He wasn't getting any. He became angry and irritable with his wife and family, and found himself increasingly isolated from other people. Later, the anger morphed into panic attacks and a feeling that his life was coming apart. His three-year-old daughter found him on the steps of their house one day, weeping. She put her arms around him and told him everything was going to be okay. Finally, he went for help.

Hugh Tull just couldn't stop drinking. He went to Victoria to be with his girlfriend as soon as he arrived home, but once there he spent less time with her than he did looking for other soldiers to go drinking with. "You name the bars. The Tudor House. The Carlton Club. There's just so many. So many bars." The young reservist had been known as a mellow, laid-back individual before Croatia. But on New Year's Eve he found himself drunk and dancing naked on a tabletop. A couple of months and a lot of fights later, Tull's relationship with his girlfriend was over, but his relationship with alcohol continued.

The issues were no less acute in the regular forces, except that those soldiers had the structure of their military unit for support and continuity. The battalion's regimental sergeant major, Mike McCarthy, noticed that drinking was a major problem. "The only people they can go out with, who understand what they went through, is their own section."

Phil Tobicoe had learned a lot from his experiences in an anti-armour platoon in Medak, and he thought he could teach other soldiers a few things. "I told them the book went out the window when we went into Medak. I told them how things can really get harsh." But the new trainees wouldn't listen and Tobicoe lashed out at them. "I sort of blew up. I didn't understand what was going on."

He went to see his father and his uncle, a veteran of the British army. They could only advise him to relax. "Don't drink," they told him. Tobicoe got drunk once before he realized his father and uncle were right.

He learned that many of his colleagues from the Croatia mission were leaving the service. "I watched my platoon disintegrate. Some guys did drugs, alcohol was getting out of hand, family break-ups, career problems, all kinds of service-related stuff—even one soldier running around carrying a handgun, because he was paranoid."

Mike Spellen's life slowly fell apart as well. Nightmares, sweats, sleeplessness and a complete disconnection from his family led him to leave both his marriage and the military. "I hit twenty-five [years] and I just got out. One-liner, 'To whom it may concern . . . ' and I gave thirty days' notice." Spellen started driving trucks and trying to forget. He began to hear a certain phrase that would haunt many of the soldiers who served in the Balkans. "I heard it from my own wife first—my ex-wife. And other wives and in some cases mothers and fathers of certain troops. That they didn't get the same guy back that went to war."

Dan Drew says he was burned out and desolated, especially when he was given a new company soon after he returned. "I had a company of guys I didn't want to talk to for three or four months. Those weren't my kids." *His* kids, the soldiers of Delta Company, had worked a solid eighty days with no break, and all of them had been in Medak Pocket. And now he didn't see them; many of them he would never see again.

Craig King was edgy and irritable and unable to talk about what had happened. "I told [my wife] that there was some pretty bad stuff over there but . . . I mean, would you like to have a discussion about this with your spouse?" King did an oral history of what he had seen and someone transcribed it for him. He was able to send the written account to his father before he died. But he couldn't talk about his work on the sweep team and what they had encountered.

There was no formal effort to record the individual problems the returning soldiers were experiencing, but the anecdotal information was piling up: clinical depression, bowel disorders, impotence, panic attacks and sleeplessness. Soldiers who had once loved to hunt were now startled when they heard a rifle shot. Soldiers couldn't walk out on their own lawns for fear of imaginary anti-personnel mines. But mostly the nervous conditions they suffered from were associated with death. Common odours like burning grass, singed hair and rotting garbage would overwhelm the senses and, in their minds, they'd be back in the chaos of Medak Pocket. Some got over it quickly, but for others the anxiety and depression only got worse.

**

There were sufficient signs of trauma among the soldiers that a navy doctor, Lieutenant Commander Greg Passey, conducted a study to try to figure out what was ailing them. Men and women returning from the Balkans suffered an inordinate amount of clinical depression and a condition that no one but Vietnam vets had talked about before this time—post-traumatic stress disorder (PTSD).

Passey figured that the events the soldiers had experienced were so overwhelmingly traumatic they couldn't process them. Passey sent up the first flares in a burgeoning disaster in the Canadian Forces. But his views ran up against a macho military culture that regards mental and emotional distress as a sign of weakness and inadequacy.

A strong lobby from an old guard in the armed forces dismissed theories about stress disorders and intimidated people who might have sought help for their problems. "The first people who did come forward were released from the military for being freaks," says Rudy Bajema. "One guy I know from 2PPCLI went and told them, I've got these problems. I'm beating my wife, or I want to beat my wife. And I'm having problems with my kids. Well, they just said you're out of here, buddy. You have psychological problems." PTSD became synonymous with "unfit for service" and it was the kiss of death for a career.

There were Canadian Forces medical personnel who were intrigued by the stories about the physical health of the soldiers returning from peacekeeping in the former Yugoslavia. Eric Smith, a medical doctor and a lieutenant with the navy, worried that soldiers who served in Croatia might have been exposed to toxic elements such as bauxite and PCBs. Smith served on a later tour in the Medak region and took note of the curious red soil used for sandbags, as well as the large number of damaged transformers that quite probably were leaking PCBs. Smith wrote a report warning of the possibility of toxic exposure and had a copy of his memo placed in the file of every soldier who had served in Operation Harmony. Dr. Smith was young and keen and wanted to protect the soldiers. He couldn't have known that the DND would go to extraordinary lengths to suppress his warnings.

* * *

Mike McCarthy knew the soldiers were struggling but there was no institutional way for him to find out who was having problems. "With the uniform on they were far more reluctant to come to a sergeant major and talk about an inability to get an erection, or 'I can't satisfy my wife,' or 'I'm losing my job, I lost my wife'— whatever. They just couldn't do that." And McCarthy wasn't able to track the problems for long. He was moved to another battalion by the following summer. So was Colonel Jim Calvin.

It was a purely administrative decision, but it left the battalion without any continuity or memory in the command ranks, no one at the senior level who might have noticed that many of the soldiers were changing, becoming uncharacteristically impatient and edgy, that marriages were breaking up, that people were depressed. And there was no one to explain that the soldiers were probably like that because, for a number of months in 1993, they had been caught up in a vicious ethnic war. Calvin was no longer in a position to run interference for his soldiers. But he would soon have more immediate problems of his own.

* * *

Throughout the 1990s the Somalia affair continued to absorb much of the time and energy of the DND, even after a new government and a new prime minister, Jean Chrétien, took power. The Chrétien administration picked up where the Campbell regime left off. A new defence minister, David Collenette, launched a broad-based commission of inquiry into the Somalia affair.

The scandalous problems in the armed forces were actually convenient for the new finance minister, Paul Martin, who was savaging government spending in an effort to reduce the deficits that ballooned in the Mulroney years. The defence budget was a sitting duck. There was little public sympathy for the Canadian Forces in those days, given the horrors of Somalia. Martin could hack away at it without fear of a political backlash.

Reporters remained fixated on the foibles of high-level targets like the two generals Jean Boyle and John de Chastelain, and the former deputy minister Robert Fowler, as the Somalia Commission of Inquiry turned up files and documents that had been clumsily concealed or altered. The military paper chase was material for front-page stories for months.

The Canadian military had a sad legacy of self-serving leadership at the most senior levels; keeping the nose clean and the backside covered were proven survival tactics. It was a system that rewarded obedience and perpetuated the culture of secrecy that had resulted from years of Cold War paranoia.

Many claim that the already bumbling and top-heavy institution lost its direction irrevocably two decades earlier in 1973 when the Department of National Defence merged with the military command of the Canadian Armed Forces and created one, large, banal bureaucracy, housed in a new, monster edifice nicknamed "Disney on the Rideau." The new building didn't mean there were any new ideas. Very few of the top officers seemed to realize that the Cold War was over, the world had changed, secrecy was no longer acceptable and the destruction of files would be revealed, sooner or later. The Somalia affair brought all the rot and incompetence out into the glaring light of day, and it would ultimately have a cleansing effect. But in the 1990s, the process felt as invigorating as swallowing Drano. And all the while Paul "the Axe" Martin was taking the armed forces apart.

Rudy Bajema claims Medak was subjected to official censorship but he can't put his finger on where the directives were coming from, or why. "Why didn't someone come forward and say, 'Something extraordinary just happened and we want to talk about it'?" Bajema blames Colonel Calvin for not taking the lead. "I don't know why Calvin didn't say something. He just settled into a groove."

Calvin shrugs off comments that he may have been part of the failure to get the story out. He says he was a colonel living in dangerous times; the media and the bureaucrats were looking for targets. It was years before Calvin made any public pronouncement on the events, much to the frustration of many of his officers and soldiers.

Occasionally, there were small leakages of information, in which the possibility of a larger story was either ignored or lost in the smoke of misunderstanding. Bryan Bailey, commander of Charlie Company, was shocked to see a story in a Winnipeg newspaper alleging that his men had violated the Geneva Convention when they used a .50-calibre machine gun to shoot at Croats.

It was a reference to Tony Spiess shooting back at the Croats during the events of the fifteenth of September. According to the story, which allegedly came from a reservist, the soldiers had broken international law when they used a weapon that's considered to be an anti-personnel weapon in a peace-support situation. "Entirely wrong. Poorly researched," Bailey says. Use of the weapon for defence was clearly within their rules of engagement for the mission and for peacekeeping in general. Otherwise, why would they even have the guns?

Bailey was furious that the soldiers had no way of responding to falsehoods in the article. He wanted the battalion to take the paper to task but Calvin refused. Bailey says Calvin told him it would only prolong the media attack by adding fuel to the fire. Better to leave it alone. Bailey had no choice but to obey his senior officer, but he was disappointed in Calvin.

Calvin's advice to keep a cool head may have been right. The charges and accusations of poor judgment by the officers in charge of 2PPCLI were only starting to roll in, and overreacting could have made it worse

Shawn McKinstry, the operations officer for C Company, remembers in the final days of the mission that Calvin told the soldiers not to be ashamed of anything that happened in Croatia. Bryan Bailey had told the company to make sure no one ever trivialized their accomplishments in Medak. McKinstry wasn't sure what they were talking about at the time; he couldn't imagine that the battalion wouldn't be celebrated for the job they had done. Then back home, he found himself on a training course where a full colonel, whom he will not name, made a disparaging reference to "a little skirmish" that the Patricias had found themselves in during their Croatian deployment. McKinstry recalled the words of Calvin and Bailey—that they should let no one trivialize the events—and he raised his hand to offer a full explanation of the little "skirmish." But he says he was cut short. The colonel politely took McKinstry aside later and told him that, while his version of events was probably accurate, this wasn't an appropriate time to discuss it. McKinstry was flummoxed. He realized the colonel was trying to do him a favour and that there seemed to be a gag order on the Medak story.

Worse was to come. The DND began a series of investigations into perceived failures by the officers commanding the battle group. In the normal course of events, Calvin would have been promoted after returning from Croatia. He wasn't, and it was definitely an unusual slight. Instead, he found himself—and his officers—under attack.

The investigations focused on the leadership of Calvin and Major Dan Drew, how they handled the discipline problems in the final weeks of deployment. The fight between soldiers on the night of the Delta Company smoker was among the first disciplinary issues to come under review. The two soldiers in the punch-up had been antagonistic throughout the tour in Croatia. Private Jason Woolley thought his superior had singled him out for harassment. Master Corporal Craig Van Dongen claimed he was just trying to make Woolley a better soldier. When the tension between them came to a head the night of the smoker, Woolley had a significant advantage because Van Dongen had been injured and had his shoulder in a sling. The fight ended after Woolley pounded Van Dongen's head against a concrete floor, leaving the young man with serious injuries.

The probe by the National Investigative Services (NIS), a branch of the DND, only started in 1995, after Van Dongen disclosed the incident during psychological counselling. The therapist reported it and the NIS blamed Calvin for not bringing criminal charges against Woolley.

Calvin freely admits that in order not to delay their departure, he made a decision to disregard the fight. In his judgment it would not have been in the best interest of the forces or the public to pursue a court martial in the case at such a difficult time, because it might have created even larger problems. It was a big decision, given the severity of Van Dongen's injuries, but for Calvin it was only one of many large decisions he had to make in those final days.

The way that the injured soldier had been handled after the incident was also controversial. Mike Spellen became involved in a dispute with Steve Atkins, the Delta Company medic: Atkins wanted a proper ambulance for the injured man, but Spellen wanted to take Van Dongen away immediately in a jeep. Spellen prevailed, and Van Dongen survived the Ilitis jeep ride. But now there were charges that the soldiers had been too drunk to make rational decisions. The buck stopped with Calvin. He had permitted the smoker. He had authorized the drinking limits. And now he would be held accountable.

In the course of the review of these incidents, latent resentment against Calvin and his officers emerged. Simmering frustrations suddenly exploded in an attack on their leadership. "I was accused of not transporting the injured soldier out with a helicopter. I didn't even have a helicopter, for Christ's sake," says Calvin with clear exasperation.

He was also called to account for Major Dan Drew's pistol salute to the company's reservists. In that case, he successfully argued that he had properly handled the matter by punishing Drew in the field. For his part in the incident, Drew would be hounded for several more years.

Many of the disciplinary complaints arose from perceptions that the troops had been placed in dangerous situations unnecessarily. But the entire mission had been unusually dangerous. Calvin had put the success of the mission ahead of the safety of his soldiers—a military principle that many officers would endorse, but controversial for a peacekeeping mission. He'd been following orders from Jean Cot to establish an UNPROFOR presence in a place that had defeated the French only months earlier.

Suggestions of incompetence quickly expanded into full-blown charges, and it became apparent that the process was part of a witchhunt. Senior officials were determined not to be caught out by another Somalia. They were going to find any transgressions and deal with the culprits before the media did. Dan Drew was accused of working the men too hard, but also of excessive leniency (when it came to alcohol). He was accused of pistol-whipping a soldier, but the charge died when the "victim" wasn't able to remember the incident. There were questions about racism, an ugly reality that officials had been confronted with during the Somalia inquiry, and were now hypsersensitive about.

For Dan Drew, the last straw was a complaint to the defence minister by a Croatian-Canadian living in British Columbia. Canadian soldiers, according to the complaint, had executed Croat prisoners. The minister took it seriously. Drew says that when he got a call from headquarters about the charge his response was "Tell the minister to grow some nuts." He was already having problems with investigators from the Judge Advocates General (JAG) office and the National Investigative Service—now they got worse. Past issues over alcohol and his tough leadership style led to suggestions that he was unfit for service.

Colonel Joe Sharpe, the air force officer who would subsequently conduct a definitive investigation of the mission in Croatia, believes that Dan Drew was singled out by bureaucrats because of his military style. "Dan is a soldier's soldier, period. Through the bureaucracy's eyes, he's absolutely the last man you want in uniform, but if I had to go to war as an infantryman," says Sharpe, "I would want to be with Dan Drew."

Before long the bureaucrats were trying to fire Drew.

What now seems strange is that nobody was paying any attention to the mission itself and, particularly, what the soldiers had been asked to do and what had happened in Medak Pocket.

Nobody wanted to know about the firefight of September 15–16 or about the possibity that there had been Croatian casualties that night. Interviews with senior officers who were in the military at the time are revealing: they seem to vaguely recollect hearing that something worthy of attention happened during Colonel Calvin's mission, but no one can quite remember what it was.

***

At the end of April 1995, Croatian tanks swept through western Slavonia, recapturing a large swath of territory. They called it Operation Storm. All but 2,000 of the 20,000 Serbs in the region fled to Serb-held Bosnia where they took over the homes of Croats and Muslims who had been expelled from there. Croats quietly moved into abandoned Serbian houses in western Slavonia.

There is now evidence that they had the active support of the United States. In late July 1995, Gojko Susak advised the U.S. ambassador, Peter Galbraith, that the Croats planned a decisive move to take back territory they had lost in the early fighting. Susak had been given a warm welcome in Washington when he had asked for help the previous March. The U.S. couldn't offer official assistance because of the arms embargo, but Pentagon officials directed Susak to an outfit called Military Professional Resources Incorporated.

MPRI is a military consultancy with a permanent staff of several hundred and a resource base that includes 2,000 former military officers up to the ranks of general and admiral. With their help, the Croatian military started planning their endgame. After the disappearance and presumed slaughter of 8,000 Bosnian men and boys at the hands of Serb forces in Srebrenica in August 1995, Washington abandoned any pretence of impartiality: they wanted the Serbs defeated militarily.

Whether through tacit or explicit signals, the U.S. conveyed to the Croats that they now had a free hand to do what they had to do to take back Serb-held territory. It looked aside while Gojko Susak imported MiG-21 fighter planes, helicopters and guns from Iran, Turkey and Ukraine, despite the arms embargo that the Americans had endorsed.

On August 4, 1995, with American-led air support and U.S. mercenaries on the ground, Janko Bobetko launched Operation Storm (the name echoing that of the U.S.-led Desert Storm in the 1991 Gulf War). In a matter of hours the Croatians, outnumbering the Serbs 150,000 to 40,000, had smashed through crumbling Serb defences in the Krajina, including the Lika Highlands and Medak Pocket. On the second day of the operation they entered Knin and raised the checkerboard flag of Croatia in the centre of town. Walls were plastered with triumphant pictures of Franjo Tudjman in a victorious pose.

There was no doubt that the West, and principally the United States, approved the operation (though Moscow opposed it) and helped in the execution. The territory rightfully belonged to Croatia and the international community had promised its return. What had prevented the approval of this operation up to now was the concern that the Croats would not protect their Serbian minority, a concern that was rooted in the grim reality of Medak Pocket.

Military observers in the Krajina said that Operation Storm had a textbook U.S.-military design. Colonel Andrew Leslie, a Canadian soldier acting as chief of staff at the UN mission in Knin, told journalists that "The plan of attack could have gone to any NATO staff college in North America or Western Europe and received an A-plus."

It was easy to justify the Croatian attack. But what happened next is impossible to defend. Serb civilians in the region were promptly abandoned by their corrupt patrons in Belgrade. UN personnel in the area were confined to their compound, while Croat soldiers drove Serbian residents from their homes. More than 100,000 Serbs left the area within days in what is now considered the largest single forced displacement of civilians in Europe since the Second World War.

They fled for complex reasons: because they knew that Yugoslavia (Belgrade) would no longer protect them; because Serb leaders in Knin had fed them three years of propaganda about the murderous Ustashe; in some cases because the Serbian army, to create a humanitarian crisis, forced them to flee, much as they would do a few months later in Sarajevo.

But aside from all the internal politics and fearmongering, the Krajina Serbs fled because they had seen what the Croats were capable of. The massacres in Medak were still fresh in their minds. UNPROFOR attempted to provide safe corridors, but Croatian civilians attacked the departing Serbs with stones and farm tools, killing some of them. Croatian soldiers, moving into the abandoned farms and villages, repeated the acts of barbarity the Canadians had witnessed in Medak but on a larger scale. Canadian general Alain Forand, commander of Knin UN headquarters, counted twenty to twenty-five bodies on the street in one patrol.

The Croats detroyed or damaged about 20,000 homes and they killed the elderly and infirm who could not join the exodus. One UN report later described the corpse of an elderly woman, bound with fishnet, a rubber tire hung around her neck before she was set on fire. An old man was burned to death nearby. Franjo Tudjman had assured the Croatian Serbs—and the Western world—that Serbs were welcome in his Croatia. But the Serbs knew otherwise.

***

Operation Storm rekindled the Patricias' contempt for the Croats and renewed the horrors of Medak. There is overwhelming evidence that the brutal character of the Balkan wars of the nineties was driven by Belgrade's quest for Greater Serbia. Franjo Tudjman and moderate Croats tried, in the early days of Yugoslavia's break-up, to find compromises on the ethnic questions, but Milosevic stonewalled their efforts. But during the course of the war, Croats showed themselves to be every bit as remorseless as the Serbs in their ethnic cleansing. And from the vantage point of the soldiers of 2PPCL, they looked like the aggressors. The Serbs became the white hats.

Jim Calvin believes to this day that Operation Storm rendered his efforts, and the Patricias' losses in Croatia, useless, because the Croats simply destroyed everything his soldiers had managed to salvage or to protect. Mike Spellen laments that the Serbs in Croatia had become sitting ducks, lulled into a false sense of security by the UN Protection Force. He wondered if any of the people he met, or others who might have escaped the Medak attack, survived Operation Storm. "I like to think they all got out okay. But I also know that's probably not the reality."

* * *

In the months and years after the war in Croatia, health problems among the 2PPCLI soldiers became more acute. Shawn McKinstry was among the many who developed gastrointestinal disorders, but he was aware of people who were significantly worse off. "I know a couple of individuals—I won't give out names—that have been described as non-functioning. They can't hold a job. No stability. And I think . . . at least part of that has to be their experiences in Croatia."

Geoff Crossman, the man who delivered the bodies to Kelly Brett in the morgue, has his own gut problems, and also knows four people from Operation Harmony who developed life-threatening ailments, including cancer.

Mike Spellen has heard stories of soldiers from Operation Harmony who have isolated themselves in remote parts of the country. One sergeant major reported discovering one of his former soldiers panhandling in downtown Ottawa. Spellen found one of the Medak soldiers living among the homeless in Winnipeg, and moved him into his own house. For three weeks, Spellen tried to help him get back on his feet, but one day he found him gone. "There was a note on my desk saying, 'Thanks for everything, Mike. Just too big a city for me.'" True to his military training, the man had neatly made his bed before he left.

Many soldiers simply tried to carry on. Phil Tobicoe, whose father and uncle had told him not to drink, found that he just couldn't talk about his experience. He had stood up to a gang of Serbian paramilitaries who were threatening Croats in Sector South and he had picked up bodies in Medak Pocket. Now he suffered his nightmares in silence.

Other soldiers who shared the experience in Croatia turned to Tobicoe for help, assuming that his silence meant that he was coping. But he wasn't. Tobicoe heard that one of his former colleagues had snapped and had been committed to a mental institution, and he worried who was next. His new colleagues, whom he had tried to talk to about Croatia, mocked Tobicoe and the others, calling them "war heroes." They would say, "Why don't you war heroes give us a hand?" and then laugh at them.

Tobicoe didn't know what to make of it when his physical symptoms began. His health started to deteriorate, his skin broke out, his joints were swollen and he found that he was slowly going blind. Tobicoe's mother was deeply disturbed, especially when she learned her son's application for a veteran's pension had been turned down—even though his doctors reported that Tobicoe was suffering a mission-related illness.

His family had a distinguished history of service in the American, British and Canadian forces as First Nations soldiers. They'd been denied pensions after their service. One uncle who had served in Korea had been buried without a tombstone after he died. The forces wouldn't supply the money to mark a veteran's grave; his family couldn't afford to. Now the biased treatment seemed to be happening again. Tobicoe plodded on, trying to keep doing the job he loved.

Tobicoe successfully avoided alcohol, but many of the others kept hitting the bottle. Hugh Tull struggled with a new-found recklessness that propelled him into extreme sports. His personal life was a shambles and he found himself incapable of sustaining relationships.

There were widespread stories of suicides and attempted suicides, but when Tobicoe inquired of his superiors whether other veterans of Medak had been experiencing difficulties he was advised that he was the only one exhibiting physical and mental disorders.

For Joe Sharpe, a retired colonel who would became the guardian angel of the soldiers from Medak, the biggest failure of the DND wasn't in the crude attempts to cover up the story of Medak or in the feverish paper shredding at headquarters. It was in the way the system treated them as they began to fall ill. "They said, 'I'm sick, there's something wrong with me.' And the system said, 'Well, in that case, we can't afford to have you around,' and they threw them away. We just discarded them and said, 'Not our responsibility any more. Let's bring in some new people and get on with business.' And that's where the real culpability lies."

***

Matt Stopford didn't care what excuses the army gave him for ignoring his illness. Stopford was certain his physical ailments were related to Medak Pocket. The strapping soldier with the heavy beard had gone from robust health to serious disability in the years after his tour in Croatia. His joints ached so badly he could hardly walk. He had severe headaches and he was going blind in one eye, as a result of conjunctivitis.

Stopford had been the no-nonsense warrant officer in Delta Company who had spurred the men on as they filled sandbags with the curious red dirt from God knows where. The heat had been intense and the water supply dubious but they were caught in the crossfire of Serb and Croat hostilities and had no choice but to build and fortify their bunker.

Now Stopford was sick and he wanted compensation. In response, the army transferred him out of Calgary to Trenton, Ontario, and released him twenty-five days later, just three months short of his twenty-year service mark, when he would have become eligible for a larger pension. The administration told him if he was disabled he was no longer fit for service, and dismissed him. The bureaucrats even attempted to deny him severance pay. It was 1999, six years after his tour of duty in Croatia; they didn't believe that his illness could be service-related. Stopford could collect only $1,200 a month in pension and no disability. He was unable to work.

Stopford wasn't the only soldier who had been shown the door by the department after complaining of an illness. But he became the first to fight back. Stopford did what had long been taboo within the tight "family" of the Canadian Forces, but which was becoming more common as the fabric of the military family unravelled in the 1990s: he went to the media. The gruff, bedraggled image of Matt Stopford with his black eye patch became the public face of hundreds of soldiers who had served in Croatia.

By the late nineties American doctors had noted widespread illness, including neurological disease, among veterans of the 1991 Gulf War. They were even calling it the Gulf War syndrome. Stopford suspected he was suffering something similar, possibly related to environmental toxicity overseas. A few wildly speculative articles appeared—one by Scott Taylor of *Esprit de Corps* magazine, who claimed the soldiers had been exposed to radiation and toxins from a bauxite-uranium mine, neither of which is mined in Croatia. But there was bauxite in the environment.

Dr. Eric Smith had certainly worried about that possibility. He had seen smashed PCB transformers and the battle-damaged aluminum smelter near Obravac that Padre Bob Sparks had investigated.

Jim Calvin had been hearing vague rumours of serious problems among the people who had served in Croatia. In 1998, he sent a letter to the head of the army, asking him to investigate the reports of widespread illnesses among his former soldiers. Nothing came of it. Calvin decided to take on the department. He had nothing to lose: his career had been stalled since Medak anyway. He appeared before the parliamentary Standing Committee on National Defence and Veterans Affairs (SCONDVA) and spent several hours telling the story of Medak Pocket.

Calvin brought an entourage of other witnesses, including his wife, Elise, who had headed the families committee in Winnipeg, plus a number of soldiers who described their mental and physical conditions. The parliamentarians were shocked, mostly because they had never before heard anything about the Medak operation and its aftermath.

Calvin had learned about Dr. Smith's memo outlining his concerns about the soldiers' health, but when he went looking for it it had mysteriously disappeared. In one of the more perplexing aspects of the post-Croatia behaviour of senior officials in the DND, someone had made the bureaucratic judgment that Dr. Smith's concerns were not "credible." The letter, placed on an unknown number of files, simply disappeared. Smith could not explain it: "I did what I thought was right, and when it left my hands, it was in the bureaucracy." The story became public. Combined with the Matt Stopford case and emerging reports that many other soldiers were suffering similar illness, the lost memo smacked of cover-up, all the more vile since the letters concerned the health of so many soldiers. Such a document would be essential for a disabled soldier to claim a pension or compensation for illnesses.

The Reform Party defence critic of the day, Art Hangar, declared the cover-up to be criminal. The defence department did an internal review to try to determine what had happened, while the scandal-sniffing media breathed down the department's neck. Captain Shane Vahey was appointed to find out how the letter had disappeared. Vahey, who became affectionately known as "Bauxite Man," went deep into the fathomless sea of internal DND correspondence, trying to find out what went wrong and who might have been responsible.

In one memo to his superiors, released under the Access to Information Act, Vahey wrote, "Apparently, Smith wrote the letter but then was compelled to water it down, and rewrite it several times before having it posted to the files of 1,200 soldiers. One source suggests that the letter was removed in order to have a different version put on the soldiers' records—except the replacement never materialized. Another source says the memo was removed because there was no evidence to support the possibility of environmental health risks in Croatia."

Vahey couldn't follow the paper trail. But around this time, *Globe and Mail* reporters Graham Fraser and Andrew Mitrovica discovered old briefing notes for David Collenette, the defence minister in 1995, prepared in the event he was challenged on the matter in the House of Commons. It's clear that the government knew about the memo warning of bauxite and PCB exposure and that the minister was prepared to argue that he was on top of the issue. Happily for Collenette, the story didn't come out for another four years, and by then Art Eggleton was the man in charge.

Eggleton's best explanation was to lamely suggest that maybe the memo didn't disappear at all: maybe it was never there in the first place. Within weeks, though, a corporal came forward to admit that he had been ordered by his superiors to remove copies of the memo from all of the files and shred them.

With the imbroglio of Somalia fresh in their memories, senior officers determined to start handling this potentially explosive issue with greater tact and maturity.

In July 1999, nearly six years after the events of Medak Pocket, the chief of defence staff, General Maurice Baril, declared that the Canadian Forces had "a moral obligation and a legal obligation" to help people who might have returned sick from CF missions. He announced a board of inquiry to look into "allegations that soldiers serving with the Canadian contingent United Nations Protection Force and assigned to an area commonly known as Sector South from 1993 to 1995 were exposed to harmful contaminants." The inquiry was to be led by Colonel Howie Marsh, who was immediately dismissed because of a conflict of interest. (It was to Marsh that Calvin had complained about the missing memos.) The task went to Joe Sharpe. At the same time, the provost marshal's office launched an independent criminal investigation into the possibility that in destroying Dr. Smith's memo, someone had broken the law by tampering with personnel files.

In an ironic juxtaposition, the monthly defence community newsletter, the *Maple Leaf,* listed a 1–800 number for soldiers who served in Croatia from 1993 to 1995 who might want to talk about their health status. Just below it was a 1–888 number for anyone who might be able to assist the criminal inquiry with information about the alleged shredding of documents in medical files.

* * *

In the first week of August 1999, Matt Stopford was nearly crippled by his illness, and confined to his home in Peterborough, Ontario, when a representative of the Department of National Defence showed up unannounced at his door. If Stopford hoped the visitor was there to offer some long-awaited assistance, he was disappointed. But what he was told by the representative was shocking.

The official had come to hand-deliver a letter from the provost marshal's office to inform him of a bizarre development in his case. Investigators had reason to believe Stopford had been poisoned by his own men while in Croatia. The letter stated that while they were building that contentious bunker in the heat and the danger, several of the men under his command had snapped and tried to either kill or disable him. They allegedly poisoned his food and his coffee.

For Stopford, the allegation was as surreal as this turn of events was ironic. After six years of deteriorating health, during which he was ignored and belittled by the government, he was now being advised that the DND was concerned about his well-being. The letter advised him to consult his doctor in the light of this new information. Stopford was stunned.

What the provost marshal, Brigadier General Patricia Samson, claimed to have heard from the members of Delta Company was that soldiers, fearing Stopford was endangering them through his aggressive leadership style, had turned on him. This was the mutiny that Mike Brown says he reported to Calvin.

Several soldiers swore affidavits stating that they had heard rumours about plans to put naptha in Stopford's coffee and battery acid in his food in order to put him out of action. The provost marshal also had at least one affidavit from a soldier who said he had personally laced the warrant officer's morning brew with Visine and naptha. The soldiers had remembered hearing that the substance would cause severe diarrhea. This might slow the hard-driving NCO down for a few rounds.

The significance of the theory was hard to miss: Stopford's condition, the most public and well documented on the record, wasn't caused by the general circumstances of the mission in Croatia; it was the result of a malicious act by particular individuals. If it was true, it meant there would be no institutional accountability.

The alleged poisoning became the subject of a criminal investigation by the DND. Patricia Samson asked Stopford not to talk to the media. After a week of silence, Stopford began to suspect that this might well be just an imaginative and cynical way to shut him up. He called in the reporters. "Instead of bringing a doctor or psychologist or somebody to come down and actually test me, they sent a cop who wanted names," Stopford told reporters.

Brigadier General Samson then upped the ante, announcing publicly that she had strong reasons to believe that both Matt Stopford and Geoff Crossman, the man who drove with the Grim Reaper, had been systematically poisoned with battery acid and naptha.

It would be hard to imagine someone failing to notice the powerful taste and smell of such unsubtle ingredients, but the provost marshal was sticking to the story. Crossman too had developed illnesses, but there were a dozen possible reasons for them, all related to his harrowing tour in Croatia. Stopford said he simply didn't believe his men would poison him. Everyone conceded that Stopford had been a slave-driver but—murder him? It was beginning to look like a tactic to derail the Sharpe inquiry before it even started.

But Mike Brown knew different. He watched the whole saga unfold in the news, not sure what he should do. Kelly Brett got in touch to suggest that they call a news conference and tell the media what they knew. According to Brown, Brett wanted to set the record straight: he could corroborate the charges of attempted poisoning but he wanted to make it clear that the poison could not possibly be the cause of all the illnesses. Brett told Brown he suspected the provost marshal was attempting to sideline the new inquiry.

Brown was highly skeptical of the plan to go public: he had no faith in the DND to tell the truth but he didn't trust the media to get it right, either. Brown says he called Joe Sharpe and told him what Brett was contemplating. Sharpe was able to persuade Brett that the best place to reveal the whole story was before the commission of inquiry.

Sharpe was worried that the poisoning charges were designed to derail his inquiry. He had just been introduced to the members of his inquiry board and they were sitting down together in Ottawa for the first time. There was a television set flickering quietly in the background. Then someone noted the familiar image of Matt Stopford on the screen. They jumped for the volume control as Patricia Samson announced that Stopford may have been poisoned. Joe Sharpe couldn't believe what he was hearing. "I was so angry I couldn't talk, quite frankly, because I saw it as a clear attempt not to sabotage the board but to go public and say, 'We know what happened, it's nothing to do with the environment, it's all to do with stuff inside the unit.'"

Sharpe almost resigned on the spot, but he didn't. "To this day, I still do not understand the coincidence of the timing" of the provost marshal's investigation. He lashed out at Samson, arguing that her allegations were unfounded. He, in turn, was reprimanded for questioning the police. Sharpe's inquiry began under a cloud.

Whether or not it was part of a conscious strategy, his board was working amid the turmoil created by two criminal investigations (for shredding medical records and for trying to poison

Stopford), and a police inquiry to determine why senior officials had ignored the 1998 letter from Calvin warning of the health problems his troops were experiencing. A retired Mountie was investigating the possibility that there was a conspiracy to cover up evidence of wrongdoing.

And Sharpe had another problem. By the time he started his work the embittered soldiers who had served in Croatia had lost all faith in anyone associated with defence headquarters, including him. The hostility was palpable as Sharpe's team began to contact soldiers to persuade them to testify. Dan Drew, who had survived repeated attempts to have him drummed out of the forces, turned up in a front-page national newspaper article declaring that the exercise was futile. There was only one problem—that the soldiers had been treated "like crap" in an effort to save money. There was nothing to investigate.

But Major Drew eventually appeared before the board, along with dozens of other witnesses. And gradually the first complete picture of what happened during the six-year-old mission started taking shape. Transcripts of the testimonies are highly censored and dozens of the witness statements were never released, but what is on the record paints an extraordinary tale.

Chris Byrne came with a prepared text, which he called "the final chapter." It was an angry presentation, full of the vitriol he had built up over years: "If I sound bitter in this statement it is because I am," he said. Byrne described the seven days that he and Delta Company spent building a bunker while under continuous artillery bombardment. Byrne accused Colonel Calvin and Major Drew of leading them into a war when they had only signed on as peacekeepers. They had no artillery and no way to fight back. "We were not peacekeepers. We were not soldiers. We were nothing over there. We weren't there to establish peace because there was no peace to begin with," he said.

Byrne warned the board that they would never hear from the soldiers with the most serious complaints. "They are caught in a system that will punish them if they show fault with the system." Byrne told the board how his own mental health had deteriorated after his return. He was still under treatment by a therapist for depression and chronic sadness.

That any of the soldiers showed up at all was in large part because of the presence on the inquiry board of a man they knew and trusted, Mike Spellen. He had his enemies in the rank and file, but he had been through it all with them, the hard days under siege in the bunker, the grim search for victims of atrocities. Spellen had been out of the forces almost since Medak and his own life was a mess. He jumped at the chance to be part of the board. Some suggested he had a conflict of interest. But Joe Sharpe knew that Spellen was often the sole reason that key witnesses appeared.

In the course of the nine-month hearing, as Sharpe and his team crossed the country, the soldiers told their stories. They brought their medical documents, their snaphots and their maps. Mike McCarthy told of the broken morale of the battalion, particularly among the reservists. He refused to blame the young men and women for being bitter. "In my thirty-two years I hope I never have to see and do things that I did down there again, and I hope that my soldiers (never) have to. I had young soldiers, very, very young, grow up very, very quickly in Sector South."

McCarthy agreed with the concerns expressed about the red soil and the possibility that they'd been handling contaminated material. "Did I see guys with their T-shirts off, sweating in forty-degree heat with this red stuff all over their bodies? Yes, I did. I saw it all. And was I concerned about issues of [contamination]? No, I wasn't. I was more concerned whether or not they were going to be alive the next day."

On September 16, 1999—the sixth anniversary of the final firefight in Medak—Jim Calvin presented his side of the story. He lambasted the Canadian Forces for failing to take care of his troops after he brought them back safely. He had lost two men to vehicle accidents and four others had been injured in the course of their time there. He accomplished a successful mission and the United Nations had recognized the accomplishment with a rare citation. Only Canada had failed the soldiers. Our own government and its DND had let them down. "*Betrayed* is too strong a word," Calvin told the board, but betrayal was what he had in mind.

Dr. Kelly Brett's testimony was the most controversial. In an echo of what Matt Stopford had heard from the provost marshal's office, Dr. Brett told stories he had heard "of graves being dug for a couple of guys in the senior ranks of the company. Guys carrying an extra couple of rounds in their pockets in case they got a chance to use them. There was a cowboy mentality out there and there was a reckless treatment of the soldiers."

But Dr. Brett blamed health problems on burnout, not toxic soil or attempted poisonings. The illnesses, he said, were the result of unreasonable exposure to danger, which in turn was the result of bad leadership. The grind of a death-defying mission for which they were not well prepared and the later indifference of their senior officers and their country were key factors in the widespread problems of the soldiers, he said. Many of the problems, from constipation to sleeplessness and impotence, were psychosomatic. "I'm not saying that there's a bunch of people out there who don't have medical problems," Brett testified. "I'm just telling you . . . that someone is attempting to treat [some conditions] as medical problems, and they're not."

Steve Atkins, the former medic for Delta Company, who had reported to Kelly Brett, brought another litany of charges, blistering Calvin and Drew for incompetence and recklessness. Atkins's testimony set off a number of new NIS investigations into the possibility that Calvin and Drew had been criminally negligent. Atkins and Brett both claimed they had raised these issues with Calvin while they were still in Croatia, but their concerns had fallen on deaf ears. Padre Mike Brown made many of the same allegations, but his testimony was later deleted from the inquiry's web site. Joe Sharpe says the DND probably did this because Brown's testimony was too controversial.

After the highly critical testimony of Brett, Brown and Atkins, Calvin was called to respond to their charges. The colonel was visibly shaken as he told the board that he had, at the time, taken account of the complaints of the doctors and of Padre Brown. But in the end, he had a job to do. The battalion had to be aggressive, it had to take risks, and he had to keep pushing the soldiers.

They were never cowboys, said Calvin. But if he hadn't ordered them into the midst of battle, their operation would have failed; as General Cot had told him, the entire UNPROFOR mission had been hanging in the balance at the time. Calvin never regretted his actions in the field, and it was only in later years that he learned how much the soldiers had come to resent him.

The most highly anticipated testimony was from Matt Stopford, the man whose obvious deterioration had launched the inquiry. "I am definitely disappointed in this puzzle palace," Stopford began, perhaps summing up what a lot of soldiers had come to think about the department they worked in. Stopford outlined the exasperating efforts he'd made to get some kind of compensation. "I stand before you today as one of the many sick soldiers that now reside across Canada pleading for a chance to testify and hopefully be looked after by the government they have shown tremendous loyalty to."

Stopford dismissed attempts to blame Calvin for the problems in the aftermath of the mission. Witch-hunting was pointless. There was only one reality that mattered: the soldiers were sent to do a job and had come back damaged by the experience; it was the responsibility of the government that sent them there to help them.

"Did we build a bunker with tainted dirt? Sure we did. But it was to save us from certain death from indirect fire. No one will dispute the fact that Medak was hell, or maybe our water was bad or burning carcasses with no place to wash is unhealthy or living in an area filled with death and destruction and vermin is bad for you."

But that's what soldiers do.

***

The board members were astonished by the intensity of anger. "We were the first people that they'd seen that they could yell at," says Sharpe, but the grief and animosity went well beyond yelling.

This was a giant *cri de coeur*. The board had issued a general call for witnesses to talk about the Croatian mission. But, repeatedly, they heard personal stories of post-mission illnesses. No one had done any prior health survey. How could they? Sharpe discovered that the DND didn't even have a complete list of all the people who had served in Croatia. Large numbers of reservists, who were possibly sick and needed help, weren't included in the records that remained at CF headquarters. The board of inquiry began a search for old soil samples that might have been sent from the red dirt at the Obravac aluminum smelter. The board also solicited its own tests of the Croatian soil and environment. The board actually managed to find one of the old samples, but all the test results were inconclusive. Sharpe broadened the scope of his commission and interviewed a cross-section of medical professionals, including specialists in the relatively new field of post-traumatic stress disorder.

In the end, the commission was unable to find evidence that the illnesses were caused by environmental factors. Toxic materials couldn't be ruled out, but because so much time had gone by it was impossible to perform the scientific tests that would provide irrefutable proof one way or the other. "We concluded that primarily they were probably the result of psychological injury, stress, operational stress injury. Post-traumatic stress disorder."

Sharpe attributed the widespread stress to a number of factors. Certainly, the difficult conditions in Croatia were number one. But he concluded that the way the soldiers were treated when they came home was also a major aggravating factor.

Sharpe believes some senior members of the DND made a conscious decision to conceal what had happened at Medak, out of fear of political fallout. One dead teenager in Somalia had shaken the defence establishment to its foundations.

Reports of twenty-seven dead Croats—in Canada, a country with a large Croatian population—was potentially too sensational to entrust to a scandal-mongering public. "I believe there was a conscious choice in the senior leadership in the department to sacrifice the long-term well-being in this group of people for the sake of the reputation and the image of the Canadian Forces at the time," he says. Whatever legitimate concerns there might have been about the image of the Canadians, the damage to the soldiers wasn't worth the benefits achieved by a cover-up.

Before the ink was dry on his inquiry report, Sharpe was assigned to another investigation. The chief of the defence staff wanted to know, after all the charges levelled at Calvin, Drew and other officers, whether Calvin really was that big a flop as a leader.

The same stories resurfaced: the Delta Company smoker, the heavy drinking, Dangerous Dan Drew's pistol shot that echoed for a decade, and the Woolley–Van Dongen fight. And another story came to light, that of a cook with Delta Company, who cut his wrists and then deliberately burned his hands on his stove, apparently so he would be evacuated out of the region.

Steve Atkins and Mike Brown both claimed they heard Dan Drew threaten to kill the cook, if he hadn't already done himself in. Drew says it was just a bit of tough love, crudely designed to bring the man to his senses. These charges were also investigated.

Drew and Calvin braced themselves for the worst. But Sharpe and his team decided it was time to end all the pointless witch hunts, which Sharpe concluded were only an effort to find a scape-goat. They concluded in a report to the head of the Canadian military that they could find nothing wrong with the way Calvin and Drew had exercised their authority. For the first time since they returned home from Europe, the two officers felt vindicated. The review group said their leadership was outstanding.

But Dan Drew's problems didn't end. Just weeks after Sharpe's special review group told headquarters that it would be difficult to find a more competent officer than Dan Drew, the major received a letter from headquarters stating he was being tossed out of the military, in a punitive release, within ten days. Drew was devastated.

A group of strong-willed officers, led by Joe Sharpe, came to his rescue, and the dismissal order was rescinded just before the deadline. But Dan Drew's morale was shattered.

* * *

Matt Stopford wasn't happy with Sharpe's findings. He strongly doubted that his health problems could all be explained by stress, but apparently that was the closest he was going to get to an official diagnosis.

The DND came through with a full pension. But Stopford concluded that if the DND was taking the position that his men had tried to poison him, they'd have to deal with the possibility that senior people knew about the plot, but failed to warn him. Kelly Brett says he told Jim Calvin in 1993, when they were still in Medak. Jim Calvin says he was never told. The military investigation into the alleged poisoning eventually ended—almost a year later—with no charges.

Inspector Russ Grabb of the RCMP said at least six soldiers and possibly as many as twelve had plotted to kill members of Delta Company but, according to those who saw soldiers' affadavits, only one person actually admitted to putting substances into anyone's coffee—a few drops of Visine. Investigators say the charges were dropped because the case was beyond the statute of limitations and because no one could prove that Matt Stopford, or anyone else, actually ingested any toxic substances. The military police say they considered charges of mutiny but abandoned the idea. Civilian police also considered pressing charges but didn't, citing a lack of evidence. Matt Stopford didn't drop it: he launched a $7.5 million civil suit against the DND claiming negligence, incompetence and breach of duty for not informing him, years earlier, that he had been poisoned.

In a cruel twist, the only person punished was Dr. Eric Smith, whose cautionary memos had been shredded in the first place. Dr. Smith was court-martialled for giving a soldier sick leave just after he bought a second-hand canoe from him. Smith told reporters it was punishment for whistle-blowing. He left the Canadian Forces a bitter man.

The Somalia inquiry ended without ever reaching a final conclusion on overall culpability, beyond that of two soldiers who were convicted for murder in the torture-death of Shidane Arone. The Chrétien government abruptly pulled the plug on the commission in 1997.

Jim Calvin was a sad and broken soldier by the time the new millennium rolled around. He had eventually become a strong crusader for his ailing soldiers. Caught between the vilification by his bitter subordinates and the deafening silence in Ottawa when he tried to present the case for them, Calvin retired. He retreated to his home on Wolfe Island, not far from Kingston. He has issued a standing invitation to any of his former soldiers to come by to visit, and to stir the ghosts of Medak Pocket. He won't say how many have done so.

* * *

Nine years, several criminal inquiries, a major commission costing millions of dollars and several deaths later, the Second Battalion of the PPCLI finally got its citation. Tony Spiess didn't sleep the night before he was to fly to Winnipeg for the big day. He was up at 4:30 A.M., just thinking about it. Wanting to see his old friends. Fearful that some might not come. Some might have changed.

Rod Dearing packed the car in Edmonton and headed to Winnipeg with his wife and a few friends. Other soldiers organized car pools and rented minivans from all over the country. Shawn McKinstry got cold feet at the last moment. He worried it would all be too emotional. But his new wife told him he was going to attend even if she had to drive him there herself. McKinstry got on the plane.

They arrived from all over Canada on a frosty Winnipeg morning. It was December 1, 2002, nine years after the events of

Medak Pocket. The soldiers were about to get the official recognition that had been deferred for almost a decade: a special Governor General's citation for their service. Finally their community, the Canadian people, were to formally acknowledge not just that they had served, but that they had served well.

In the cold corridors of the Winnipeg stadium, the soldiers milled about. It was 8 A.M. and most of them had been up late. For many it was a first reunion in nine years and they had closed a number of Winnipeg bars. They had crawled back to hotel rooms, exchanging scraps of information about the living and the dead, reliving the memories of a few months in another time that had changed all of their lives.

The soldiers swapped tales all night, embellishing reality as they went along, crafting the legends, the military mystique that inspires ordinary men and women to continue serving and sacrificing in extraordinary circumstances. Ideally, military mythology is anchored in a context of fact based on careful record-keeping and retroactive analysis. But for the soldiers who served in Medak Pocket, few detailed or reliable records have survived and there has been no military analysis. For them, their memories will have to serve as history.

It was a mishmash of units that assembled in the Winnipeg stadium that morning. Sixty-six in all—but they had once, briefly, been a single machine. Here were the Rocky Mountain Rangers, the Seaforth Highlanders of Canada, the Royal Winnipeg Rifles, the Lanark and Renfrew Scottish Regiment, the Eighth Canadian Hussars, the West Nova Scotia Regiment and the Thirty-sixth (Newfoundland) Service Battalion. And there were the regular soldiers of the Princess Patricia's Canadian Light Infantry, both retired and serving. The battle group that had found itself in the middle of a nasty little war, fought by people they didn't know over issues lost in history, were once again together. This time they knew where they were and why.

Nearly three hundred soldiers lined up in a long column, and at the head of them was Jim Calvin, a nervous bundle of emotions. Calvin was back in uniform, ready to lead a parade that should have happened nine years earlier. It was only happening now in response to enormous internal and external pressure on the Canadian Forces, and perhaps because the brass had learned a few hard lessons from peacekeeping in the 1990s.

As the accounts of illness and personal disaster among the Medak soldiers emerged, they caused a groundswell of indignation. It started after a dramatic account in the *Ottawa Citizen* of "Canada's Secret Battle." Reporters started asking questions. The Sharpe commission had been covered from coast to coast. The word was out.

The Medak Guard, as the new parade formation was called, would get a unit commendation "for courageous and professional execution of duty" during the Medak Pocket operation. The citation, to be delivered by Governor General Adrienne Clarkson, read, "Under conditions of extreme peril and hazard, facing enemy artillery, small arms and heavy machine-gun fire as well as anti-tank and anti-personnel mines, the members of the 2PPCLI battle group held their ground and drove the Croat forces back."

There was no mention of the twenty-seven Croats who might have been killed by the Canadians. The Croatian defense department denied there had even been a fight, let alone casualties, insisting never so much as a shot was fired. Oddly, in view of that strenuous denial, an officially inspired magazine account published in Croatia would criticize Canada for honouring a peacekeeping mission that had caused the deaths of people in the country they were supposed to be protecting. But Croatian disclaimers weren't going to dampen the spirits of those in Winnipeg who had been denied this moment for too long.

Jim Calvin led the soldiers he hadn't seen in years as they marched into the open stadium while a military band played "The Maple Leaf Forever." Soldiers, long out of the military, seemed awkward and out of step. Many were obviously struggling to suppress deep emotions. The early morning audience in the bleachers cheered, and an honour guard of Royal Canadian Mounted Police in full dress uniform stood at attention.

Governor General Clarkson inspected the ranks of soldiers and made the presentation; her words would live in their hearts long after that emotional day. "The simple fact remains that very few of us Canadians knew what you did in 1993. Your actions were nothing less than heroic. And yet your country did not recognize you at the time."

It was as close to an admission of neglect as any troops could get in an official declaration. But the head of the army, Lieutenant General Mike Jeffery, also surprised them with a moment of candour: "These soldiers returned home from their war to find a nation absorbed in other problems, unaware of their sacrifices and ill prepared to support them in their time of need. This made the transition back to peace very difficult and even today, many suffer in silence." General Jeffery 's words were as eloquent as they were seriously overdue.

Matt Stopford and several hundred others from the original battle group didn't make it to the parade. Some were too sick to be there, others were homeless or isolated and didn't hear about it. Even if the Canadian Forces had wanted to invite them all individually, they could not have, because they still didn't have the names of many of the soldiers who had served in the unit. And because the soldiers had to pay their own way, many simply couldn't afford to be there.

The moment was all it could be for those who made it. It was too little, but it was not too late.

"REAL MEN DON'T DO MOOTWA"

The Pentagon now termed the range of postconflict activities as "military operations other than war" referred to as mootwa. Gen. John Shalikashvili, chairman of the Joint Chiefs of Staff from 1993 to 1997, is said to have declared "Real men don't do mootwa."

—James Traub, "Making Sense of the Mission," an investigation into the attitude toward peacekeeping within the United States military, *The New York Times Magazine*, April 11, 2004

What monsters have we seen?
—Major Dan Drew, on his experiences as a peacekeeper

WE CAME AROUND a badly graded turn in the road and there it was: a tiny shrine, almost invisible, tucked in among tangled weeds and shrubbery on the side of the highway. I could see how the collision had been possible on this narrow strip of road that slaloms its way around the Velebit Mountains, especially since the driver was trying to avoid being shelled. It's dangerous to stop here even in peacetime, but we found a suitable place, probably where the rescue team parked, almost a decade ago.

The memorial is a small concrete cairn without the flowers and totems that usually festoon roadside commemorations to the victims of car accidents. I wondered how Tyrone Green, who was driving us today, had even spotted it. Captain Jim Decoste's name is inscribed on the bronze plaque above a discreet white maple leaf. A little railing surrounds the cairn with a bolder red maple leaf upon it. This is the place where Decoste died, and where two other soldiers were badly injured.

Now, in September 2002, almost exactly nine years after the accident and the events of Medak Pocket, we stood on the side of the highway, gazing at this incongruous memento of a Canadian soldier's life and death here in the middle of Croatia. Tyrone Green and Mike Spellen had returned to the country with me as my guides; we were making a documentary about the Second Battalion of the Princess Patricia's Canadian Light Infantry and its experiences in Medak.

Mike Spellen had returned to public service after his time on the Sharpe commission. He was now employed by the DND in Winnipeg, where he was trying to cope with an epidemic of post-traumatic stress disorder in the Canadian Forces. Tyrone Green had ended up at the opposite end of the spectrum, work-ing in the recruitment centre for the Canadian Forces in Vancouver. Their work had a perfect, if disturbing, symmetry: while Spellen dealt with the fallout of soldiers who had left the Forces, sick and broken, Green was responsible for finding more people who wanted to experience life as a soldier.

Spellen had a personal mission on this journey: he wanted to find the memorial to Decoste and bear witness to the place where his colleague had been killed. For Spellen the cairn was more than just a memorial to one man: it symbolized the lost youth and the shattered psyches of the hundreds of young sol-diers who had served here on the Medak mission.

Spellen was visibly overcome with emotion as he stood on the side of the road. It was not the first time on this trip that his memories had been too much for him. Tyrone Green, on the other hand, had seemed imperturbable until now. But I could see that he too was deeply affected by this reminder of a fallen comrade and his own mortality. Spellen and Green took photos and shared their grief while Croats sped by in their Mercedeses and Fiats, going about their daily business or heading out for the last beach days of autumn. They seemed only mildly curious about our little scene. After all, there are so many reminders of death in the country.

***

We drove the back roads of the Lika Highlands for days, looking for the remnants of the small villages and hamlets that the Canadian soldiers had risked their lives to protect. The maze of tractor trails and narrow lanes that Spellen and Green had become so familiar with in September of 1993 are now just a jungle of alders and vines, which in some places choke the road so completely that we had to back the car up to get untangled. People had lived in this area for centuries—tilled the land, bred their cattle and fought their enemies: the Vlachs, the Turks, the Chetniks, the Ustashe—but in times of war they had always stayed put, or if driven out had always returned to live here again. Not this time. There is no sign of human existence here now—no houses left intact, no cars, no people. The vegetation is slowly reclaiming hundreds of years of farm life.

Here and there a little scrap of humanity poked up through the shrubbery—a wheelbarrow or a rusted tractor part—and we investigated like anthropologists on a quest for a lost civilization, which in a sense we were. All of us should have known better than to stomp around in these weeds—especially the soldiers, Green and Spellen: land mines are still a very real danger. But such was our compulsion to find something human here that we disregarded our safety. In the end, we found that ethnic cleansing is a very effective exercise. No Serbs had come back to rebuild their lives in Medak. But no Croats could take over the farms either: the fields and woods are strewn with booby traps, the watersheds are poisoned, the ghosts of Medak's massacres haunt every nook and cranny.

Sveti Rok, once Camp Kananakis—the base for the Princess Patricias and the subsequent peacekeeping units for the area—was just a pile of rubble and broken, abandoned buildings, long ago looted of anything valuable. Around the camp, a small scattering of homesteads are still inhabited, almost all by Croats, although a few Serbs are living there too. We spotted a man walking past the compound and ran to meet him: a sign of life in a post-holocaust landscape. He was a shepherd, a Croat, out with his animals. He remembered when the peacekeepers were here. He remembered when all the Serbs were forced to leave. He regretted that: he lost many friends. He declared that all the leaders—Serb and Croat—should go to The Hague and be prosecuted for mass murder. The life he enjoyed before Croatia was "liberated" is gone.

An old woman was out hanging her wash in one of the half-destroyed houses that we had thought were all deserted. When I approached her to talk, I could see she wasn't old at all, at least in years. But what she had suffered had taken its toll: her dark eyes were frightened, her skin raw and ruddy and her girth a testimony to bad, starchy food. She was a Serb from Medak, though not from this village. She had ended up here after a long harrowing voyage through displaced persons camps and she was alone. She declined to tell us much more of her story. God only knew who we really were, or what further hardship we might still inflict on her.

Medak House still has its sandbags and the floors are scattered with the detritus of the peacekeeping efforts. Tyrone Green found the "out" basket he once used to file notes and reports before sending them off to company headquarters. But Medak House is no longer livable. There's no roof. Giant gaping holes allow the light and the rain to pour in on what was once the soldiers' sleeping quarters, where they were bunking on September ninth when the first shells landed. What had been the point of their efforts? What did anyone have to show for their sacrifice? Croatia has become an almost pure Croat state, but of what use is Medak Pocket, even for the Croats?

* * *

In September 2002, as Spellen and Green travelled through their old haunts, the government of Croatia nearly collapsed. The International Criminal Tribunal for War Crimes in the Former Yugoslavia charged General Janko Bobetko with crimes against humanity for his command role in the destruction of the Medak Pocket. According to the indictment, General Bobetko was the man in charge when Croatian forces attacked Medak and murdered at least one hundred Serbian civilians.

Croatia had a liberal, almost progressive government in 2002, with Stipe Mesic, the man who was forced from office by Franjo Tudjman, as the country's president. The fledgling republic was well on its way to becoming a member of the European Union and it had already won respect and recognition, however prematurely, as a modern state.

The Sabor, under the new regime, had promised full co-operation with The Hague and had agreed to hand over anyone the war crimes prosecutor indicted. That had been easy in the case of Rahim Ademi, the pudgy, dishevelled general that Michel Maisonneuve had found so annoying. Ademi is actually an Albanian who managed to climb to the top in the Yugoslav National Army and had miraculously clung to his position in the Croatian army. He was the first to be charged for his role in the events in Medak and, with few friends in high places to protect him, Ademi simply got on a plane and surrendered himself in the Netherlands. But Bobetko was a different kettle of fish: a war hero who had fought with the Partisans and then masterminded (with a lot of unacknowledged assistance from the United States) the decisive Operation Storm. Bobetko embodied Croatia's success as a nation—a founding father of the national dream. When the Croatian leadership suggested it would have to comply with the indictment or face international sanctions, the fragile coalition that had been elected in the wake of Tudjman's death teetered on the brink of collapse.

It was an odd coincidence that we were travelling in Croatia at that time, looking for the scraps and memories of the same events for which Bobetko was now suddenly indicted. Nine years had passed without any acknowledgement of the Medak operation's darker side, but now the country struggled to make sense of this stain on its national history.

After the Second World War, German citizens had been forced to march through the Nazi death camps to see what fascism had wrought, and the perpetrators of German war crimes had been tried at Nuremberg within months of the war's end. But nothing like that occurred in the former Yugoslavia. The wheels of justice turned slowly at The Hague; the citizens of the various republics had little compulsion to confront what had been done in their name during their wars of liberation.

In deciding to reject the indictment, the Croatian government gave the lame excuse that The Hague had not properly filed its paperwork. But the Sabor couldn't deny the events of Medak Pocket themselves. After all, there was incontrovertible evidence: from Rudy Bajema in his lookout post to Steve Marissink of the RCMP and his forensics, the crimes of Medak Pocket were well documented. It was one of the clearest cases The Hague had of the ethnic cleansing operations in Croatia. The Hague prosecutors had interviewed a number of the Canadians, including Jim Calvin.

We watched the news each evening on the hotel's communal television, and our translator, Natasa Barac, explained the latest developments. Croatian TV talk shows roiled with debates and interviews with experts, all concluding that Croats should refuse to turn over their famous general. Other guests in the hotel never asked why we were so interested in the minutiae of the case. The Croats in the room could not know that the events for which their war hero was indicted had so profoundly affected the lives of hundreds of Canadians, whose job it was to protect the Serbs of Medak from Bobetko's campaign.

Bobetko had more or less done himself in. *All My Battles* gives a glowing account of himself and his command role in the Medak operation; the book became exhibit number one in The

Hague. Bobetko describes how the operation was executed, names the generals who took part, and brags that it took only four hours to conduct his brilliant attack. He doesn't mention phase two of the action: the ethnic cleansing operation meant to ensure that Serbs never lived in Medak Pocket again. He also neglects to tell his readers that many of the shells his forces lobbed were not aimed at Serbs at all but at the UN soldiers who were trying to separate the two sides. And he says not a word about the fifteen hours the Princess Patricias spent in an all-out gun battle with Croatian forces, some of whom almost certainly died in the fighting. But then, neither does the Canadian government account for it.

Natasa Barac is a journalist based in Zagreb. She has little sympathy for Bobetko or for the ultra-nationalists who supported him. Tall and striking, she is the rarest of articles in the country — a Jew whose family survived the horrors of the Ustashe. Barac was no friend of nationalism and yet she understood the importance of the war and the fight for independence from the rabid project for Greater Serbia. And though a less fanatical government than Tudjman's would perhaps have tried to keep the level of violence low and would certainly have not been distracted by the doomed project to partition Bosnia, Barac believes the war was inevitable and necessary. The Serbs had taken Croatian territory illegally and she had resented the international community's refusal to countenance the Croats taking the Serbian-held area back by force. But when she learned about the ethnic cleansing phase of the Medak operation, she was appalled and came to support The Hague tribunal's indictment of Bobetko.

Barac shared the view of most in Croatia — that during the war, UNPROFOR had done little except freeze the status quo in favour of the Serbian aggressors. What surprised her about Mike Spellen and Tyrone Green was that these Canadian soldiers had become a part of her country's history without anyone hearing of it. Barac had thought the Canadians were like all the other peacekeepers and internationals: cynical do-nothings who had only made matters worse. She had never heard of the battle that Rod Dearing had led, nor of the shelling of Medak House that

Tyrone Green's platoon had endured. In fact, she doubted that the stories were true. If these things had occurred, why hadn't the UN made a big stink? Why were there no formal complaints from the Canadian government? Why was there no response from her government?

Barac couldn't doubt, however, how deeply the Canadians seemed to have been affected by the events of Medak Pocket, judging by the stories that Spellen and Green told her: lives destroyed, suicides, marriages broken. "I had no idea how far the destruction of this war had reached," she tearily told me one day. "People that aren't even Croats suffered so much."

Javor Pobric was even more skeptical. Pobric was our driver and had been my guide in the Balkans for many years. He is Bosnian, but a Serb on his father's side, though he resents the national distinction since it goes against everything he fought for in the war—a multi-ethnic Yugoslavia. Pobric defended Bosnia against the Serbian forces and he has numerous war wounds to show for it. He had been unimpressed by the UN peacekeepers in both Croatia and Bosnia and he couldn't understand what Spellen and Green were all about. If the peacekeepers had known what was going on in the Pocket, why didn't they act sooner? They had weapons; they had training; they had a moral obligation. Why did they wait until after the ethnic cleansing was over?

And as we toured the back roads of Croatia with the former Princess Patricias, Pobric had another, even more disturbing question: Did the Canadians really understand what was going on in Medak Pocket? He pointed out that some of the wrecked farmhouses still had communications wires attached to them that were probably used for military intelligence. Were these victims really so innocent?

***

For all its shoddy renovations and its notorious history, the venerable Esplanade Hotel in Zagreb remains a place of decadent comfort. An air of faded Austro-Hungarian excess still clings to the art deco lobby and mingles with the attitude of indifference toward the clientele that is a carry-over from Communist Yugoslavia. The hotel staff have the world-weariness of men and women who have seen so much that nothing can surprise them any more. They never bustle or hustle, as they do in the modern American-style hotels that have now sprung up in Croatia's capital. With a heavy sigh, the waiter tells me stories of how they couldn't get caviar or quail during the war and how they had to smuggle in the smoked salmon. It takes a moment to realize that the war years he speaks of are the 1990s.

In the evening, the hotel's grand old ballroom is occasionally opened to young Zagrebians—dressed up like Viennese aristocrats—who playact the fancy dances and dinners of the Hapsburg era and fantasize about a time of stability that probably never existed. Zagreb's railroad station is just across the plaza from the hotel; the Esplanade once provided accommodations for passengers of the Orient Express. Weary travellers might have thought for a moment that they had arrived in Vienna, so similar is the architecture and so Austrian the feel of the place, until they realized they were in a city that has aspired to be Vienna but never quite made it.

"Welcome back to Zagreb, Madame. So good to have our Canadian visitors return." The sentiment is sincere, but the words are loaded. The Esplanade became action central for the elite of repatriated Croatian-Canadians who raised money for the cause and lured emigrant businessmen back to help divide up the spoils of the post-Communist economy.

For a while, the nostalgic atmosphere of imperial twilight in an eighty-year-old hotel and in Zagreb itself was replaced by a fresh wind of change as these New World Croats returned with visions of nation-building. An Air Canada office and the Canadian embassy were installed on the mezzanine level of the hotel and a Croatian-Canadian tycoon later built a sprawling underground shopping mall beneath the adjoining plaza, complete with a bowling alley featuring pictures of Mounties on the walls and a cramped, smoky little bar called the Canadian Club that serves, of course, Canadian rye whisky.

But for all their enthusiasm for the legitimate project of an independent Croatia—and the money they brought to the cause—they couldn't prevent the country from descending into war. In fact, they were the chief contributors to that development. Serbian aggression certainly was the catalyst but the Croats did little to dispel the fears of Serbs inside Croatia who believed they would be killed. And Franjo Tudjman became the willing agent of an over-zealous diaspora in a war that left 11,000 dead and 3,000 missing in Croatia, along with several hundred thousand people displaced. And in an ironic twist the returning exiles had turned their military zeal against their fellow Canadians who had come to help them find peace. The strongest show of force Canadian soldiers have confronted since the Korean War was backed by an immigrant population that had fled to Canada a generation before to escape just the kind of tyranny that the Balkan wars produced.

* * *

Far from the decadence of the Esplanade is the rambling park-like Mirogoj cemetery in the outskirts of Zagreb. It ranges across a hillside two kilometres northeast of the city centre and is the final resting place for 270,000 Croats of all faiths and denominations. The high, fortress-like walls are covered in deep green ivy and capped by lofty cupolas that punctuate the wall every twenty metres or so. The tombs and vaults inside the wall tell the story of a more tolerant Croatian society—some have Cyrillic inscriptions of Serb Orthodox sentiment, others have the crescent moon of a Muslim grave, while most—and especially the more lavish of the tombstones—reflect the Catholic faith of Croatia's majority. The cemetery bears witness to the old Yugoslavia and its ultimately failed efforts to create a federation that was inclusive of all ethnicities.

The grave rows are densely forested with oak and maple trees, and in much of Mirogoj one can feel completely at peace. But there is one glaring contradiction to the spirit of the place: In a sterile, treeless expanse occupying the far corner are hundreds of graves of young men killed in the Croatian war of independence.

The dates chiselled into the granite of the tombstones range from 1991 to 1995. The vast majority of those buried here are Catholic Croats but there are Muslim and Orthodox graves as well: powerful testimony to the people's belief, in the early days of Croatia's national struggle, that the new state would be for everyone who no longer wanted to live under Belgrade's thumb, not just for Croats. Images of the dead are etched into the shiny black marble facades—boyish, grinning faces, full of mischief and hope, the birth dates betraying the overwhelming youth of these dead men.

There are two much larger monuments in this soldiers' graveyard. One is a giant cross, forged out of brass and encrusted with what appear to be bullets, shells and bombs moulded out of black lead. The other stands in the opposite corner; a cold, art-less tomb of granite and marble, it is inscribed simply "Gojko Susak, 1945–1998," with a quotation from St. Luke: "When ye shall have done all those things which are commanded of you, say, We are unprofitable servants: we have done that which was our duty to do." Susak died young after a long battle with cancer. The tomb tells you nothing about the man who, perhaps more than anyone other than Tudjman, who is also buried in Mirogoj, was central to the success of Croatian nationalism; the man who would do anything in the service of "what was our duty to do" in carving out a Croat state in the former Yugoslavia.

You will learn nothing here about the man who sold pizzas in Ottawa before he became the Prince of Darkness, Croatia's defence minister and the right-hand man of Franjo Tudjman, father of the nation. The U.S. secretary of defence in 1998, William Perry, attended Susak's funeral in Mirogoj Cemetery, where he lauded the Croatian defence minister as a man of integrity and gave a eulogy in which he quoted from Shakespeare: "He was a man. Take him for all in all, we shall not look upon his like again."

* * *

Jim Calvin is still waiting for his day in international court. The Hague investigators have interviewed him about the Medak operation as they gather evidence to show that the ethnic cleansing was systematic, and organized out of Zagreb, principally by Janko Bobetko. But the portly old General Bobetko will never go to The Hague: he passed away not long after the indictment, at the age of eighty-four.

Tudjman, Susak and now Bobetko are deceased, taking with them most of the secrets of Croatia's war. Rahim Ademi was, by most accounts, kept out of the loop on all the planning, but Mirko Norac certainly wasn't. General Norac was responsible for the artillery attack on Medak Pocket, and was convicted in a Croatian court of murdering fifty people in Gospic in one of the few prosecutions of Croats by Croatian courts. While serving his twelve-year sentence, he was also indicted for crimes against humanity by the war crimes court in The Hague, joining Ademi. At the time of writing, the UN is in the process of dismantling the war crimes tribunal while trying to persuade reluctant governments of the former Yugoslavia to pursue the indictments themselves. That seems highly unlikely, given the strong biases of the respective governments.

Calvin passes his time fixing up old cars and working on the municipal council of Wolfe Island. The man who only joined the army in order to get an education is bitter and sad today. During a final interview for this book, Calvin broke down and wept as he discussed his failures: first, his inability to protect the people of Medak Pocket and second, his inability to protect his own soldiers from the fallout of the Medak mission.

Calvin was transferred to a staff position a year after returning from Croatia and he says no one in the battalion had enough knowledge of the events to shield soldiers like Danny Drew from all the inquiries. "They had no one. It just wasn't right . . . I'm so sorry. . . ." Calvin paused, overcome with emotion. "They did everything that was demanded of them.

Everything that any citizen could have asked of their forces. And then the military police with their inquiries . . . all those bastards . . . it was just terrible. And there are people who will never recover from that. It's just . . ." Calvin wiped away tears, before concluding the interview with these plain words: "The Croats never did as much damage to us as our own organization did when we came home."

* * *

Among military personnel, the term "peacekeeping" is rarely used. Peacekeeping is a United Nations word, a euphemism that governments employ to reassure their citizens that the missions on which their soldiers are being sent are not dangerous or life-threatening in any way. Both the Canadian and the American defence departments use the term this way, instead of the more technical and candid "mootwa"—military operations other than war. But even mootwa is misleading, because it too implies there is no war involved. In the 1990s, Canadian soldiers often found that when they deployed on "peacekeeping" missions, they landed in the midst of someone else's ongoing war and were unavoidably engaged in the fighting.

The United States government, under successive administrations, insists that the U.S. military's purpose is "to fight and win wars." Anything else is "mission creep." George W. Bush and the Pentagon have stated that they want to avoid exercises of "nation-building," the effort to put a post-conflict country back together again: a central premise of mootwa, or peacekeeping.

The U.S. military policy of fighting wars but not guarding peace goes a long way to explain why the invasion of Iraq in 2003 was so successful, but the occupation of Iraq in 2004 was a fiasco. Americans are warriors, not peacemakers.

Canada has assigned itself the role of peacemaker: it's in our mythology, our history and our foreign policy, but as a nation we are colossally deluded about what the role really entails. That delusion has meant that Canadian soldiers have repeatedly been sent to face the horrors and violence of wars in foreign countries, and have actively fought in those wars without Canadians ever hearing much about it. The time has undoubtedly come for Canada to figure out what role the Canadian Forces should play in the modern world, but also to acknowledge and understand what the Forces have been doing, on difficult missions their fellow citizens have paid scant attention to since the end of the Cold War.

Real men do mootwa. And they pay dearly for it.

ACKNOWLEDGEMENTS

The story of Medak Pocket began to haunt me many years ago. At various Canadian military events I was covering, or at the base camps of peacekeeping missions, I would hear anecdotes about the mission in Medak Pocket from the soldiers who had lived them; just as often I heard them from someone else, tales passed around like folk legends, which in fact they had become. I found a few probing reports of the Medak mission in newspapers but the stories left me with more questions than answers. It was clear to me that the whole saga needed to be told.

Without the dozens of Canadian soldiers who gave me their first-hand accounts of those days in Croatia in 1993, this book couldn't have been written. Many of our interview sessions were painful and disturbing; I owe an immense debt of gratitude to those who agreed to let me explore their memories and by extension their psyches. These soldiers also shared diaries, letters home and personal photographs, all of which were invaluable. Many soldiers didn't want to talk to me and I completely understood. Many others came forward to share stories that I could not find room for in this account, but I hope one day someone will undertake to create a thorough archive of their oral history. There is appallingly little documentation of the events of Medak Pocket.

My first excursion into the Medak region was to make a CBC television documentary. The producer was Robin Christmas, who did much of the difficult driving. The superlative camera work was by Brian Kelly, one of the best shooters in the business, who has been my companion for many difficult

Balkan excursions. Jay Bertagnolli's sunny personality and dogged determination won the trust of many interview subjects who were crucial to the documentary as well as the book. I also want to thank Jonathan Whitten, executive producer of CBC's *The National*, for giving me the opportunity to make the Medak film despite the very difficult financial times the CBC finds itself in. Also my gratitude goes to the CBC's Pam Clasper, whose incessant digging on the Internet found us just about everything ever written about the Canadian experience of Croatia.

Trying to determine what is the truth in the former Yugoslavia is perhaps the most difficult exercise any journalist could pursue. The treacherous and murky waters of Balkan politics and history require excellent guides and I had some of the best. Enormous thanks to Natasa Barac for her questioning, skeptical mind and her relentless digging for the truth of these events. Javor Pobric has been keeping me honest in the Balkans for many years now and he did not let me down on this excursion. Suzana Vasiljevic is a new guide for me and I hope to do much more work with her. Mladen Mali and Tamara Indik were readily available for several consultations, offering vast knowledge of Croatia and its conflicting political ambitions—as well as its idiosyncrasies. Ivo Goldstein explained the complexities of Croatian history and I thank him for his patience when I couldn't quite understand. Norman Cigar dredged his notes and his memory for some important information; Miran Sopta agreed to talk to me when his instincts told him not to. Mate Mestrovic filled in the blanks that no book or written account has yet provided.

I could never have embarked on a project such as this without the Knezevic family, though regrettably I had only the spirit and not the intellect of Ivo to help me this time. *The Ghosts of Medak Pocket* is dedicated to him. Great thanks to Gordana for always being my backbone and the voice of reason in the midst of the crazy moments; to Boris and Igor for painstakingly translating and interpreting many documents; and to Olga, whose wit and humour keeps me inspired.

Susan Young and Victoria Vasileski managed to penetrate all but inaudible interview tapes, recorded in smoky bars and noisy rooms. I don't know how they did it but I thank them for it. I'd also like to thank Mike Bechthold for the map of Medak Pocket reproduced at the front of this book.

Craig Pyette managed to keep track of me—and the manuscript—as both travelled the world. Scott Sellers is the best in the business at promoting people's books and I know I will be in good hands once this book is published. My biggest thanks go to Anne Collins, the publisher of Random House Canada, without whose untiring support and assistance books like this one would never be written or published. Her ability to make a messy manuscript into a comprehensive narrative is truly awesome.

Don Sedgwick and Shaun Bradley have been there for me every step of the way, providing moral support, business acumen and friendship. My husband, Linden MacIntyre, who provides everything from mugs of tea to brilliant insight, was the essential companion for this project. I couldn't have finished without him.

Finally, I want to thank the Canadian Forces and especially the men and women of Princess Patricia's Canadian Light Infantry. All Canadians owe them a tremendous debt of gratitude for their efforts to protect people in other countries caught up in wars that usually have nothing to do with them—except that we are all part of humanity and worthy of living in security.

SOURCE NOTES

PROLOGUE

The account of the attack of September 9, 1993, from the Canadian soldiers' point of view, comes from original interviews with those who were there and from the transcripts of sworn testimonies from those who participated in the Board of Inquiry into Potential Exposure of Canadian Forces to a Contaminated Environmment, 1999, better known as the Sharpe inquiry.

The brief history of the Krajina and medieval Croatia comes from interviews with the historian Ivo Goldstein, as well from his book, *Croatia, A History.* I also consulted *Croatia: A Nation Forged in War* by Marcus Tanner, and several reference books on the Ottoman and Hapsburg empires.

CHAPTER ONE: HOMELAND CALLING

The source of the historical material in this chapter came from: *Yugoslavia as History: Twice There Was a Country* by John R. Lampe; *The Balkans 1804–1999: Nationalism, War and the Great Powers* by Misha Glenny; *The Serbs: History, Myth and the Destruction of Yugoslavia* by Tim Judah; *Milosevic: A Biography* by Adam Lebor; *The Death of Yugoslavia* by Allan Little and Laura Silber; *Paris 1919: Six Months that Changed the World* by Margaret MacMillan; *Origins of a Catastrophe* by Warren Zimmerman; *Homeland Calling: Exile Patriotism and the Balkan Wars* by Paul Hockenos; *Croatia, A History* by Ivo Goldstein and *Croatia: A Nation Forged in War* by Marcus Tanner.

Additional historical material came from the on-line archive called The Pavelic Papers, which contains a wealth of translated douments about the Ustashe.

Material on the Croatian diaspora came from a variety of sources published by the Croatian community of Canada regarding settlement and census figures in the diaspora, much of it distributed by the Norval Centre. I also interviewed Miran Sopta, Mate Mestrovic, Ante Beljo, Vinko Grubisic, and others who did not want to be named. Information on Gojko Susak and his role in the war came from *Saturday Night* magazine, Croatia's *Globus* newspaper, the official Susak biography, *Minister of Defence: A Memoir of Gojko Susak*, and a documentary on the diaspora's contribution to the war by CBC's *the fifth estate*, which also allowed me access to the full interviews on which the program was based. Material about the criminal activities of Otpor and other Croatian diaspora outfits came from Canadian newspaper accounts and also from U.S. newspaper coverage of the pertinent RICO trials.

CHAPTER TWO: NO PEACE TO KEEP

I conducted interviews with Stipe Mesic, Stepjan Kljuc and others who were part of the Croatian government during the war and prefer not to be named. I also consulted transcripts of interviews with Anton Tus and Martin Spegelj. Material on the formation and deployment of the peacekeeping mission to Croatia came from the United Nations website, and the websites of the Canadian Forces and the Canadian Department of National Defence. Books I relied on in this chapter include many of those cited in the notes for chapter one, as well as *Unvanquished: a US–UN Saga* by Boutros Boutros-Ghali and *Peacekeeper: The Road to Sarajevo* by Lewis MacKenzie.

CHAPTER THREE: THE GHOSTS OF KAP'YONG

To describe the contemporary situation of the Canadian Forces I relied on *The Patricias: Proud History of a Fighting Regiment* by David J. Bercuson; *Maple Leaf Against the Axis: Canada's Second World War* also by Bercuson; and *Somalia Cover-up: A Commissioner's Journey* by Peter Desbarat. Other support material came from the DND and the UN websites; documents on the Somalia affair released after Access to Information requests and also on-line reports from the Somalia review conducted by the Canadian government.

The soldiers' accounts come from original interviews and also from the sworn testimonies of the witnesses to the Sharpe inquiry.

CHAPTER FIVE: FRONTIER WARFARE

Most of the chapter comes from original interviews and from the sworn testimonies of witnesses to the Sharpe inquiry. I also consulted transcripts of the hearing concerning the events of Medak Pocket before the Senate Committee on National Defence and Veterans Affairs.

Additional material on the Croatian side of the story came from original interviews with members of government as well as accounts from Norman Cigar, the author of *Genocide in Bosnia: The Policy of "Ethnic Cleansing."* Cigar is a professor of National Strategy at the United States Marine Corps Command and Staff College, and he has also consulted for the International Criminal Tribunal for the former Yugoslavia.

Other source material includes Ambassador Warren Zimmerman's *Origins of a Catastrophe; The Death of Yugoslavia* by Laura Silber and Allan Little; Croatian newspaper accounts; and the official biography of Gojko Susak.

CHAPTER SIX: INTO THE FIRE

This chapter largely derives from original interviews with the players. Errors and inconsistencies are entirely the fault of the author but where the eyewitness accounts slightly contradict each other—particularly in timeline—I left the contradiction. There is little printed record of these remarkable days. Curiously, the more interesting the events, the less documentation exists or has survived. The operations officer for the 2PPCLI, Shane Brennan, says there were simply very few written reports filed. Brennan compiled what he could of the accounts from the soldiers and supplied them to Colonel Jim Calvin for his final report. The firefight between Charlie Company and the Croats described here is almost entirely pieced together from the memories of people who were there.

Sean M. Maloney and John Llambias's fascinating oral history book, *Chances for Peace: Canadian Soldiers in the Balkans: 1992–1995*, with its section on the Medak operation, was an invaluable reference. The authors note that some of the witnesses they interviewed did not want to be named in the text, a detail that only underlines how suspicious many of the soldiers are of chroniclers and journalists. It was certainly my experience.

In addition to more than a dozen interviews from the ranks of the 2PPCLI, this chapter also relied on testimonies from the Sharpe inquiry and on interviews with Lieutenant General Michel Maisonneuve, Major General John Arch MacInnis and the Croatian general, Petar Stipetic. Croatian President Stipe Mesic provided an interview, as did other Croatian politicians and officials who prefer to be nameless. I arranged for Janko Bobetko's chapter on Medak in his autobiography *All My Battles* to be translated into English, as well as accounts of the Tudjman papers published and analyzed in the *Feral Tribune*.

The indictments at the International Criminal Tribunal for the Former Yugoslavia include detailed descriptions of the events of Medak, which I relied on in this chapter, along with the UNPROFOR archives at the UN.

Material from Jim Calvin's final After Action Report, filed three weeks after the battalion returned home in October 1993, was finally made public in its entirety through an Access to Information request in the spring of 2004 and was used in this account.

Additional material came from HINA, Croatia's official news agency, and from Reuters reports.

CHAPTER SEVEN: SCORCHED EARTH

The account of the aftermath of the Croatian assault on Medak Pocket comes principally from the accounts of the Canadian soldiers who entered the Pocket and from the 2PPCLI logs, diaries and situation reports. Descriptions of the war crimes come from the detailed information contained in the indictments filed at the International Criminal Tribunal for the Former Yugoslavia. The Tudjman defence counsel tape reported on here was translated and published in *Harper's Magazine*.

CHAPTER EIGHT: WITCH HUNTS AND PAPER SHREDDERS

In this chapter, I have relied on original interviews with the soldiers, testimonies from the Sharpe inquiry and statements made before the Senate Committee on National Defence and Veterans Affairs. Through Access to Information, the government has released about three hundred pages of material that trace the DND investigations into the red soil, the Eric Smith memo and the Matt Stopford affair. There is additional material on the various investigations on the DND website, specifically the section devoted to the Judge Advocates General department.

The story of Operation Storm came from numerous journalists' reports, mostly in the *New York Times*, and from *Death of Yugoslavia*. Material on Gojko Susak's relationship with the United States administration comes from Paul Hockenos's book *Homeland Calling*, and also from Susak's official biography and Croatian newspaper and magazine accounts.

INDEX